WEST HAM
IN MY DAY

WEST HAM
IN MY DAY

By Tony McDonald

FootballWorld

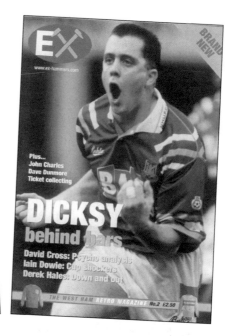

First published in England in August 2007 by

FootballWorld

Tel: 01708 744 333
www.footballworld.co.uk
www.ex-hammers.com

©Copyright Football World

Printed by Biddles Ltd, King's Lynn, Norfolk

Distributed by Football World
103 Douglas Road, Hornchurch, Essex, RM11 1AW, England
Email: editorial@footballworld.co.uk

Set in Times Roman

ISBN 978-0-9551176-8-8

www.ex-hammers.com
Plus..STUART SLATER, ALLEN McKNIGHT,
STUART PEARSON, BOYS OF '86

The life of
BRIAN
BRIAN DEAR ON WHAT
REALLY HAPPENED AT

www.ex-hammers.com
Plus..BOBBY HOWE and TREVOR HARTLEY,
KEITH COLEMAN, TREVOR DAWKINS

Top
MARK
WINGER WARDIE
REFLECTS ON HIS ROLE
IN '86 AND PREPARES
TO GO DOWN UNDER

www.ex-hammers.com
Plus..BILLY JENNINGS,
ALAN DICKENS, MEMORABILIA

Eddie
BOV
Midfield
iron Man's
honest

www.ex-hammers.com
Plus..VIC KEEBLE & JOHN DICK,
KEVIN KEEN, MEMORABILIA

BONZO
Exclusive with our
Ca

www.ex-hammers.com
Plus..MARK ROBSON, COLIN MACKLEWORTH,
MEMORABILIA and much more...

BONZO
Exclusive with our
former boss

"I NEVER ENJOYED
MANAGEMENT"
Part 2 of our Billy
Bonds special

THE WEST HAM RETRO MAGAZINE No.13 £2.50

www.ex-hammers.com
Plus..PAT HOLLAND, PAUL ALLEN,
MEMORABILIA and much more...

The Auction
of the Year

LUDO
Exclusive with our
big Czech mate

THE WEST HAM RETRO MAGAZINE No.14 £2.50

CONTENTS

ACKNOWLEDGEMENTS

A sincere thanks to all the following for their help in making this book possible:

Terry Connelly, Tim Crane, Danny Francis, Terry Roper, Neale Harvey, Susie Muir, Jack McDonald, Tony Hogg, Steve Blowers and Anne Walker.

A special big thank you to all the former West Ham United players who kindly gave up their time for the interviews that appear in this book. Their co-operation is very much appreciated.

And for their help with photographs: Steve Bacon, Arthur Griffiths and John Helliar.

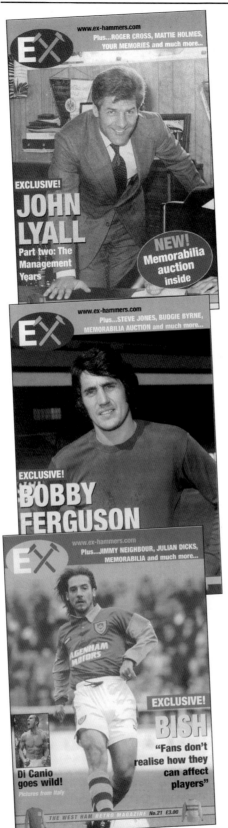

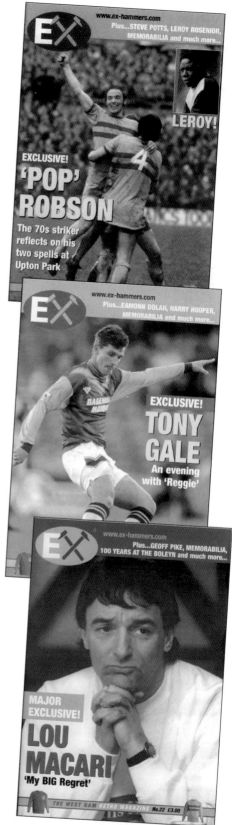

www.ex-hammers.com
Plus...ROGER CROSS, MATTIE HOLMES, YOUR MEMORIES and much more...

EXCLUSIVE!
JOHN LYALL
Part two: The Management Years

NEW! Memorabilia auction inside

www.ex-hammers.com
Plus...STEVE POTTS, LEROY ROSENIOR, MEMORABILIA and much more...

LEROY!

EXCLUSIVE!
'POP' ROBSON
The 70s striker reflects on his two spells at Upton Park

www.ex-hammers.com
Plus...STEVE JONES, BUDGIE BYRNE, MEMORABILIA AUCTION and much more...

EXCLUSIVE!
BOBBY FERGUSON

www.ex-hammers.com
Plus...EAMONN DOLAN, HARRY HOOPER, MEMORABILIA and much more...

EXCLUSIVE!
TONY GALE
An evening with 'Reggie'

www.ex-hammers.com
Plus...JIMMY NEIGHBOUR, JULIAN DICKS, MEMORABILIA and much more...

EXCLUSIVE!
BISH
"Fans don't realise how they can affect players"

Di Canio goes wild!
Pictures from Italy

THE WEST HAM RETRO MAGAZINE No.21 £3.00

www.ex-hammers.com
Plus...GEOFF PIKE, MEMORABILIA, 100 YEARS AT THE BOLEYN and much more...

MAJOR EXCLUSIVE!
LOU MACARI
'My BIG Regret'

THE WEST HAM RETRO MAGAZINE No.22 £3.00

9

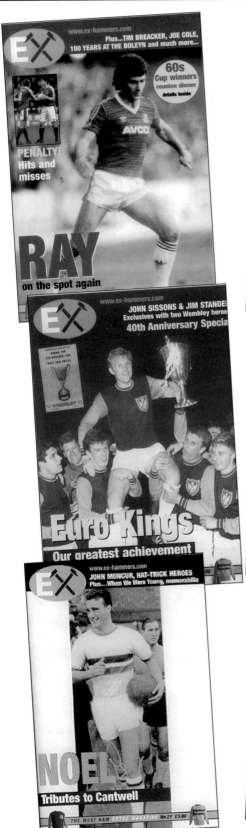

INTRODUCTION

IN MY DAY is a compilation of some 26 exclusive interviews conducted with former players of West Ham United whose careers spanned five decades, from the 1950s to the millennium.

The interviews first appeared in issues of the monthly *EX* magazine, which we at Football World launched in November 2002. They have been edited for the purpose of this book and, in most cases, new pictures of the subjects (many of them rare) have been included.

From 50s goalkeeping legend Ernie Gregory to the Italian maestro Paolo Di Canio, there should be plenty here for Hammers supporters of all age groups to enjoy.

In many ways this book serves as a fascinating, and at times revealing, history of how our club has evolved over the past half century – the contrasting characters who have passed through the claret-and-blue gates and the atmosphere, both buoyant and gloomy, that has existed within the club at various times. It is also in itself a fascinating commentary on how football has changed over the same period.

And certainly not always for the better, it has to be said.

Regular readers of *EX* are already well aware of my sometimes cynical references to modern football and the money that has infected so many aspects of what was once the working man's game, when players still inhabited the same planet as the people who paid their wages. We would need another book to fully cover everything that is wrong with the greedy, seedy business this sport has become since the infusion of Sky TV's millions in the early 90s.

Indeed, it was the rampant self-indulgence of the modern footballer that proved the inspiration for *EX* magazine in the first place. Sick of reading or listening to banal interviews with current players (and not just those at West Ham) who have nothing of interest to say and who are low on genuine talent but very big on ego, we thought it would be nice to track down and interview people – some long forgotten – who really did have lots of interesting things to say about their time at West Ham.

Ex-players (hence the mag's title) who genuinely cared for football, fully appreciated the benefits the game had brought them and also the club who gave them their chance to shine as professional footballers. In some cases, the former Hammers featured in *IN MY DAY* were paid only the maximum wage, or they earned a pittance compared to the ridiculously overpaid and overhyped players who have been cosseted aboard the Premier League gravy train in recent years. Most of the former players you will read about in this book played for the love of the game – money was never a motivating factor and agents did not exist.

And the great thing was, these men – most of them once stars in their own right but some now unrecognisable if you happened to pass them in the street – were just as keen to talk to us as we were eager to interview and reminisce with them! Most of them were genuinely flattered even to be remembered. Many of them invited us into their own homes to talk. This in itself is a refreshing departure from the culture of celebrity and 'bling' favoured by today's pampered *prima donnas*.

Producing 43 issues of *EX* to date has been very much a team effort, a labour of love for all of us involved. It certainly would not have got off the ground without the help and enthusiastic efforts of my good friend and fellow West Ham supporter Terry Connelly, who has been a trusted ally to many ex-Hammers over a long period – many of whom he first met in the course of obtaining their autographs as a kid. Knowledgeable TC has been watching the best and worst of West Ham for more than 50 years and is far better qualified than most fans to pass judgement on the merits (or otherwise) of the players who have worn the shirt during this lengthy period.

Another great mate of mine and Terry's, Tim Crane, who writes the memorabilia column in each issue of *EX* as well as contributing other features and interviews, has also been with me all the way since we launched. A keen historian and incurable football romantic, Tim's enthusiasm for all things West Ham United past knows no bounds and he is the proud possessor of the most impressive West Ham trade card collection in existence!

More recently, Terry Roper has been a very welcome addition to the *EX* editorial team and, again, a more enthusiastic Hammers devotee you could not find. Danny Francis (who travelled to Rome to interview Paolo Di Canio), Tony Hogg, Steve Blowers, Stuart Allen, John Helliar and John Northcutt have also played their part and, like the three T's, have done so enthusiastically and without financial reward. I can't thank them enough for their support.

For us it has been an absolute pleasure to sit down with so many one-time West Ham favourites, many of them big names in their day, and recall the good times and the bad they experienced at Upton Park and after leaving the club. By virtue of the fact that they are ex-players, the people interviewed on the following pages have been able to speak very freely and candidly about their careers, the players they played with and the managers they played under, without fear of upsetting their old employers. At times their honesty is compelling.

And the fact that *EX* is published independently of the club means we don't have to tow the party line in the same way that the official publications inevitably do.

The magazine – the only retro publication of its kind covering a Premiership club – has been warmly welcomed by many people inside the club and by those with past West Ham connections. A number of ex-players (and one former director) have themselves since become subscribers to the mag!

Undoubtedly the proudest moment in respect of *EX* was the celebration dinner we organised, in May 2005, to mark the 40th anniversary of the European Cup Winners' Cup victory. Dismayed that the club had no plans to honour the survivors of the greatest night in Hammers' history, we took the bull by the horns and put on a four-course reunion dinner at the International Hotel in London Docklands, jointly hosted by Martin Peters and Tony Cottee.

We invited every surviving member of both the 1964 FA Cup and 1965 ECWC-

The cup-winning heroes of 1964 and '65 reunited at the EX 40th anniversary gala dinner in London Docklands, May 2005.
Back row, left to right: Ken Brown, Joe Kirkup, Alan Dickie, Jim Standen, John Bond, Jack Burkett and Martin Peters.
Front row: Eddie Bovington, Peter Brabrook, Brian Dear, Ronnie Boyce and John Sissons.

Below: Bondy keeps Martin Peters and Joe Kirkup amused before dinner.

winning teams, together with their wives and partners, and paid for their overnight accommodation. We also footed the bill for John Sissons to fly in from South Africa, Jim Standen from California and Joe Kirkup from France. Of the players, only Sir Geoff Hurst couldn't make what turned out to be an unforgettable occasion. Stephanie Moore (another avid *EX* reader) was sorry that a prior engagement meant she was unable to attend, Ron Greenwood was too unwell to make it, but it was a delight to welcome along Barbara and Anthony Sealey, wife and son of the late Alan Sealey, the two-goal Wembley hero of '65.

It wasn't intended to be a profit-making venture, but some 200 supporters attended and you couldn't have put a price on the sheer joy the evening brought to the former players and their families, as well as everybody else present. For one more night, 40 years after what was for most the finest achievement of their career, they were feted stars again – just as they deserved to be. We were all honoured to be in their presence on this special occasion but such is the genuine warmth, humility and gratitude of these guys that *they* were the ones who felt most honoured of all.

The pleasure the anniversary dinner gave the ex-players, was worth every late night spent toiling over a computer keyboard and every home match day my partner Susie and I spent shouting on street corners around the Boleyn Ground in our efforts to flog the bloody magazine!

I'm not sure there are too many among the 35,000, who religiously give their unconditional support to the club at each home game now, with much, or even any, interest in the actual history of the club and the players who came before them. It's become very much a live-for-today world. I suspect that most of the people we have been aiming *EX* at have long since given up attending matches, for whatever reason, and our problem has been trying to reach those fans from bygone eras who have drifted away and are content to follow West Ham from the comfort of their sofas. However, the support and encouragement we have received from our small band of loyal readers has always been very much appreciated.

So, too, is the enthusiasm shown by many former West Ham players and managers, whose genuine interest has been vital to the mag's growth over the best part of the past five years. The magazine has brought together many former West Ham team-mates who had previously lost touch with each other, and that has been gratifying.

EX lost one of its biggest supporters when John Lyall sadly died of a heart attack in April 2006. The memorable summer's day in 2005 Terry Connelly and I spent in the company of the respected former Hammers manager, as privileged guests at his Suffolk farmhouse where we got through seven hours of interview tape (it ran in two of our best-selling issues), is one I will cherish forever. John loved reading his copy of the magazine and he couldn't have been more sincere when he offered to help us in any way possible. He happily posed for a photograph holding copies of the magazine, for use in a subscriptions advertisement, and was keen to meet Terry and I for more informal talks about what he still referred to as 'his' club.

I took John up on his kind offer to help when we first conceived the idea of re-producing a number of the magazine interviews in a more permanent book form, by asking him to contribute the foreword. This he was very happy to do and his neatly handwritten copy duly arrived before publication date, originally set some 18

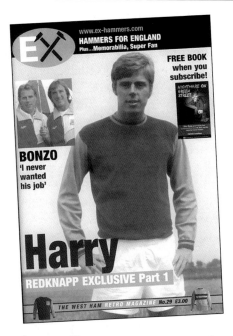

months ago. For one reason or another, we put the book on hold and, instead, continued to produce more issues of the magazine – which has now moved to a quarterly frequency – both before and after John's sudden and untimely death. I thought it appropriate, though, to publish his original copy on the following page, to emphasise just how supportive of us John had always been.

It was a real coup, too, when Harry Redknapp invited us inside his mansion on the exclusive Dorset coast to be interviewed about his time as both player and manager at Upton Park. Our special interview with Billy Bonds, another helpful ally throughout, also ran over two issues, while the man who preceded Bonzo in the Hammers hotseat, Lou Macari, readily agreed to talk on the phone from his Cheshire home. The list of players we have met and interviewed for *EX* reads like a West Ham who's who. Soon after they returned to Upton Park in their managerial roles in December 2006, Alan Curbishley and Mervyn Day both happily agreed to be exclusively interviewed by us.

Now it's certain that many of you reading this won't have even heard of *EX* magazine and have therefore not yet sampled this nostalgic delight! Where have you been for the past five years? Well, don't worry! Most back issues are still in stock and for the cost of just £3.50 per 40-page issue (in the UK), a year's subscription will ensure you never miss another copy in the future (see details in our advert at the back). We are fortunate that our club has a rich history, thanks primarily to the World Cup-winning trio, and *EX* is a pleasant way to relive those days gone by.

In the meantime, we hope you enjoy the interview extracts included in this first edition of *IN MY DAY* and a welcome look back at a number of the characters who helped to shape our club over the past 50 years. Happy memories!

Tony McDonald
Hornchurch, August 2007

John Lyall pictured on the day EX visited him at home in August 2005.

FOREWORD

SINCE *EX* magazine was launched, independently of the club, in November 2002, we have read many articles by ex-West Ham players. I know so many of those players enjoy contributing and reading and beyond that have a genuine fondness for the magazine.

From the outset the magazine's personnel have gained the trust and respect of the players and it is to their great credit that *EX* is read with great enthusiasm by the players themselves.

Whilst so many modern day magazines promote the 'star players', EX has endeavoured to interview not just the big names and internationals, but the 'lesser lights' too. This has resulted in some great articles and reminds us that the club belongs to us all.

The publication is greatly helped by the fact that both editor Tony McDonald and historian Terry Connelly are West Ham United through and through. (I did in fact play with Tony's father, Terry, in the West Ham youth team in the late 50s).

They both are fiercely proud of the West Ham history and tradition. To that degree they have made every effort to talk to previous generations of players (such as Ernie Gregory, Vic Keeble, Mal Musgrove, Frank O'Farrell and Harry Hooper) to help their readers learn more about former Hammers players and managers.

As further proof of their commitment to the club, the people behind *EX* undertook the risk of funding a gala dinner to honour the cup-winning teams of 1964 and 1965. The evening was a great success and raised a donation for the Bobby Moore fund for cancer research. I should add that the magazine is always available to assist Stephanie Moore's fund-raising activities.

Having read every issue since the origin in 2002, I am most surprised that the *EX* mag is largely a labour of love for those who put it together. I would have thought that as the magazine is an excellent read, it would be greatly enjoyed by all true Hammers fans. We are lucky to have such a publication available to us.

In wishing everyone involved with *EX* success, I look forward with great enthusiasm to receiving and reading the follow-up volume two of this book in the not too distant future.

John Lyall
September 2005

● *The late John Lyall played for West Ham United in the early 60s before managing the Hammers from August 1974 until May 1989. He led the club to FA Cup success in 1975 and 1980 and (in 1986-86) their highest-ever league position.*

Dr Oliver Thomas, former club doctor and director, takes a look at Ernie's injured arm. It was Dr Thomas who introduced steak to the players' pre-match diet.
Hammers 1951-52 – Back row, left to right: Tommy Moroney, Derek Parker, Dick Walker, Ernie Gregory, Malcolm Allison, Harry Kinsell and Frank O'Farrell. Front: Steve Forde, Tommy Southren, Jim Barrett (jnr), Bill Robinson, Gerry Gazzard and Terry Woodgate.

Chapter 1

ERNIE**GREGORY**

"When I coached the keepers myself years later, I also used a sandpit, but the lads didn't want to know because the sand went all over them! But in my day, we always used the sandpit for goalkeeping practice – you could dive all over the place without hurting yourself"

THERE are none better qualified to talk about the evolution of West Ham United than Ernie Gregory, the loyal one-club man who served the Hammers as man and boy.

He joined the club as a 14-year-old in 1935 and made 382 league (a then club record) and 24 cup appearances between 1938 and 1959.

When Ernie made his final appearance as first team goalkeeper, he was almost 38-years-old and had played 406 times between the sticks, gaining a second division championship winners' medal at the end of his last full season.

But after 24 years and more of unstinting service as a player, Gregory was not cast aside by the club to whom he had devoted his life. Under first Ron Greenwood and then John Lyall he became a key member of the club's backroom staff.

Manager of the old 'A' team, reserve and youth sides, Ernie had already been honoured with The Football League Long-Service Award well before finally conceding that a dodgy knee (it has since been artificially replaced) convinced him it was time to give up coaching the keepers at Chadwell Heath and take things a little easier. He became a specialist goalkeeping coach at West Ham way before the majority of clubs had even considered such a role within their coaching set-up.

The greeting is warm and the hands distinctively large as Ernie Gregory rises from his favourite armchair in the living room of his Goodmayes, Essex home to welcome *EX* into his unique and fascinating world of West Ham United memories.

Once in the company of this 85-year-old Hammers legend you are quickly reassured that there is still claret-and-blue blood pumping through his veins.

As Cockney as pie and mash and jellied eels, Ernie Gregory is an intrinsic part of West Ham United's fabric. He talks lovingly of the great players and characters he shared a dressing room with. As he explained, one of them actually took pity on him at the start of his career.

Ernie said: "My first game after joining the Irons was in the traditional 'Possibles v Probables' pre-season friendly. I was still only 14, up against the likes of Jimmy Ruffell, Len Goulden and Jim Barrett."

Get Big Ernie talking about winger Jimmy Ruffell and you'll never stop him.

"What a player he was," says Ernie with a twinkle in his eyes. "Jimmy got the ball, went past the lot of 'em and as he got in the box, he looked up and must have

J. RUFFELL, West Ham United.

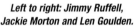

Left to right: Jimmy Ruffell, Jackie Morton and Len Goulden.

thought to himself: 'I can't shoot at the poor sod from this close range'.

"Instead, he turned round and dribbled the ball back to the edge of the box and shot from there. I managed to tip his effort over the bar – it's a story Jimmy always liked to tell."

With pre-war great Ted Hufton having firmly established himself as first choice No.1, and Herman Conway following him between the sticks in the mid-30s, Ernie and some of his fellow young Hammers were farmed out to Leytonstone, where he won the Isthmian League championship in 1935.

Ernie never saw Hufton in action – he admits that, as a kid, he always preferred playing to watching – but he said of Conway: "They brought Herman from Gainsborough and although he must have been a good keeper, he did tend to punch the ball rather than try to catch it. But manager Charlie Paynter made a point of telling me: 'Don't let me see *you* punch the ball when it's there to be caught'."

According to Ernie, Paynter believed Hufton was the greatest Hammers keeper of all-time, although he later paid Gregory the ultimate compliment by saying that he was not far below Ted's class!

Ernie's proud record of 406 first team appearances would have been significantly greater but for the intervening war years. His first team debut was delayed until December 28, 1946 – a 4-1 home win over Plymouth Argyle in Division Two. He played the last eight games of that season but didn't miss a single match the following campaign.

Only injuries, not lack of form, displaced him from the side – he missed all of the 1954-55 campaign, when George Taylor deputised – until Noel Dwyer, Brian Rhodes and Lawrie Leslie took it in turns to succeed the veteran custodian.

Ernie's 406th, and final, first team appearance came in a 2-1 home defeat by Leeds United on September 5, 1959. He was two months short of his 38th birthday. The following year the club awarded him a testimonial match, with the Hammers facing LDA of Costa Rica.

So who did most to help him on his way during the early years?

"I was coached regularly by Dave Bailey, the understudy to Ted Hufton," said

Ernie. "He was also a terrific goalkeeper who specialised in handling low shots – he'd make a cup-shape with his hands.

"He looked after me off the field, too. At lunchtimes, if we had a few bob, Dave, 'Woody' (the groundsman), team-mate Ron Cater and I would go over the road for a meat pudding, or up to Sandy's on Green Street for egg and chips or a Chelsea bun. Then we'd go back to the ground and practice on the field at the back of the old West Stand. There was a cinder track and, out the back, a training field with trees and a sandpit area by the goal.

"When I coached the keepers myself years later, I also used a sandpit, but the lads didn't want to know because the sand went all over them! But in my day, we always used the sandpit for goalkeeping practice – you could dive all over the place without hurting yourself.

"Dave Bailey worked me well and in the end I became better at taking the ball on the deck than 'upstairs'.

"I used to mark an area in front of the six-yard box, to help me work out the angles. Keeping is all about knowing your angles. And spreading. I was also good at spreading (the art of diving at an opponent's feet)," added Ernie.

He gained one England 'B' cap, against France in 1952, and only the brilliance of so many of his early post-war contemporaries denied him the full cap many say he deserved.

"I was a great admirer of Frank Swift," he continued, while pulling yet another old newspaper clipping from a drawer. Ernie has collected a number of cuttings to remind himself of the former greats and as he handed me one relating to the Manchester City legend, he said: "Big Swifty was great, played for England, but he was tragically killed in the Munich disaster."

If Swift was Ernie's all-time goalkeeping favourite, who gets his vote as the greatest Hammer of all-time? Despite almost a lifetime at the Boleyn, there is no hesitation. His eyes sparkle again at the memory and he says: "Len Goulden was the greatest-ever to play for West Ham. I was there for 60 years and I never saw anyone better than little Lennie.

"You had to see him to believe it. He was about five-feet six but he could jump as high as a six-footer. A West Ham boy through and through and a great ball player, he could pass the ball anywhere you liked. He played with Jimmy Ruffell and Jackie Morton – two more great players.

"I was brought up with ball-players and Len was the best of 'em, but we've not had a good ball-playing midfielder in this country since Gazza."

Cherished memories and the all-time Irons greats continue to trip off Ernie's tongue. "Tommy Moroney – ooh, what a player, I can see him now . . . he could shovel the ball anywhere he wanted it to go. Imagine how good he'd be on the lovely pitches they play on today. A wonderful passer of the ball, Tommy was one of the first boys to come to us from Ireland, just after the war, and he lived in digs in East Ham.

"Dicky Walker was the greatest centre-half they ever had after he replaced Jim Barrett in 1936."

Fast-forward to the 60s, by which time Ernie had finally hung up his boots and

West Ham line-up before their game at Bury in September 1955. Back row, left to right: Dave Sexton, John Bond, Ernie Gregory, Malcolm Allison, Noel Cantwell and Frank O'Farrell. Front: Malcolm Musgrove, Harry Hooper, Billy Dare, Johnny Dick and Ken Tucker.

taken over as coach of the 'A' team that had one or two future legends in the making. He recalls: "Another great player was Trevor Brooking who, after training, would ask me for a lift to Barking station.

"Billy Bonds was also right up there. I remember watching him with Ron Greenwood, playing for Charlton in a five-a-side tournament at Earls Court. Ron pointed him out to me and soon afterwards signed him for £49,000. Smashing player."

Ernie confirmed that Bonzo was, literally, also out on his own when it came to endurance training. Whenever bad weather forced a session to be switched from Chadwell Heath to Upton Park, Ernie recalls: "I used to train them in groups of five and six, had them running up and down the steps of the old Chicken Run for 25 minutes. Billy would always lead the way and he'd run all day."

Ted Fenton succeeded Charlie Paynter as manager in 1950 and there is no doubt that he made a string of astute signings, notably Vic Keeble, Johnny Dick and Malcolm Musgrove who were outstanding in the 1957-58 Division Two championship-winning side. But like most managers of his era, Fenton was no tracksuit boss and was content to let senior players Malcolm Allison, Noel Cantwell and John Bond – The ABC of West Ham – formulate tactics and establish what in the late 50s became famously known as the West Ham Academy. As all West Ham fans with any sense of history well know, along with the likes of Dave Sexton, Frank O'Farrell and Jimmy Andrews, Allison, Cantwell and Bond would devise tactical innovations by moving salt and pepper pots around on the dinner tables upstairs in Cassettari's Café, which is still serving meals in the nearby Barking Road.

"Malcolm was a fantastic trainer and a great talker," Ernie agreed. "Football is an easy game but you have to know *how* to talk football. Malcolm was a good coach, very innovative, but he wasn't the only one at West Ham then who knew what he was talking about. We *all* went on courses to get our coaching badge.

"In our day we'd play in threes, always working the angles. I'd give the ball to Bondy and he'd give it to Andy Malcolm. Today they play too many square balls, whereas we played angled passes."

Although he is happy to give the influential Allison due respect for his coaching credentials and achievements, Ernie does not credit him as the architect of the side that finally won promotion to the top flight in May 1958 after an absence of 26 years.

"Malcolm had TB and had packed up playing that season," Ernie points out. "Kenny Brown took over from him at centre-half and, with John Bond and Noel Cantwell, they were our defence. I used to say to Brownie: 'You just fill in the hole, I don't want you to play too much football there'.

"Kenny was a good centre-half but Bond and Cantwell were the best two full-backs in the country. They'd put spin on the passes they played down the line. And if they looked like being tucked up, they'd clip it back to me!"

Opponents couldn't ruffle Ernie but Bond and Cantwell toying with opponents in their own penalty area might have hastened the greying process for the veteran keeper!

"I think Noel could have been the best centre-half in the game," he adds.

There were innovators on and off the field at the Boleyn in the 50s. Ernie points out that West Ham were ahead of the rest in the culinary stakes, too. He says the credit for introducing juicy steaks to the players' pre-match diet should go to club doctor and director, Dr Oliver Thomas.

"We'd previously usually ate fish or chicken and toast, but Dr Thomas advised us all to eat steak and rice two hours before kick-off instead. All the other clubs copied us after that," reveals Ernie.

"We were also the first club in the country whose players wore Adidas football boots, the lightweight ones. We wore all the continental stuff – small shorts, shiney shirts, the lot.

"I always wanted to play in black, like the continental goalies of that time, but the English football authorities wouldn't allow it. They said I couldn't 'cos referees always wore black and therefore my kit would've clashed with theirs.

"I liked to wear lightweight gear. I never played in a vest, just a goalie's shirt, and I was one of the first to have my shirt-sleeves rolled up above my elbows.

"We wore string gloves but only when it was wet – you needed the string to help grip the heavy, slippery ball. It was the German keeper, Sepp Maier, who started the fashion in the early 70s of wearing the big, padded gloves they all use today."

Ernie was somewhat of a fashion rebel in his time, though. Disappointed that he wasn't allowed to wear all-black kit, and unimpressed with the club's standard issue with its claustrophobic polo neck design, he had his devoted wife, Yvonne, knit him

Above: Ernie dives full length in the Upton Park mud as a watchful Malcolm Allison looks on.
Left: Ernie pictured at a West Ham home game in 2005.
Below: Holding aloft the FA Cup, just before the official squad picture was taken in the summer of 1964. Trainer Bill Jenkins and coach Albert Walker are also in the foreground.

the home-made green shirt he wore for matches.

Not that he ever thought about leaving the club who signed him as a boy.

"I always thought West Ham was the greatest club going, that's why I never went anywhere else," he says. "Arsenal, Man United and Newcastle came in for me – I could have gone to any of them but I was already getting maximum wages at West Ham, so why move?

"When I turned pro at 17, I was paid a fiver a week, plus a tenner signing-on fee. The highest amount I ever earned was £20 per week just before I finished playing, which was good money at the time."

And how Ernie earned it. Among the bravest of the brave, he was a regular fixture in the A&E department of the London Hospital, where he received treatment for several career-threatening injuries.

"I broke my left shoulder, elbow, scaphoid . . . well, take a look at that finger," he says while pointing at the deformed little digit on his right hand.

He explained: "Eric Westwood, of Man City, kicked right across the finger and I thought I was going to lose it. I was in hospital for 10 days but, luckily, it didn't have to be amputated.

"I had an operation to have the scaphoid bone in my left wrist removed because the injury affected the blood flow to my hand. They said I wouldn't play again. We didn't have a physio then, just Billy Moore the trainer, and I was up the London Hospital every day for weeks trying to get it right. I fixed it myself in the end. I've still got nerves there but I've lost the feeling in that finger.

"I also busted my nose playing against Luton – I still get occasional nosebleeds from that one.

"George Taylor was the reserve keeper when I played and it was thanks to me that he stayed at the club for 15 years. Every time West Ham went to sell George, I got injured, so they couldn't let him go!"

Ernie rated Arsenal's Ted Drake, Leeds United's John Charles and Len Duquemin of Spurs as three of the most formidable opponents he faced, while he says Aston Villa's Trevor Forde was the hardest. "They all used to hit you left, right and centre," he grimaced, bearing the scars to prove it.

Remembering his final days as a player, Ernie says: "We were playing up at Burnley and this fella got through but as I came out to spread myself and smother the ball, he kicked me in the leg. I thought it was broken.

"I went out of the first team picture and I thought that was it – until they asked me to play for the reserves at Portsmouth. Harry Hooper senior was our trainer that day. The crosses were coming over and although I knew what I *wanted* to do, I could no longer do it. I told Harry I'd had it and said the same to our chairman, Reggie Pratt.

"I played for the reserves and the 'A' team in the old Metropolitan League but, after 21 years as a pro, I decided the time was right to stop.

"Yvonne and I talked about starting a grocer's business but Reg and fellow director Len Cearns thought it would be a good idea for me to stay in football. I had my full coaching badge, so I decided to remain at the club. I took over the 'A' team and we had a good side, including the likes of Martin Peters – he was king – plus Ronnie Boyce, Johnny Lyall, Joey Kirkup and Brian Dear."

Unshakably loyal and a man of high principles and dignity, Ernie will not direct personal criticism at the keepers who have been coached by him in the past or lesser talented men who earn fortunes from the modern game today. But he clearly believes that there are precious few around now to compare with the likes of his own hero, Frank Swift.

"Too many of them want to stay rooted to their line instead of coming out to take the ball at its highest point," he says. "And when they do come out for the ball, they end up punching heads instead!

"I always used to drum it into Mervyn Day to take the ball at its highest point. If the keeper allows the ball to drop any lower than that, the centre-half may as well clear it with his head instead.

"Another common failing I see today is the way keepers allow their own defenders to back onto them. The space immediately in front of the goal should belong only to the keeper."

Greenwood clearly valued Ernie's opinion highly. "Ron sent me to see Jim Standen play for Luton Town Reserves. Ron had already watched him and soon afterwards we signed him for £6,000. But it wouldn't be unusual for, say, six different people from the club to go and watch a player before he was finally signed."

Ernie tracked Mervyn Day's first youthful steps with Chelmsford and London Boys before recommending him, aged only 18, as the permanent replacement for the fading Bobby Ferguson at Upton Park in the early 70s. Day was hailed by Greenwood as not only West Ham's established keeper for the next 10 years, but also England's. But a crisis of confidence prevented Day from fulfilling his early promise and he made way for QPR's Phil Parkes before the end of the 70s.

"John Lyall knew he had to go out and pay big money for a keeper like Parksey," says Ernie. "I coached Phil for 10 years and there were days when he didn't want to do it, but on other days he'd be out there training for hours. For a man of his size, his agility was fantastic.

"Ludo (Miklosko) was the same. By then I was working only part-time, coaching two mornings a week, but I asked the little fella (Lou Macari): 'Have you been out to Czecho to sign him yet?' I said: 'You should do, for the money they want for him!' Ludo's fitness and character were just right.

"Parksey and Ludo were the best I worked with at West Ham. Mervyn was very good too . . . but none of 'em could lace my boots!" he laughs.

Peter Grotier had competed for Fergie's No.1 shirt before the overnight emergence of the teenage Day in the early 70s. "Good keeper, Peter . . . if only he'd been two inches taller," says Ernie.

"I always maintain that a good height for a keeper is around the 6ft-to-6ft, 2 inches mark. Keepers who are bigger than that tend to wait until the ball drops before they try and catch it, which can cause problems for them.

"But now I'm 85 years of age, an ol' cowson, so what do *I* know!"

Chapter 2

VIC**KEEBLE**

"On a Saturday morning Jacko and me would both be up in secretary Eddie Chapman's office to borrow a few quid – we were always skint! Johnny and I were earning about £20 a week, top whack, but we could easily lose that gambling every week"

VIC Keeble, one of the greatest strikers in West Ham United's history, was a prolific goalscoring star well before Ted Fenton brought him to Upton Park in October 1957 for a transfer fee of £10,000.

Fenton and Keeble went back to 1948, when Ted was player/manager at Colchester United and he discovered grammar school pupil Keeble playing for the local King George V Boys' club.

Keeble left his home town club, who were then in Division Three South, for top flight Newcastle United in 1951. He had spent only one full season in Colchester United's first team but he had made a big impact with 23 goals in 46 appearances, etching his name into U's history books as the first player to score a hat-trick for the Essex club (in a 3-0 win against Plymouth Argyle). It was obvious he would excel at a much higher level.

After Fenton was recruited by West Ham to succeed Charlie Paynter as manager at Upton Park in 1950, Ted's replacement at Colchester, Jimmy Allen, gratefully accepted a £15,000 fee – huge for a club of that size – and waved his 21-year-old star on his way to glory in the black-and-white of Newcastle United. It was a move that suited all parties, not least Vic, while Fenton would also benefit greatly from the big man's presence when they were reunited later that decade.

At St. James' Park, Vic formed a potent attacking spearhead with Geordie legend, Jackie Milburn. It speaks volumes for Vic's quality that he established himself alongside England ace 'Wor Jackie' in a team of proven internationals while the Magpies were soaring as one of the great cup sides of that era.

In addition to the iconic Milburn, Newcastle boasted an array of other accomplished stars, including right-half and skipper Jimmy Scoular, wingers Bobby Mitchell and Lenny White, with Bob Stokoe marshalling defence in front of Scottish international keeper Ronnie Simpson.

Keeble scored 67 goals in 120 top flight league and cup matches for the Magpies and was the fastest player to score 50 goals in a Newcastle shirt until Andy Cole beat his record (albeit most of Cole's coming at second division level). The pinnacle for Vic was an FA Cup winners' medal in 1955, when Newcastle beat Manchester City 3-1 – their third Wembley triumph in five years and the last major domestic trophy

Vic wearing the white away strip introduced by manager Ted Fenton in the late 50s.

the success-starved Geordie fans have had to celebrate. No wonder Keeble enjoyed his five-and-a-half years on Tyneside, although he still welcomed a move much nearer to his Colchester home.

"I was a little bit unlucky with injuries at Newcastle. I had a bad back," said Vic, pinpointing a chronic problem that surfaced early in his career. It cost him his first team place at St. James' and would return with a vengeance to finish him as a player at West Ham just a few years later.

The respected soccer scribe, Bernard Joy, heralded Keeble's arrival in E13 in the hope that he would emerge as the centre-forward to finally emulate the 1930s scoring exploits of the legendary Vic Watson. The similarities didn't just end at their shared Christian name and East Anglian backgrounds.

"I came to West Ham in October 1957 when they were fourth from bottom of the second division," recalled Vic. "The atmosphere in the camp was not as good as it should have been. They wanted somebody who was strong and good in the air."

Billy Dare started the 1957-58 season in fine style, scoring six in the first four matches, including all three in a 3-2 win at Bristol Rovers. He added five more in September before Keeble arrived to forge his famous partnership with Johnny Dick. For all the early success he enjoyed on the ground, diminutive Dare couldn't possibly possess the same aerial threat as Keeble.

Vic explained: "Billy was one of those little fellows who played for himself, whereas I was a bit different. I used to get the ball down and play it to the other forwards – and let them know I was a target man."

West Ham didn't have to wait long for a return on their 10 grand investment. In the fourth minute of a friendly against Sparta of Rotterdam, a benefit match for former skipper Dick Walker, Keeble opened the scoring. More significantly, given how the season and his Hammers career would pan out, he flicked the ball on for strike partner Dick to complete his hat-trick in a leisurely 5-0 win.

Dick and Keeble would become a match made in heaven.

"I then made my league debut the following Saturday (Oct 19), against Doncaster Rovers, who had Harry Gregg in goal before he went to Man United. He dropped the ball over his head and I dived and headed it into the empty net. It must have been the easiest goal of the season. We won 1-0 and didn't look like getting beat after that – it just got better and better."

Indeed, Keeble's debut match-winner against Doncaster at Upton Park sparked the promotion surge that saw Hammers embark on a remarkable run that included only one defeat in 21 league games. Lincoln City, Bristol Rovers and Swansea Town all conceded six goals at the Boleyn, while Huddersfield Town and Stoke City were hit for five before Fenton's men set a new club record by roasting Rotherham United, 8-0, in March '58 as the promotion push went into overdrive.

Although the influential club captain, Malcolm Allison, had missed all but five matches very early in the season while recovering from tuberculosis, his tactical blueprint for success was carried out by the players. Inside-forwards Dick and John Smith flourished alongside the lanky, stooping Keeble, while wingers Malcolm Musgrove (nine goals) and Mike Grice also provided a constant, quality supply line to the front men.

"The biggest game in the promotion season was the last one at home, against Liverpool. We drew one-each, with Bondy scoring from a freekick. We drew up at Anfield, too, so they were two important results. The other one big occasion was, of course, the last game of the season – our 3-1 victory at Middlesbrough.

"We always felt Fulham and Blackburn would both fade away and that Liverpool would end up being our main promotion challengers. I think four teams could still have gone up on the last day of the season – and it was Rovers who were eventually promoted with us."

Keeble put the seal on the championship, and Hammers' return to the top flight

Vic with the rest of the 1958 second division champions, who scored 101 goals on their way to the title and a return to the top flight after an absence of 26 years.
Back row, left to right: Andy Malcolm, Ken Brown, John Bond, Ernie Gregory, Noel Cantwell, Bill Lansdowne and Malcolm Pyke. Front row: Mike Grice, John Smith, Vic Keeble, Johnny Dick and Malcolm Musgrove.

after an absence of 26 years, by netting the third and his 19th league goal in 29 matches at Boro. Scottish favourite Dick, who was also on the scoresheet along with Musgrove, finished the league campaign with two more than his partner, but they were from 41 appearances.

"A draw would have done us for promotion but we needed a win to clinch the championship," recalls Vic. "I don't remember feeling any great pressure on us, though, not like there would be today when the stakes are so much higher."

With the title in the bag, Hammers returned from the North-East in jubilant mood but the celebrations were not over the top, as Vic recalls: "I didn't drink then – in fact, I didn't start drinking wine until I was 40-years-old and I never smoked either – so we didn't go wild. Even when we went dog racing in the evenings, we'd usually drink only tea and eat a meat pie between races."

The triumphant win at Middlesbrough's Ayresome Park ground was reward for a superb, all round team effort in which everyone played his part during the season. Although Allison was cruelly denied much of a playing role, the tactics and style of play he preached as the widely acclaimed founder of the Academy were a fitting testimony to his enormous influence.

But as the Eastenders finished a point clear of Blackburn Rovers (56 points), who in turn edged out Charlton Athletic (55) and Liverpool (54), promotion was also a great credit to Ted Fenton. The manager showed diligence and persistence in going back to Newcastle three times before he finally landed the signature of Vic Keeble, the catalyst for promotion.

If Fenton lacked tactical nous, he knew there was no shortage of sharp football brains he could turn to within the West Ham dressing room, with or without the stricken Allison, who was at a convalescence home in Midhurst, Surrey from September until he returned to Upton Park the following March to admire the eight-goal rout of Rotherham from the directors' box.

"Basically, Ted let the players get on with it," says Keeble. ''Noel Cantwell, our skipper, would always be the one to start us off. We'd have a talk at the beginning of the week and discuss the following Saturday's game. Ted would always ask Noel what he thought but we'd all have an input. Bondy, especially, would have his say. The team spirit got better and better as things went on. The banter in the dressing room was always good."

Another 29 years would pass before West Ham fans could rejoice in a 40-plus goal partnership – the Tony Cottee/Frank McAvennie pairing of 1985-86 – and Vic talks in almost reverential terms about his remarkable understanding with the man he affectionately called 'Jacko'.

He recalled a bizarre tale involving the two goalscoring heroes and firm friends: "We were playing an evening match at Upton Park but that afternoon Johnny and I had gone down to Folkestone for the horseracing. Unbeknown to us, in the stop press of the *London Evening Standard* it was reported that we had both been killed in a car crash!

"We arrived at the Boleyn Ground for the game a little bit late, by which time the club had received thousands of calls from worried fans asking what had happened to us. We didn't know anything about the so-called car crash, so when we got to the dressing room there were people shedding a few tears of relief.

"Johnny and I were a bit inseparable – we loved dog racing. After training on Tuesdays we'd catch the last two races at Dagenham or Hackney Wick. I liked going to Walthamstow best, though – that was *my* track. Our trainer, Billy Moore, used to go along there, too. Not that he mixed with us but we would see him regularly at Walthamstow, where he knew one or two of the greyhound trainers.

"In football, they used to say there were three distinct groups: drinkers, gamblers and the lads who go home.

"At West Ham in my day, the gamblers were Jacko, Malcolm Allison, Noel Cantwell, myself and, to some extent, John Bond. Little Harry Cripps liked a bet, too. He was the slowest player I'd ever seen but he didn't half do well when he went to Millwall.

"Andy Malcolm liked a glass of beer, and Michael Grice would also go up west with Allison and Cantwell.

"The quiet lads were 'Muzzie' (Mal Musgrove), Big Ernie (Gregory), Billy Lansdowne and Ken Brown.

"Johnny Smith was a bit of a loner in some ways. I think he liked to gamble but he never came out with us. John went to Tottenham but he couldn't get far there because Danny Blanchflower was pure class and went on to play for a couple more seasons. I don't think Smithy would have got much help there either. He needed to be encouraged to get hold of the ball. He was a good, fit lad, though, who really

*Outside Peterborough Cathedral where they had just attended Noel Cantwell's funeral in September 2005.
Left to right: John Lyall, Vic Keeble, John Bond, Martin Peters and Brian Dear.*

enjoyed training.

"Jacko used to do his wages gambling every week. On a Saturday morning we'd both be up in secretary Eddie Chapman's office to borrow a few quid – we were always skint! Johnny and I were earning about £20 a week, top whack, but we could easily lose that gambling every week.

"Once, Malcolm Allison, Noel Cantwell, Johnny and myself had built up a kitty with about £150-to-£200 in it – a lot of money back then. I'd had a tip from a stable lad at Newmarket for a horse called Red Moon, which was running at Bath at odds of 20-1. I told the lads and they insisted that I went to the track with 100 quid to back this horse.

"We were due to be training at Grange Farm that morning, so I phoned in and said I wasn't feeling too good. I went off to Bath instead to place our bet! I put tenners on here and there with different bookies at the course to get us the best possible odds. The horse ran fairly well but came in fourth, so we'd lost.

"The day had a happy ending, though. I drove from Bath to meet the lads at Wimbledon dogs that night and at first they weren't very happy at all after the earlier loss. But we won £150 that evening to make up for our disappointment on the horses!

"A Jewish bookie, Louis Baum – a lovely fella – used to accept Johnny's bets.

"I didn't meet Johnny until I got to West Ham even though, ironically, he'd been stationed in my home town of Colchester when he was in the Army doing his national service.

"He was a Scots-Cockney and I don't care what anybody says, he was the most popular player, among his team-mates, that West Ham had in my time there – and that includes Bobby Moore. *Everybody* loved Jacko. He used Cockney rhyming slang a lot and was always joking about. The young players loved him, too, because he'd always make them laugh.

"On the field, things were perfect between us. We never needed to discuss how to play either during training or just before a game. We just slotted in so well with each other and our partnership was completely natural.

"In the promotion season of 1957-58 we beat Blackpool 5-1 in the third round of the FA Cup. I got three and Jacko scored two that day but our right-back, George Wright, played Stanley Matthews off the park. Afterwards, Jacko sent me a little picture of Stan that he'd cut out of a newspaper and he'd written on it the message: 'To think, we played on the same pitch as this fella'.

"We all looked up to Matthews. Although you knew what he was going to do with the ball, you still couldn't stop him doing it.

"Jacko had a terrific left foot and was unlucky not to have gained more than the one Scotland cap he got. He was very good in the air, too.

"I did a little bit of driving after I stopped playing and whenever I was in London I would always call in and see Jacko. He would tell me the same stories over again but I'd still laugh at them – it was the *way* he told them."

But while Keeble and Dick rightly earned most plaudits for the 101 goals scored by the Irons in their promotion season, Vic singled out an unsung hero for praise.

"I thought Ernie Gregory was our best player. He was a bloody good keeper, brilliant on his angles," says Vic. "Ernie was a bit of a loner really but I always reckoned he was the main reason we won promotion. He should have received more credit for his efforts.

"I actually put together a brochure on our promotion-winning season, with all the money we earned from it going into the players' pool. I was a fairly bright lad and wrote all the player profiles and captions to the pictures myself."

Vic's favourite of his 19 goals in the promotion campaign? "It was a header I scored at Leyton Orient, from a cross by Muzzie, in our 4-1 win." Gregory in fact started the move with a throw-out to the wing.

As Hammers prepared for their first season back in the top flight since 1932, Keeble was confident the team would be more than capable of merely surviving among the big boys. A 2-1 opening day win at Portsmouth, with Keeble and Dick both on the mark, proved a foretaste of what was to follow. Indeed, four wins in the first six matches cemented Irons' place in the top half of the first division table and laid the firm foundation to achieve a very creditable sixth place at the end of 1958-59. Despite the step up in class, Dick (27) and Keeble (20) amassed 47 league goals between them.

Like the majority of observers, Vic admits he did not fully appreciate the significance of Bobby Moore's debut against Manchester United on September 8, 1958. "It was just a question of whether Malcolm Allison was fit enough to play or young Bobby came in for him. You didn't think much of it at the time," he recalled.

The phenomenal Dick/Keeble partnership was broken up for the first time at the start of March '59, when Vic damaged a cartilage and had to limp off on the day

Johnny hit a hat-trick in a 3-0 home win over West Bromwich Albion. He aggravated the knee a month later in an abortive comeback bid at Leicester and had to sit out the rest of the season as John Bond successfully moved up front and young Joe Kirkup came into the right-back spot.

"I tried another comeback on the summer tour of Germany but I was still hobbling about and Bondy went mad at Ted for even thinking about playing me."

Standing six-feet tall and weighing 11st 7lbs in his prime as a professional, Vic says he owed his natural strength to schoolboy rugby. "I wasn't a bad stand-off half and it taught me how to take knocks and how to give 'em back."

He needed to be powerful, too, to withstand the no-nonsense treatment dished out by the centre-halves of his day. "Maurice Norman of Tottenham was the hardest I came across," he said.

Keeble recalls one hectic Saturday in his early youth that typified his thirst for sporting competition: "I played rugby for my grammar school in the morning, then cycled to Castle Point in the centre of Colchester to play for King George V Boys' Club in an Essex football five-a-side tournament. From there I cycled 10 minutes to Lands Lane, where I played for Colchester Casuals against Lakenheath. I went home for my tea and then went out again that evening to play table tennis for Colchester against Chelmsford. I didn't think anything of it."

However, maybe all the intense activity eventually took its toll on Keeble ailing back. He played only 15 games, scoring six times, in 1959-60 and never appeared for the first team again after the visit to Leeds United on January 16, 1960. The club signed Dave Dunmore as his replacement in the No.9 shirt, in a swap deal that took John Smith to Spurs, as Keeble had to accept that his illustrious goalscoring days had come to a premature end.

Summing up his own attributes as a player and the reasons why he was forced to quit at the age of just 29, Vic says: ''I was pretty good at heading the ball – I thought I was the best header of a ball there was at the time – and I'd say I was also good for other players around me. I'd tell them when to hold the ball and went to release it – I was a good general for them.

"But I swear I wasn't as good at West Ham as I'd been at Newcastle, because I suffered a lot of back trouble. I had a collapsed disc, which originated in my playing days at Colchester. It 'went' again once at Newcastle and when I left West Ham in the summer of 1960 I went home and I literally couldn't move.

"I was put into plaster from my neck to my waist and spent about six months flat on my back. My back righted itself – touch wood – but I knew I wouldn't be able to play football again.

"West Ham weren't really all that good to me about it – only Noel Cantwell, Malcolm Allison, Bondy and Jacko came to see me. Ted Fenton never came to my house to see if I was recovering and despite talk of the club giving me a benefit game, it never materialised. But that was how it was in those days. If you weren't on the retained list, you were out. It was so impersonal back then.

"My back didn't get much better. I couldn't run properly, so I had to find something else to do. I was lucky that a job came up at the Essex Chronicle newspaper group, where I wrote a column on Colchester United for the *Colchester*

Vic pictured when EX interviewed him at his Earls Colne, Essex home in January 2004.

Express. I was also involved in advertising and circulation and spent five or six years with the paper."

From writing about the U's, Vic returned to Colchester United in the capacity of commercial manager, initially with the supporters' club. "I had six or seven good years there, we went from strength to strength and I earned more money then than I did in my playing career," said Vic on returning to the club where it all began for him as a young apprentice in 1948, the year of the club's famous FA Cup run to the fifth round.

"After six or seven years back at Colchester, I moved on to a similar role – this time as secretary and commercial manager – at Chelmsford City, where it was a struggle for the club to make ends meet."

Although now retired, Vic does "a little bit of driving" to earn a few bob for himself. He keeps fit and active by taking Maggie, his German Shepherd, for long daily walks around their home village of Earls Colne.

Vic was also known for his penchant for sports cars . . . and casual footwear.

"Oh yes, everybody used to laugh at me when I'd arrive for training in my carpet slippers. I wore them because it made driving more comfortable.

"I used to pick Geoff Hurst up every day for several months when he was a youngster. Our Grange Farm training ground was a hell of a place to get to from Chelmsford, where Hurstie used to live. His dad, Charlie, played for Chelmsford City and I used to pick up Hurstie in my Austin Healey Sprite, at the flyover by the Britvic pub.

"I loved sports cars – I suppose I was a bit flash! Of course, all the cars were on HP – no one owned them outright. Except Kenny Tucker, who had shops in Barking Road and could afford the best.

"Tucker used to wind all the lads up with his money. He'd bring a great, big wad of notes into the dressing room before training and, with the rest of us looking on enviously, he'd ask the trainer to look after his cash for him."

Sadly, shortly after *EX* visited Vic to carry out this interview, he was stunned by the death of Carole, his second wife of 26 years, due to cancer.

But Vic Keeble, now 77-years-old, can reflect happily on his days as a West Ham star, the man who was the catalyst for the club's return to the elite almost half a century ago.

"I thoroughly enjoyed my time as a player at West Ham. I was much more content there than I had been at Newcastle," he said.

Chapter 3

RONNIE**BOYCE**

"I always had a fear of failure and was a bundle of nerves before every game. I'm a natural worrier anyway – I inherited that from my mum – and it was just how I was"

AS the editorial plans were drawn up for a special edition of *EX* to commemorate the 40th anniversary of the first major honour in West Ham United's history, there was really only one man we could consider when it came to lining up our main exclusive feature.

Ronnie Boyce is Hammers' original Cup final hero, the man whose injury-time headed winner against Preston North End at Wembley on May 2, 1964 brought the FA Cup to Upton Park for the first time.

A local lad who grew up close to the Boleyn Ground in East Ham and followed the Irons as a young fan in the 50s, the classy midfielder was just 21-years-old when he became the toast of East London.

Having already gained most headlines with a double strike in the magnificent semi-final win over mighty Manchester United at Hillsborough a few weeks earlier, Ron went one better by grabbing the clincher in a thrilling 3-2 victory beneath the Twin Towers.

After goals from John Sissons and Geoff Hurst had twice pegged Preston back either side of the break, Boyce famously latched on to Peter Brabrook's inch-perfect right-wing cross in the dying moments and planted a firm header past goalkeeper Alan Kelly and into the bottom corner of the net, to send the claret-and-blue half of Wembley wild with delight.

And four decades on, the man who went on to become one of the club's longest-serving and most loyal members of staff was only too happy to co-operate when we requested an opportunity to sit down and gather his own personal memories of his finest hour.

We arrive at the six-acre farm in deepest Norfolk, where Ron and his wife Dawn (together with eldest son, Gary, his wife Claire and their three children Holly, Esta and Jack) – are in the process of converting the property into two separate family homes and a holiday guest-house.

After giving us a guided tour of this lovely place, Ron seems almost almost surprised that we should even be interested in talking to him about a game of football almost half a century ago.

As one of the select band of players who have guaranteed themselves a place in football's hall of fame by scoring the winning goal in an FA Cup final, you might

Ronnie Boyce, supported in attack by Johnny Byrne, scoring Hammers' third goal against Stoke City in March 1964 – a good year for Ron for various reasons.

think that Ron would be able to call upon an almost photographic recollection of his big day, or a well-rehearsed script full of anecdotes and tales slightly exaggerated after years of after-dinner speaking and countless conversations with starry-eyed fans.

Far from it. When asked if he keeps any memorabilia from the final, Ron mutters something about possibly "having a few bits," before Dawn disappears into a spare room and returns with the actual number eight shirt he wore that day . . . and the Cup winners' medal itself!

"Oh, I knew they were around here somewhere," he says with endearing modesty. And not surprisingly, Ron is just as humble when coaxed into talking about the day he made match-winning history for West Ham United.

The passing years may have dimmed the memory somewhat but, with the help of several informative prompts from Dawn – who can recall the facts of her husband's early career more clearly than he can! – there is a twinkle in Ron's eyes as he casts his mind back to that momentous May-day weekend.

"It's surprising, I look back and it was probably the most important game of my career – the one I'm remembered for more than any other. But, other than my goal, I really can't recall too much about it!" he laughs.

"Maybe it's because we went on to play in another cup final the following year? People ask you questions and you have to start thinking about which was which, you know, who played in one and who played in the other.

"I didn't feel I had a particularly good game in '64 but I happened to be in the right place at the right time with just a few minutes left. It was getting a bit desperate and

Cup winner: Ronnie starts his famous run around the net after scoring very late in the 1964 FA Cup final.

everyone was tired. I think it was Geoff (Hurst) who managed to get a move going before pushing the ball out wide to Peter (Brabrook).

"He put in a terrific cross from the right and the thing that always sticks in my mind is that, when I headed the ball, I could see it going in, yet it seemed like an eternity before there was any reaction from the crowd.

"I knew for sure the keeper had no chance of getting to it but it just seemed like time stood still for a few seconds, and the crowd erupted. The noise hits you and everything else happened so fast.

"I ran round the back of the goal – people say I was one of the first to celebrate scoring in that way – but it wasn't a planned celebration. It was just momentum that took me behind the goal.

"Funnily enough, I was visiting my younger son, Tony, recently and he had been watching a video of the game. He said to me: 'Dad, you don't half look funny' because I sort of skipped round the net after scoring!

"Other than that, I can't remember much else about it – I don't even recall if it was the West Ham fans who were at that end of the ground when I scored. In those days most of the supporters wore a shirt and tie, not the club colours, so there wouldn't have been as much colour in the stadium as there is now.

"I also remember Preston winning a free-kick just outside our box a minute or so after I had scored the winner, and I was thinking: 'Don't let this go to extra-time!'"

Thankfully, Hammers – led by the imperious Bobby Moore, who was about to lift the first of three trophies in successive years – held on for their first major triumph under manager Ron Greenwood.

Ronnie and Eddie Bovington hold the Cup after victory over Preston. Others in view on the lap of honour are (left to right) Johnny Byrne, Jack Burkett, Jim Standen, John Sissons, Ken Brown and Geoff Hurst.

While the Saturday night celebrations may have been somewhat blurred by the champagne and beer that flowed freely, Ron admits the scenes that followed the next morning, when the victorious Hammers paraded the cup through the streets of the East End, remain much more vivid.

"The celebrations afterwards were great. We had a brilliant reception at the Hilton, then we went to some nightclub that Budgie (Byrne) had recommended," he recalls.

"Nothing could beat the following day, though, when we took the cup back to the town hall on an open-top bus. It's funny, I remember coming down past Aldgate and at that point there was just a sprinkling of people waving to us. I was thinking: 'Blimey, this is gonna be a wash-out!'

"But as soon as we got to Stratford, it all started. We went past the Black Lion (pub) at Plaistow and the people outside there handed us a crate of lagers. People were kissing me on the forehead and the atmosphere when we got to the town hall was tremendous. The whole thing was unbelievable, such a wonderful experience.

"Soon afterwards, I passed my driving test and then married Dawn in the summer, so 1964 was quite an eventful year for me one way or another!"

At this point, Dawn once again helpfully interjects to remind Ron that he actually passed his driving test a year later, in 1965, a few weeks after the birth of their first son, Gary.

A puzzled Ron turns to his wife: "Really? Are you sure? I've always told people that three great things happened to me in 1964 – I scored the winning goal in the cup final, passed my driving test and then married you . . . in that order!"

One of the nicest and most unassuming people you could wish to meet, Ron has certainly never let his professional achievements diminish his down-to-earth character, and he insists that scoring the winner in an FA Cup final wasn't the life-changing experience it would be nowadays.

"For me, nothing changed," he shrugs. "I didn't notice anything different about the way people approached me, but then things were different in those days.

"We lived on the County Park Estate in Hornchurch, which wasn't as full of West Ham fans then as it is now. The likes of Martin, Hurstie, Dearie (Brian Dear) and Sisso (John Sissons) all lived there as well, although Dawn and I were the first couple to move on to the estate and the last to leave it!

"But we didn't enjoy the kind of attention and commercial spin-offs players enjoy now. We produced a book to commemorate our Wembley win that made us all a few bob. We sold some ties and did a milk advert straight after the game that showed us drinking it from the cup.

"That was it, though, and the players weren't given anything else in the way of bonuses or rewards. In fact, I ended up having a bit of a dispute with the club in the summer, when my contract was up for renewal. In those days, of course, there was no such thing as freedom of choice, so when your contract expired you just waited to see what the club would offer you the following year.

"You'd go up to the ground and there would usually be a long line of players waiting to go in to the manager's office, to find out what they were being offered, or whether

Although there were few Hammers' fans around Upton Park when the team returned to the Boleyn Ground on the same night they won the European Cup Winners' Cup, there were many thousands lining the streets of East London to cheer their claret-and-blue heroes on the day of the official civic reception.

Left: A ticket for the 1964 FA Cup final.
Right: How the front cover of the '64 final programme looked.

THE FOOTBALL ASSOCIATION CHALLENGE CUP COMPETITION

FINAL TIE

PRESTON
NORTH END   v   WEST HAM
UNITED

SATURDAY
MAY 2nd
1964

Kick-off
3 p.m.

WEMBLEY
OFFICIAL PROGRAMME . . . . . . ONE SHILLING

they were going to be released.

"I can remember being told that I would be kept on but I didn't sign the contract at first and Eddie Chapman, the secretary, put a bit in the local paper saying something along the lines of: 'Because he's scored the winner in the FA Cup final he thinks he's a lot better than everyone else.'

"I didn't take his comments badly – I was more embarrassed than anything else, so the first thing I did was get back down the ground and sign the new contract they had offered me! That was how things were then – clubs had all the power.

"I wasn't earning big money at the time, but it was certainly more than the average man on the street was getting paid and we had a comfortable lifestyle. I suppose it was in the £20-£30 a week mark, when a fiver a week would pay for bills, shopping, fags, everything we needed . . . with change left over. I remember Ernie Gregory moaning: 'The bloody money you lot are earning!'"

No-one could doubt that Ron and his team-mates earned their rewards. Having secured the club's first-ever involvement in European club competition with victory over Preston, Ron Greenwood's men really put the name of West Ham United on the global football map with a stylish victory in the European Cup Winners' Cup the following season.

That memorable 2-0 triumph over Germany's TSV Munich 1860 at Wembley, with 'Ticker' Boyce the heartbeat of a brilliant team performance, was the culmination of a memorable campaign that began with a slice of Boyce history. For in September 1964, Ron notched the only goal in Hammers' first round, first leg win against La Gantoise in Belgium, making him the first West Ham United player to score in European competition.

"Yeah, I remember it, a near-post header," he smiles. "We enjoyed the European trips because it was something new and the matches suited our style of play. I learned a great deal from the experience and it certainly improved me as a player.

"I would say that the second round game against Sparta Prague, in Czechoslovakia, was my best-ever performance for the club.

"Mooro was injured, so I was asked me to fill in for him at the back. I'd never played in that position before but Ron thought my reading of the game would stand me in good stead. Although we lost 2-1, I had the game of my life. We'd won the first leg 2-0, so went through on aggregate. It was a wonderful result for the club.

"Most people remember the final, though, and I would have to say that was the best game of football I ever played in. It was a great match between two teams who wanted to play the game the right way. Munich helped to make it such a great spectacle with the players they had, too.

"Personally, I wouldn't say it was one of my greatest performances, and it surprised me a bit to hear Brian Dear say that he thought I was our best player on the night. Again, I look back and can't really remember too much about what I did in that match.

"I made Alan Sealey's first goal but nothing else really sticks in my mind. It was just a superb all-round team performance.

"Afterwards, the scenes were nothing like what they were following the FA Cup final, though. We arrived back at Upton Park at about 2am and there was nobody around – it was like a ghost town. We just got off the coach and went home – as if we had returned home from an away league match. I suppose our supporters weren't around the ground because they were all still celebrating up West!"

For Ron, it was the ultimate reward for all the hard work he had put in since arriving at Upton Park as a hopeful schoolboy in 1957, when he first began to absorb the ideas that would shape his own playing style and lead to a long coaching career with West Ham.

However, he also admits to fighting a few psychological battles to overcome nervousness and lack of self-belief in order to succeed at the highest level.

"I first came to the club at the age of about 13," he remembers. "I was invited along by the chief scout, Wally St Pier, and began training on Tuesday and Thursday nights under the tunnel at Upton Park.

"Noel Cantwell and Malcolm Allison were our coaches and, although we didn't really have the facilities to do too much, the training was always enjoyable and everything was geared to improving your touch and fitness.

"In those days, you could leave school in the fourth year and, if you were at a football club, join their groundstaff. My mum wanted me to take my 'O' Levels, though, so I followed her wishes and stayed on for the fifth year to sit my exams.

"I remember being on holiday when mum sent me my results. I'd taken eight exams . . . and passed none! It was a wasted year at school, because I was always going to join West Ham. Although, saying that, I never saw myself as being good enough to become a professional footballer. In fact, it's fair to say I never saw myself as being successful at anything!

"I always had a fear of failure and was a bundle of nerves before every game. My routine before home matches was to eat a piece of boiled fish at midday round at Dawn's mum's house in East Ham, then I would walk to the ground and get there for about quarter-to-one.

"I suppose it was just the fear of putting in a poor performance that made me so nervous before a game. I'm a natural worrier anyway – I inherited that from my mum – and it was just how I was.

"If I hadn't been nervous or uptight, I probably wouldn't have performed as well as I did. Some players liked to be relaxed before the match, but not me."

Ironically, Ron made his first team debut against Preston North End, as a raw 17-year-old on October 22, 1960, in what turned out to be manager Ted Fenton's final season in charge of the club.

"I'd played as a 16-year-old against Millwall the previous year in the Southern Floodlit Cup, so I had that experience of senior football.

"I don't remember too much about my debut against Preston, except that we won 5-1 and Malcolm Musgrove scored a hat-trick. Then the next game I played, a few months later at Leicester, we lost 5-1!"

Welcome to the rollercoaster ride that is West Ham United!

"Being so young, I wasn't considered ready for regular first team football and I played just a handful of matches over the next couple of years. I only got my opportunity after Phil Woosnam was sold to Aston Villa."

That was in November 1962, by which time Greenwood was firmly settled in the Upton Park hotseat. The first 'outsider' in West Ham's managerial history had no qualms about handing the Welshman's creative midfield role to young Boyce, who took his chance with both hands.

"Ted Fenton was a lovely man but not really what you would describe as a coach," says Ronnie. "Ernie Gregory always said that Ted would have made the best chief scout ever, because he brought some magnificent players to the club.

"Then Ron came in and it was a complete change. He was a training ground manager, a teacher of the game, and once you took part in a training session under him it opened your eyes.

"He was very good at putting his ideas across and explaining the reasons behind them. People said that his man-management could be a bit suspect sometimes but I never had any problems with him. I always thought he was good for making players feel confident by the way he spoke to you about the game.

"If you listened to what he said, you couldn't fail to agree with his views on football. He had such a great knowledge and I always found it very easy to understand what he was trying to get across."

After starring in the trophy-winning seasons of 1963-64 and 1964-65, Ron was dealt a frustrating blow the following year when a troublesome back injury, sustained during a round of golf, restricted him to just 16 league appearances and ruled him out of the majority of the European Cup Winners' Cup campaign that saw Hammers, as holders, make it to the semi-finals, where they lost to Borussia Dortmund.

"I missed quite a lot of that season due to the back injury. We had played an evening game on a Monday night and, the following day, I went for a game of golf. The next morning, I woke up and could hardly move. I was literally twisted up in pain and it turned out I had a back spasm that developed into a disc problem. It took a few months to get it right again and Bill Jenkins, our physio, had me doing all sorts to try and fix it.

"I remember he told me to open up the loft hatch at home, rest a pick-axe handle across the hatch and then hang from it with both hands while Dawn grabbed my legs and stretched me downwards, in order to straighten my spine!

"Although my back injury was eventually cured and I returned to the first team, it was a problem that has caused me some discomfort in later life. I had to have a hip replacement a few years ago.

"Thankfully, though, that was the most serious injury I encountered. I had my fair share of niggly problems, muscle strains and cuts to the head, that sort of thing, but nothing to keep me out for longer than a few games."

And had it not been for the injury that virtually wrote off his season in 1965-66, who knows what Ron might have achieved that year?

Had he continued the rate of progress that led to him being named man-of-the-match against TSV Munich at Wembley in 1965, in what many consider to be the greatest West Ham match ever played, it's fair to suggest that Ron may have been in

Two-goal hero Alan Sealey and Ronnie lead the celebrations after the classic victory over TSV Munich.

the running for an England call-up prior to the 1966 World Cup.

As modest as ever, though, 'Boycie' refuses to entertain such a notion and insists he was just happy to share in the success that surrounded Upton Park in the swinging mid-60s.

"We had three good years, '64, '65 and '66, when we also reached the League Cup final and the semi-final of the European Cup Winners' Cup. And of course Mooro, Geoff and Martin won the World Cup with England.

"I don't remember wondering what it would have been like to have been be part of that England success. It was just great for the three lads who were involved – I didn't really have any ambitions of playing for England myself. I was on the bench for the under-23 side against Turkey but that was the closest I ever got. I've always said I got half a cap!"

After recovering from his back problem, Ron returned to become a first team regular again in the late 60s but, with a new era dawning under Greenwood at the turn of the 70s that saw several new signings try – and fail – to replicate the success of their predecessors, he became more of a fringe player.

He admitted: "I lacked pace, which didn't help, and I had a few injuries, so I could understand why I was playing less. The game got quicker, and that might have caught up with me a bit, but I was just happy to be at the club and earning money.

"I wasn't the type to go knocking on the manager's door and demanding to play – that just wasn't me."

There was still time for one more act of glory, though, and what a moment. When Hammers travelled to Manchester City for a first division fixture on March 21, 1970, new signing Jimmy Greaves was the centre of attention following his switch from Tottenham Hotspur that had seen Martin Peters head in the opposite direction.

However, despite grabbing a brace on his debut in a claret-and-blue shirt, Greavsie was upstaged by Ronnie, who struck an amazing wonder goal that any self-respecting Hammers fan over the age of 40 will remember instantly.

His reflex volley, following City keeper Joe Corrigan's drop-kick to the halfway line, is a strike that will forever be remembered by anyone lucky enough to be at Maine Road that rainy day, or who marvelled at it later that evening while watching the televised highlights on *Match of the Day*. Ron admits his long-range goal is normally the second subject raised in conversation with Hammers fans after his winner in '64.

"It was certainly a unique goal and the funny thing is that Hurstie saw Joe Corrigan a few weeks after the match and was giving him a bit of stick about my goal. Joe said to him: 'What I couldn't fathom was why there were two balls on the pitch'. He'd kicked one and thought another had been thrown in to his net!

"It was just one of those opportunities that pop up very rarely. As the ball dropped to me, I could see Joe facing the other way and I just had a go for it. I definitely meant to score, though," Boycie insists.

"For years afterwards, whenever we went to Maine Road, the old groundsman used to shout: 'Here he is!' and mark out the spot on the pitch from where I'd scored my goal!"

A sprinkling of appearances followed in the next couple of years, before Ron

Ronnie pictured at home in May 2004 with the original shirt he wore in the 1964 FA Cup final.

stepped down to reserve team football and then, in 1975, began a long and successful coaching career.

But just who was it that thought up his nickname of 'Ticker?'

"I honestly don't know where it came from," says a fairly bemused Ron. "I think it was a press thing – Ron Greenwood might have said something about me being the heartbeat of the team, and there may have been a 'Ticker' headline somewhere after that, but I'm not sure.

"I suppose it was an apt nickname for me, though. I made a living out of playing one and two-touch football. I had strengths in as much as I could anticipate well and read the game – and I learned that just from playing in the holding role Ron wanted me to play."

To suggest that he made a living from the game just by playing one and two-touch football is of course under-valuing and over-simplifying the enormous contribution made by Ronnie Boyce during his 15 years as a professional at West Ham. But you won't hear this humble man claiming to be anything other than a lucky guy who just felt honoured to wear the Hammers shirt.

He may be best know for his contribution to our 1964 FA Cup victory but Ronnie revealed to *EX* the little-known secret of his link to the 1923 White Horse Final at Wembley.

Born and bred in East Ham, it isn't surprising to know that Ron grew up in a Hammers-supporting family, but his connection with the club goes much deeper.

"My family were always West Ham fans and my grandfather, Amos, was actually a turnstile operator at the first-ever FA Cup final at Wembley in 1923," reveals Ron.

"He always used to tell me the story about how he had one of those old market pouches stuffed full of money, but he couldn't get into the ground because there were just too many people already inside – so he didn't see the game.

"My grandfather was a West Ham fan through and through. In fact he worked for Thames Ironworks and purchased two shares in West Ham United back in the 1920s. They were handed down to my dad and now I've got them.

"My dad, Bill, was also invited to a trial at West Ham but it was back in the days when it was much more important to get a trade or a steady job first."

Ronnie Boyce, now 64, left Upton Park in unhappy circumstances in 1995, when he received a derisory pay-off from the club that treated him shabbily after all the loyal and distinguished service he had given them over the previous 35 years and more.

He stayed in the game through various scouting jobs before heading to Tottenham Hotspur as chief scout under manager George Graham and then Glenn Hoddle. He left White Hart Lane in the summer of 2003 and, along with his family, is now fully devoted to running their six-acre farm, near Fakenham in Norfolk.

"It's a lovely, peaceful area and the local people are very friendly. There are a few Hammers fans out this way, too!"

Chapter 4

EDDIE**BOVINGTON**

"I finished Bryan Douglas as a player when I tackled him from behind and he tore his cruciate knee ligaments. He did play again but he was never the same player. I regret it. It wasn't right and I'm not proud of it. Doing something like that to a fellow pro is nothing to be proud of"

WHEN Eddie Bovington got the call from manager Ron Greenwood to return to the side for the visit to Blackburn Rovers in December 1963, it was a change that would alter the course of Hammers history as well as reignite the tough-tackling midfielder's ailing career under a manager with whom he admits he never saw eye to eye.

Hammers had been battered 8-2 by Blackburn at Upton Park on Boxing Day, '63, but Greenwood made only one change to his side for the return clash at Ewood Park just two days later.

Out went promising right-half Martin Peters. In came the much more robust Bovington.

Greenwood made it plain to the Edmonton-born youngster exactly what he expected from him. He wanted him to stop the threat of Bryan Douglas.

The cultured inside-left had orchestrated Rovers' romp at the Boleyn but, tightly man-marked by Bovington, he didn't get a kick in Lancashire as West Ham claimed an unlikely 3-1 away win that altered the course of their season.

Bovington, who had made his debut in a 5-3 defeat against Manchester United at Old Trafford on Easter Monday, 1960, kept his place for the rest of that season. Four league wins in their next six matches lifted Hammers to mid-table but, more significantly, they were on their way to their first FA Cup final success.

Bovington is the first to admit that he was not a typical West Ham player in the mould of Bobby Moore, Peters and Johnny Byrne. He was a ball-winning grafter, a good, honest pro who did his job simply and effectively. When Greenwood reluctantly compromised his skillful footballing philosophies to add reinforced steel to his midfield, Eddie was the enforcer he turned to. And it worked a treat.

For the first three-quarters of the 1964-65 season, Eddie's no-thrills approach earned him ever-present status while the creative Peters could only get in the side as an adventurous left-back. But, with the European Cup Winners' Cup final only eight weeks away, unlucky Eddie suffered a broken kneecap in a home game against Sunderland and had to sit out the epic Wembley showpiece against TSV Munich 1860. It was Peters' turn to sip champagne that night.

He recovered to start the following season but with Peters destined for World Cup glory in '66, Eddie could never re-establish himself in the No.4 shirt and from then

The Smiling Assassin! Eddie did an important job at the heart of midfield.

on he had to be content with sporadic appearances.

Now 66-years-old and living in comfort at his lovely home in leafy Epping, Essex, Eddie reflects with mixed feelings on his decade at West Ham, his only professional club before he quit league football at the young age of 28 to manage his father-in-law's retail clothing business.

Looking back on the turning point of his career, he said: "It wasn't Martin Peters' fault that we were slaughtered 8-2 by Blackburn and, to be honest, I didn't expect to play up at Blackburn two days later. But his misfortune was my good luck.

"As Bryan Douglas told me after the game, I didn't let him have a kick of the ball . . . although I still didn't expect to play against Charlton in the third round of the FA Cup the following week. But we put a few good results together and I suppose Greenwood felt that he couldn't really change a winning team."

Eddie's apparent lack of faith in himself and the willingness of Greenwood to pick him regularly is a recurring theme throughout this interview.

"I wasn't sure I'd play in the FA Cup final at Wembley," he admitted. "There was a long time – some six weeks – between us beating Man United in the semi-final and the final against Preston, so it only needed a few bad defeats in that period for Ron to want to change the side. Anything can happen in football.

"I remember being badly beaten at Everton in the final league match of the season, when Roy Vernon was putting it about a bit until John Bond reminded him that we had a Cup final to come and that we weren't going to risk injuries! I think we were a bit half-hearted that day, to be honest.

"Ron announced the Cup final side just before we played in John Lyall's testimonial at Upton Park on the Monday before Wembley, and I was obviously relieved and delighted to keep my place."

Eddie admits that a lack of self-confidence might have held him back at times.

He says: "Once you know you are playing in the side on merit, and not because of injury to others, you feel much more comfortable and confident in yourself. I got to the stage that season where I felt that if I had played well, I *would* be in the side again the following week.

"Until I got injured in March '65, I played every game of 1964-65 and enjoyed the best period of my career," he recalled.

While his team-mates were away in Lausanne, playing the quarter-final of the ECWC, Eddie was stood on the steps of the London Hospital, his knee in plaster, awaiting a lift to take him home. "I had to ring the ground because there was no-one around to collect me – they were all in Switzerland!

"I was fit enough to play in the European final but because I hadn't appeared in any league games since my injury, I knew I wouldn't play at Wembley. Martin moved to right-half, which opened the way for Jackie Burkett at left-back.

"I didn't find it particularly hard to watch the final from the Wembley stands, because I felt I'd played my part in helping the team to get there. It was a great final between two very good sides."

Having fully recovered from his serious knee injury to play in 44 league and cup games in 1965-66, including a rare headed goal against Cardiff City in the League Cup semi-final, Eddie appeared 34 times the following campaign before seeing his first team involvement restricted to just six outings in 1967-68. His relationship with Greenwood, never harmonious, deteriorated further as he declined a move that the West Ham boss hoped would generate funds for him to strengthen the team.

"Ron wanted to get some money in and he agreed a £25,000 fee with Fulham for me to go there. Jack Burkett was also offered for sale and eventually went to Charlton. I spoke to Fulham, then managed by Bobby Robson, but the deal wasn't right for me. I was being offered £10 a week less than the £50 I was on at West Ham, with no signing-on fee, so I turned it down and decided to stay put. Ron didn't like it.

"By then I was also working part-time in the afternoons in my father-in-law's clothing business – he had shops at Wood Green and Archway – which I saw as my long-term future.

"Ron phoned me and wanted to know why I hadn't made the move to Fulham, so I explained the situation to him. I had two years left on my West Ham contract and I would have been crazy to have left to take a 20 percent cut in my weekly pay.

"Like most of us at the time, I had gone in to see Greenwood for more money after the European final win when, in agreeing to sign a new two-year deal plus a two-year option, my money went up from £30 to £50 a week. I bit his hand off at the offer because it was a lot of money then. We also got an extra tenner a week first team appearance money, plus bonuses for progress in Europe. It gave me a good standard of living.

"My relationship with Greenwood was never good, we just failed to click from the time he arrived. I had signed pro a year before he became manager and was earning £14 per week. He offered me £16 but I said 'no' and asked for £20. I trained hard in pre-season and then Ron agreed to pay me what I had asked for, but I don't think he liked a young whippersnapper standing up to him. I wasn't prepared to be dictated to, though, if I felt I was worth more than I was getting.

"Ron put me on the transfer list in '67, and there was talk that I might move to Blackpool or Northampton, while Rotherham was also mentioned. But once he knew I wasn't going anywhere, he recognised that I had trained hard – I always loved training – and accepted I might as well stay at West Ham as cover for Martin and Bobby Moore. It didn't suit me but I had to face facts.

"Being brutally honest – and you should always hold up your hand and be truthful with yourself – Ron couldn't possibly value me as highly as Martin or Bobby, could he? That was fair enough."

Eddie pointed to the 1965-66 League Cup competition to further underline his perceived low rating in Greenwood's eyes. He said: "I played in every game of each round up to the final, scoring in the first leg of the semi against Cardiff. But he dropped me for the first leg of the final, at home to West Brom. I came back in for the second leg but I couldn't understand why he'd left me out of the game at Upton Park.

"I don't think our personality clash was the reason he decided not pick me, though. I believe he left me out because he just didn't think I was good enough. He never told me that was the case, but that's how I saw it anyway.

"I remember playing well in the first match of the 1967-68 season, at home to

Liverpool's Roger Hunt loses his balance as Eddie nips in to snuff out the danger, watched by Ken Brown.

Sheffield Wednesday, which we lost 3-2. It wasn't my fault we were beaten – Bobby Ferguson was responsible for two of the goals on his debut – but I was the only one dropped for the next game, against Burnley at Upton Park. So I told Ron what I thought, which only soured things between us even more.

"He dropped me again but said I'd be brought back the following week, but how could he promise that? If the team won their next match, as they did, he couldn't then change it again, could he?

"That's where I wished Ron had been more straightforward and not pussyfooted around. It's best to be honest with people, even if they don't want to hear what you've got to say. At least that way everybody knows where they stand.

"It's like Simon Cowell on *Pop Idol*. It's no good him telling some silly bird, who can't sing, that she's hasn't done too badly. It's pointless for all concerned. But a lot of managers are frightened to tell their players that they're not up to it.

"That injury in '65 was definitely the defining moment of my career, though, because I had established myself as a regular before it happened."

Despite his 'hard man' tag, Eddie could also play a bit himself and he regards a comparison with his right-half predecessor, Andy Malcolm, as a compliment. "I don't think Ron liked the way Andy played either – he preferred Martin Peters – but it's nice if one player's style can complement another.

"Andy was a nice man and a good player. He used to mark the likes of Johnny Haynes, Jimmy Greaves and Denis Law, who I later man-marked as well. But Andy was skillful, too."

Eddie is honesty personified as he reflects on his ball-winning role in a West Ham side otherwise brimming with more naturally gifted players.

"I wouldn't say I was skillful but my main asset was that I was prepared to give

Happy Hammers in the summer of 1964. Bobby Moore, Eddie Bovington (Mooro and Bov were often room-mates on away trips), John Bond, Peter Brabrook and Tony Scott relax in front of a cricket sightscreen at the club's Chadwell Heath training ground.

100 percent *all* the time," he admits. "It's no good kidding yourself you're a Stanley Matthews when you're not! My job was to win the ball and give it to players who could use it to the best possible effect. Having good players around me, like Budgie Byrne, helped me – there's no doubt about it."

Who were Eddie's most difficult opponents, the inside-forwards who caused him most problems?

"I had to try and mark Dennis Violet at Man United on my debut and he was very quick. John White and Greavsie of Spurs were good, too. Jim was hard to mark, you always had to be on your toes against him. Today you'd struggle to pick out even a few good, creative players but back then there was a lot of good ones around. The likes of Haynesy, Ian St. John . . . they were so quick and really made you think.

"But the best I played against was George Eastham of Stoke. In one game against them at Upton Park, we were 3-0 up at half-time and thought we were cruising. I hadn't given George a kick but I couldn't get near him in the second half and it was largely my fault that we lost 4-3. I had stopped doing what I had been doing well in the first half and George caused us loads of problems."

Although Eddie is proud to have played in Hammers' first FA Cup-winning team, he took more personal satisfaction from his performance in the semi-final victory over Manchester United at rain-soaked Hillsborough.

"I had to mark Bobby Charlton," he recalls. "United were odds-on to win at Sheffield and it was unbelievable that we beat them. They were so cocky before the game and I can remember Bestie and one or two others in the United side chatting-up the Dagenham Girl Pipers as we were lining up in the tunnel before going out onto the pitch."

With no prospect of winning back a regular first team place at Upton Park, Eddie considered, and then ruled out, a move to lower league Colchester United, and one or two non-league options, before turning his back on the professional game a few weeks after his 28th birthday, in May 1969.

West Ham offered him a free transfer but he was learning his business in the clothing trade and quickly identified where his future lay.

Eddie's only football involvement after leaving West Ham was back with his old Sunday morning club, Park United, in the Edmonton District League. "I paid five bob subs a week and it was great fun being back with the same fellas I'd played with as a 14 or 15-year-old kid before I joined West Ham.

"Later on, I also played for a Polish ex-pats team at Wandsworth – I can't recall the name of the team but they paid me eight pounds a game. They sent the money to me in the post each Friday. That was okay until a team-mate accidentally kicked me in the ankle and damaged my ligaments!

"I didn't become disillusioned with the game. I loved football but I knew that after leaving West Ham there was only one way I could go. I was lucky I had the clothing business to go into full-time, so I didn't have to scrape a living from the game playing out my last days in the lower divisions. I don't regret that decision because I wasn't going to be joining Manchester United or any other club as a top player. Nobody of any note wanted me.

"Having said what I have about my time at West Ham, I still maintain they are one of the best clubs a young player can go to. The opportunities and the way the young players were looked after, it was a good place to be at."

Eddie remembers with affection his early days on the Boleyn groundstaff. "Fun days," he enthuses, "when Mooro, Hurstie, Harry Cripps, Jackie Burkett and the rest of us used to sweep the terraces and under the stands after training. There were so many old fag butts discarded under the Chicken Run, it's a wonder it never went up in flames. It used to smoulder underneath there!

"It was good experience and, after all, it wasn't really working, was it? My mates were all earning two pounds and 10 shillings a week as apprentices, while I was getting six quid – a fortune back then. We used to have a real laugh.

"Although I've moaned about some aspects of West Ham, it was still the best time of my life. We won things during the time I was there, the club's first successes for many years, and it was good to be part of it. The club won promotion from the second division in my first season there, which gave the whole place a boost.

"To be honest, living in North London, I was torn between Tottenham and Arsenal as a kid. My uncle took me to Highbury a few times and I'd often go to Spurs with my mates. I didn't even know where or who West Ham was – they were second division!"

Eddie first came to West Ham's attention when he attended a trial with his friend, Alan Durrant (who went on to play for Bristol Rovers) and then played against Fulham in an end-of-season South-East Counties League game before being invited back to train with the Hammers under the watchful eye of Malcolm Allison.

"We used to get on the coach to go to training at Grange Farm and I was in awe of the first team stars. Everyone loved Jackie Dick – a real gambler, who'd creep out the back door at the ground on a Friday to avoid the bookies he owed!

"When Vic Keeble arrived he was already a big star to us, having played in the Cup final for Newcastle. He had a sports car and wore smart jumpers like Andy Williams. He had such a casual way about him, nothing flustered him.

"And Noel Cantwell . . . he was a proper man.

"I think back to the gear we wore for training – big thick, dark grey rollneck jumpers that seemed to weigh four tonne. And you were lucky to be given a pair of tracksuit bottoms!

"I was a bit star-struck by the kids playing alongside me in the youth team because most of them were already England Schoolboy internationals – Mickey Brooks, Johnny Cartwright, or 'Didi' as we knew him, Andy Smillie and Derek Woodley. I felt like a fish out of water at first.

"After I got in the first team, my best friends at the club were Bobby Moore, Budgie, 'Sammy' Sealey and Peter Brabrook. We were always together and enjoyed a drink. Geoff, Martin and Ronnie Boyce liked to play cards. With a bunch of 15 players it's impossible to get on very well with everyone but, mostly, we all got on. There were never any rows or feuds.

"We were responsible with our drinking. I only drank once a week unless we were playing away and then we'd have a few light ales the night before a match. Greenwood didn't have a problem with us drinking. A few people abused it from time to time but, by and large, we were sensible. Besides, pubs shut early in those days and the latest you'd been in a club would be 1.00am.

"We travelled to all our away games by train. We'd be in the buffet car on the way home, enjoying a meal and a few beers, and the fans would sometimes mingle among us. I don't think Ron was comfortable with some of the fans who wanted to dominate the scene – and I made him right about that."

You wouldn't expect honest Eddie to be anything but forthright in his opinion of modern-day football. "I hardly ever bother to turn on the telly to watch football now," says 'Eddie the Bov', as he is affectionately known to his close friends.

"I sit up in the stand and see 20 players compressed into a 15-yard area, either side of the halfway line. Goalkeepers boot the ball the length of the pitch and they all fight for it. It's what I call 'fightball' – no-one wants to put their foot on the ball and slow the game down.

"Greenwood used to want our keeper to throw it out to one of our full-backs. He'd say: 'If we've got the ball, why punt it up in the air and give ourselves only a 50/50 chance of winning it?' *Why* do teams do that now?

"It's sounds like I'm jealous and embittered but that's not the case. I've been to West Ham as an occasional guest of Terry Connelly's in the last few years, but it just doesn't appeal to me much. Andy Gray and Richard Keys rave on about in on Sky but then they have to, otherwise people won't turn on to watch or subscribe to the channel.

"I don't know what it is but today's players have everything going for them. They are using a lighter ball than we played with, the pitches have no mud on them and are prepared like billiard tables. Perhaps the game's too fast?

"When you think back to what the forwards who played in my day had to put up with, when defenders were allowed to tackle from behind. I did it myself – it was the way the game was played then. Every team had it's ball-winner who would go through the back of players to try and get the ball. Looking back now, it was a terrible way to play.

"But I was never booked or sent-off once in my career. You had to break someone's leg to be sent-off!"

Again, with refreshing and candid introspection, Eddie reflects on a dark moment in his career he would much rather forget. When asked if he had ever badly hurt an opponent, he replied somewhat sombrely and without a trace of satisfaction: "I finished Bryan Douglas as a player when I tackled him from behind and he tore his cruciate knee ligaments," admitted Bov.

"Bryan did play again but he was never the same player. I regret it. It wasn't right and I'm not proud of it. Doing something like that to a fellow pro is nothing to be proud of.

"The worse thing about it is that Bryan was a class player and a very nice bloke.

"Yet despite the way we were allowed to tackle in those days, there are more injuries now than ever. Pitches are better than they've ever been but we keep seeing cruciate injuries. I think it might be down to the fact that players now wear blades instead of rounded screw-in studs. The blades seem to stick in the turf more, they don't turn with the movement of the foot.

"Players spend a lot of time stretching before a game but there are still a lot of muscle injuries. And yet we never warmed up the way they do now – we'd just go into the gym underneath the main stand, do a few stretches and kick a ball up against the wall.

"And today's players warm-up too early. They come out onto the pitch for 10 minutes, but then go back into the dressing room, sit down again and so all the work they've done is useless. I always hated coming back out again after the 10-minute half-time break. I'd rather have turned straight back round.

"At West Ham now they've got a sports scientist, physios and a couple of masseurs, so how did Rob Jenkins cope in his day?"

Despite selling Jays, the clothing retail business which he took over from his father-in-law in 1985, Eddie still works five days a week for a clothing manufacturer in Walthamstow, East London. He usually starts at around seven in the morning and works through to 5pm.

The walls of his stylishly furnished Epping home are neatly decorated with framed photographs of his family, his devoted late wife, Pauline, daughters Lorraine, Sue and grandchildren, James, Scott and Chelsey. There are also pictures of his playing days at West Ham. Eddie has kept cuttings and, with the help of his friend, *EX's* Terry Connelly, he now has an even more illustrative record of his time in the claret-and-blue.

What frustrates Eddie most of all now is that he can no longer enjoy his love of cross-country running which has kept him in remarkably good shape – a slender 10st 3lbs compared to his regular playing weight of 11-and-a-half stone – and also brought him a new sense of personal pride and satisfaction. The medals he won as

The B-team line-up at their FA Cup reunion dinner at Preston in May 2004. Left to right: Ronnie Boyce, Ken Brown, Eddie Bovington, John Bond and Peter Brabrook. Below: Later that same evening, 'Eddie the Bov' renewing acquaintance with Cup final opponent Nobby Lawton, the former Preston captain.

a cross-country runner for Woodford Green Athletics Club are testimony to his determination but, unfortunately, a knee problem has curtailed his running activities in recent years.

Chapter 5

MARTIN**PETERS** MBE

"People say I was upset because I was always regarded as the 'third one' of the West Ham World Cup-winning trio, but that was definitely never the case"

ITHOUGHT I'd timed my arrival at the Holiday Inn hotel, Brentwood to perfection, a bit like Martin Peters 'ghosting' into the opposition's penalty box. It was just a minute before midday, the agreed time of our meeting. Well, who could possibly be late for one of West Ham's three World Cup-winning legends.

But as I entered reception, the man himself was already there, halfway through dialling the *EX* magazine office number on his mobile to check on my whereabouts. I should have known he would be early . . . Martin Peters was famously described by Sir Alf Ramsey as being "10 years ahead of his time".

That enduring comment was made by the England manager after Peters had scored in a 1-1 draw against Scotland at Hampden Park in 1968 – one of his 67 full international caps – and Martin has only relatively recently come to accept it as a compliment from a man not renowned for showering his players with praise.

It was Ramsey, following some heavy prompting by West Ham manager Ron Greenwood, who catapulted Martin to fame and an everlasting place in sporting history by giving him his England debut against Yugoslavia at Wembley on May 4, 1966, just weeks before the World Cup finals started. Hardly a day goes by now without somebody reminding him of the glorious feats of that momentous day beneath the Twin Towers, when Peters and his Hammers club-mates, Bobby Moore and Geoff Hurst, became enshrined in football folklore.

Yes, that day when West Ham United won the World Cup!

Our meeting, not far from Martin's home at Shenfield, Essex, had to be slotted into a hectic schedule of England '66 reunion dinners and book shop signings following the recent publication of his autobiography, *The Ghost of '66*.

"I'm very busy right now but it's always a great pleasure to attend dinners with the other players from that World Cup team. We all try to keep in touch as much as possible and get together every year, although there is always a lot on in a World Cup year," he says.

"About nine years ago, Geoff and I started our own '66 reunion that is attended by the 10 surviving players from the team, plus a few other members of the squad, and their wives."

Martin and his team-mates must have relived their finest two hours a million times, so did anything 'new' ever come to mind amid all the talk and television programmes centred around English football's greatest day 41 years ago?

"Not really, but Geoff and George (Cohen) and I got together the other day and there was a screening of the actual game going on in the background. All of a sudden I'd see a certain bit of footage from the match and say something like: 'That wasn't too good, George'. He'd then say: 'That was a crap cross, Martin!'. And Geoff would add: 'Oh, I should have hit the target there', so we laugh about little things that happened."

One vivid memory Martin has, but one that is rarely spoken about when reflecting on '66 and all that, is of an incident that happened the day after the final. He explained: "My wife, Kathy, and I were being driven back from the ITV studios, where I'd been for an interview, when we were involved in a minor accident. A car whacked us from the back and although it was nothing major, the next day there was a newspaper headline: 'World Cup star in motor accident'.

"People ask me if my life changed after '66 and, of course, it did but not to a great degree. Bobby, Geoff and myself had three weeks off and then we were back training again with West Ham for the start of the new first division season.

"Bobby became more of an icon, because of the way he was and the way he was with Tina – they were the Beckhams of that era, although not living to the grandeur or earning the money that David and Victoria are now!"

Martin's 'reward' as one of the Hammers' holy trinity was a pay increase from his previous basic of £45 a week. He was just 22-years-old and admits: "I was young and very naive. I had a meeting with Ron and he said the club was prepared to offer me such and such. I can't remember exactly how much more he offered me – it could have been a rise to 60 or 70 quid a week – but the point is I would have taken it whatever it was.

"If I'd had the nerve and wherewithal when I got older, I would have been better off. I was just happy to be part and parcel of, firstly, West Ham United and, secondly, the England World Cup-winning team. To be earning £45 a week and then going into ask for, say, £145, was something I just wouldn't have done.

"We didn't have agents in those days and there was no-one around to advise me. Jack Turner, who helped a number of West Ham players to purchase houses, came along a bit later on. If I'd gone in and asked Ron for more money, I'm sure he would have done as much as he could without stretching the budget too far!

"Ron ran a fairly tight ship in those days, although in saying that I didn't personally worry about money too much.

"Our West Ham team-mates didn't treat us any differently after the World Cup. They were pleased for us, it reflected well on the club again off the back of winning the European Cup Winners' Cup and the FA Cup in the previous two years, as well as having reached the League Cup final in '66 and the semi-final of the ECWC again the same year. We did okay in cup competitions, but in the league . . . " his voice drifts away.

Hammers fans who were fortunate enough to witness the Moore-Hurst-Peters era of the 60s are still scratching their heads to this day trying to understand why a team so rich in world class talent never challenged for the league championship. In the seasons either side of the '66 World Cup Greenwood's team finished no higher than 12th (1965-66) and 16th – a mere seven points clear of the relegation zone

Above: Bill Lansdowne, Martin Peters and Eddie Bovington working with dumb bells as part of manager Ted Fenton's tough pre-season training regime at Grange Farm, Chigwell in August 1960.

Below: Listening intently to coach Albert Walker, secretary Eddie Chapman and chief scout Wally St Pier are the youths of 1960-61. Left to right: Brian Dear, John Charles, Mick Beesley, (Frank Caskey hidden), Eddie Presland, Ronnie Boyce, Dave Bickles, Derek Woodley, Roger Hugo, John Starkey, Martin Peters and Reggie Leseuf.

Above: Martin wearing the classic 60s home and away kits.
Left: A ticket for the 1965 European Cup Winners' Cup final.
Below (inset): How the front cover of the '65 ECWC final programme looked.
Below: Martin Peters and Alan Sealey turn away to celebrate Hammers' second goal in the Wembley final against TSV Munich.

(1966-67). The highest placing the Hammers achieved with its three most famous players in harmony was eighth, in both 1961-62 and 1968-69.

The period of his 11 years at West Ham that Peters recalls with most affection is the 1964-65 campaign that ended with that epic European final victory over TSV Munich 1860 at Wembley when, for many, the slender figure in the No.4 shirt was the most outstanding player on the field, which is saying something given the sheer quality on show (from both teams) that evening.

Martin admits he was "hurt" when he was made a scapegoat and dropped from the team that went on to defeat Preston North End in the previous season's FA Cup final. That day, as he walked forlornly back to the dressing room unable to fully share in the glory of the club's first major domestic cup success, having watched Eddie Bovington play instead of him, he received some consoling words of encouragement from Ron Greenwood: "You will play at Wembley more times than I have eaten in the stadium restaurant," the manager reassured him.

It was a prophetic statement but one that must have been of little comfort to Martin at the time. West Ham had been battered, 8-2, by Blackburn Rovers in East London on Boxing Day and yet, inexplicably, he was the only player Greenwood dropped from the team to face Rovers again at Ewood Park just two days later. This time, with Eddie Bovington coming in at right-half, West Ham snuffed out Blackburn's best player, Bryan Douglas, and won 3-1. 'Bov' kept his place in the side and although they could still not finish any higher than 14th in the league, West Ham won the Cup without Peters, who played no part in the competition.

"I was also left out of the first five games of the following season," he points out ruefully, before highlighting his supreme versatility. "When I did start, it was at centre-half, alongside Bobby. I played a couple of games there as Ken Brown's replacement and then at left-back against La Gantoise in the ECWC. In the home leg I scored an own goal!" he recalled with less satisfaction.

When Moore was secretly receiving treatment for testicular cancer that winter, Peters then switched to left-half as cover for the stricken skipper, including both legs of the European tie with Sparta Prague. For the quarter-final against Lausanne, Peters found himself reverting to left-back as a replacement for the injured Jack Burkett. It wasn't until the more combative Bovington injured his knee in March '65 that Peters reclaimed his favoured No.4 shirt, operating in the heart of midfield in both semi-final matches against Real Zaragoza and the final against Munich.

He came very close to scoring West Ham's second against the Germans at Wembley, before Alan Sealey netted his second. Peters and Ronnie Boyce controlled the game from midfield. Both were outstanding, although Martin says modestly: "I remember it as Alan Sealey's final. He was pretty quick early on down the wing and Sammy's first goal was a great one. His second was lucky – from a freekick we'd worked out. Mooro knocked it over, it came between Alan and somebody else and just hit me on the leg. It rebounded kindly for him to slot in.

"It was a brilliant night for me, but not performance-wise. One game in which I thought I played really well was against West Bromwich Albion on Good Friday, 1965. I scored our first goal and knocked a couple in for Brian Dear . . . but Brian

His most famous goal . . . Martin scoring England's second in the 1966 World Cup final.

scored five that day in 20 minutes!

"It was great to go back to Wembley in '65 and actually play in the final, having missed out there the previous year when substitutes weren't allowed. I was moaning about being left out of the side in '64 but, looking back now, I was only a 20, a kid, although a lot of things had happened to me by then. I'd been playing regularly for England under-23s, scoring twice on my debut, had got into the West Ham side and spent six weeks out with a broken leg after Mooro kicked me in the back of the calf during training.

"So when I was the only one to be left out after we lost 8-2 to Blackburn, I naturally thought I couldn't have been the only one to have played badly on the day." He adds with a hint of sarcasm and a tongue-in-cheek smile: "It *must* have been my fault because they then won 3-1 with Eddie playing!"

Despite his bitter disappointment during that uncertain period in his career, Peters says the thought of seeking a move to another club hadn't entered his head. He had undoubtedly been a victim of his own remarkable versatility – once, he even played in goal for the first team!

"You could say I was fortunate, or even unfortunate, to be able to play in every position," says Martin, who Ramsey picked on the left of a three-man midfield as his 'wingless wonders' beat West Germany in extra-time playing their new 4-3-3 system. "I think that's what Alf meant when he said I was 10 years ahead of my time – I was able to adapt to whatever role I was asked to play. I never, ever asked him what he meant by it, though, I was just happy to hear him say those words.

"Being two-footed, I could cope if I had to play left-back, or if I was asked to play right-wing, where I could put in a decent cross. I could also be a half-decent target man up front – Ron tried me there a couple of times and so did John Bond after I

Martin was the most naturally talented of the famous three.

joined him at Norwich – but I was never quick enough to play there. I was crap up front, to be honest, but I filled in at centre-half several times.

"I did once ask Ron which position he thought was my best but he didn't answer me. I don't think he knew himself for sure. Anyway, I finished up back at right-half and stayed there for virtually the rest of my career."

Peters' versatility saw him take over in goal against Cardiff City during the Easter period in 1962. Keeper Lawrie Leslie suffered injury against Arsenal and completed the home game as an outfield player while left-back John Lyall deputised for him. Peters had made his debut in the No.4 shirt in a 4-1 home win over Cardiff on Good Friday, April 20 but when Hammers visited Ninian Park the following Monday, stand-in debutant keeper Brian Rhodes dislocated his shoulder. With no substitutes, and Lyall missing from the team that day, it was the tall 18-year-old Peters who replaced Rhodes with half-an-hour still to play. Cardiff scored only one past him, though, before completing a 3-0 win.

"The second Cardiff match was only my third game for the first team. I played at right-half, left-back and then goalkeeper, in three games, in the space of four days!"

Even the experience of being asked to pull on the green jersey didn't faze the unflappable Peters.

He continued: "Sometimes I used to play in goal during training – in fact, I once started a youth team game at Welling as goalkeeper. But someone scored straight from a corner, so that shows you how good I was! I also went between the sticks for the Reserves, so the position wasn't new to me when I covered for Lawrie against Cardiff that time."

Peters rightly acknowledges Greenwood as the man who did most to shape his career. After the mundanity of more physical training under Ted Fenton, the man who signed him as a professional in 1959, Peters was among the most receptive to Greenwood's far more cultured approach to the beautiful game. Despite occupying more positions than can be found among the pages of the *Karma Sutra*, Martin blossomed under Ron's stylish ideology of how football should be played.

He became one of the most accomplished all round midfielders in the world, scoring freely with either foot and a good many with his head too. Martin's renowned speciality was his innate ability to arrive late, and unmarked, in the box to finish off a move.

Few who were at the game will ever forget the exquisitely timed right-foot volley he struck to score from John Sissons' precision left-wing cross in a thrilling 4-0 home win over Leicester City in November 1968.

A quiet, modest man who has always let his skill on the football field do most of his talking for him, did Martin ever suffer a lack of self-confidence or doubt that he would go all the way to the top?

"I never thought like that as a youngster," he responds. "I just wanted to get in the West Ham first team – I didn't dream I'd play for England. When I got picked for England under-23s by Walter Winterbottom, I was actually third choice. The other two guys were both injured and I scored a couple of goals down at Plymouth against Belgium – I was lucky to get a chance at 18."

Martin was in the mould of a Roy Keane, Frank Lampard (jnr) or Steven Gerrard in terms of box-to-box stamina and effectiveness – but he had much more subtlety than all of those three and was a far more accomplished all round performer. He explains: "I was a long-distance runner, winning lots of races at school, and I had a good engine. But I couldn't beat Brian Dear in the cross-country runs!

"Brian and I joined West Ham at the same time and came up through the ranks together. He was a very good goalscorer in his youth and he really should have done better in his career. I played with him for England Schoolboys and he scored all our goals against Scotland and Wales, but he was gutted to be left out of the big Wembley game.

"He was a bit cheeky but he still scored plenty of goals for West Ham. He was a predator and although he didn't always work well in the team unit, he did a great job when he came into the ECWC campaign in '65.

"John Sissons was another who I thought should have gone on to enjoy more success than he achieved. He had a great time early on in his career and I always thought he would become an England player, but his career dwindled away."

Martin was the first of the World Cup-winning trio to leave Upton Park, when he joined London rivals Tottenham Hotspur just before the transfer deadline in March 1970. It was a British record £200,000 deal, with legendary Spurs goalscorer Jimmy Greaves going in the opposite direction, but it attracted none of the hype that surrounds every major move today. In fact, the respective managers, Ron Greenwood and Bill Nicholson, shook hands and agreed the deal in private, in a car parked outside Walthamstow greyhound stadium!

And with his second World Cup finals tournament just 12 weeks away, Peters signed his new contract alone in Bill Nick's little office at White Hart Lane, without the presence of an agent or financial advisor. Nowadays, youth team hopefuls employ agents to represent them.

It's been suggested that he wanted to leave West Ham to escape the giant shadows cast by his England colleagues, Moore and Hurst, and to grab more of the limelight himself. But Martin strongly refutes the notion and says he needed a new challenge at a club that was more likely to win trophies and challenge for the league title.

"I think it was one day before the transfer deadline that I got a phone call from Ron saying that Bill Nicholson wanted me over at White Hart Lane to talk about a move, with Jimmy Greaves set to join West Ham. I went to Tottenham and when I got there Bill said that it was basically a done deal already. He pointed out that Tottenham had been in a bit of a lull, that they hadn't won anything for *three years!* They'd won the Cup in '67 but he said their team had 'gone a bit iffy.'

"Bill asked me: 'How much do you want?' I just said I wanted exactly the same money as I'd been on at West Ham, which was £147 a week. As I hadn't asked for a transfer, I knew I would also receive five percent (£10,000) of two hundred grand, which was quite a lot of money in those days. I was still in awe of someone like Bill Nicholson, as indeed I was Ron Greenwood.

"People say that I was upset because I was always regarded as the 'third one' of the West Ham World Cup-winning trio, but that was definitely never the case. Bobby was captain of England and by 1970 had become an even bigger footballing icon. Geoff had scored three goals in the World Cup final and was still banging them in left, right and centre, so I was quite happy to be, if you like, 'the third one.'

"Geoff said it the other night, strangely enough, and I know that Bobby has also said it before . . . they both felt that, technically, I was the better player of the three of us, which I take as a great compliment."

Despite his somewhat dour public persona, Martin has an engaging and dry sense of humour and he joked that his goal in the final was actually the most important of England's four against the Germans on July 30, 1966. "Well, if I hadn't scored our second goal, we would have lost 2-1!" he smiles.

"I was glad I went to Spurs at the age of 26. Ron had given me the base of my career, but I felt that after 11 years at West Ham it was time for me to take on new ideas and different opinions. Bill was a bit like Alf Ramsey in that he didn't coach me or try to change my natural game – it was Eddie Baily who did all the coaching at Tottenham."

It was a good move for Martin Peters, although not West Ham. While Martin went on to cement his place in the England midfield for another four years and win the UEFA Cup and League Cup twice (the second time, against Norwich City, as captain) in the next three years, Greaves' struggle mirrored Hammers' own battle at the wrong end of the table. Within 10 months of signing, Greaves – along with Moore – was in disgrace with Greenwood for being caught up in a late-night drinking session prior to an FA Cup tie at Blackpool and, with his career in rapid decline, heading towards alcoholism. While Spurs finished 1970-71 third in the table, behind Arsenal and Leeds United, West Ham plunged deeper to only one place clear of relegation.

But Peters admits that he didn't have it easy trying to win over his new supporters in North London, who were more demanding than those to the east who had not seen as much silverware, let alone been spoiled by two Double-winning sides. "I was bought to replace their hero, Jimmy Greaves, the greatest British goalscorer there has ever been. I scored after about eight minutes of my Spurs debut against Coventry City but we lost 2-1. Jim scored twice on his debut for West Ham, who won 5-2 at Manchester City!

"It took me a time to win over the Spurs fans. We played West Ham in the first game of the following season, drew 2-2 and Jimmy scored the equaliser. So people were looking at me a bit suspiciously until I got on a good scoring run. We finished third in the league and started to win trophies again.

"I became a stronger person at Tottenham, where the players – especially the likes of Joe Kinnear, Cyril Knowles, Terry Naylor and Jimmy Pearce – were piss-takers and you had to stand up to them and learn to cope in that environment.

"I thought I'd be a West Ham player for life, and I felt the same way when I was at Tottenham – until it all changed again when Bill resigned and Terry Neill came in."

After five years with Spurs, Martin moved on to Norwich City in 1975 and starred in a City side managed by his former West Ham team-mate John Bond and coached by another ex-Hammer, Ken Brown. The six seasons he spent at Carrow Road were some of the happiest days of his career, when survival in the top flight was regarded as an achievement in itself. Norwich fans voted him the best player ever to pull on the Canaries shirt and, in a further mark of recognition, the club awarded him a testimonial in 1978.

"I spent longer at Norwich than I did at Spurs – five-and-a-half years – and was successful there too, but in a different way. All they wanted to do was keep the club in the first division and we did that.

"I enjoyed it at Norwich but my wife, who is an East London girl, hated it. Within days of us winning promotion, I was off to Kenya for three weeks on tour with the players, leaving Kathy at home with our two young kids. We lived there for eight-and-a-half years altogether, in a nice house with a swimming pool – the only pool we've ever had, which was particularly nice in that very hot summer of '76. We made some good friends in Norfolk but Kathy missed Essex so much."

You couldn't blame Martin for thinking he would be one of the world's most coveted and costliest players if he was still gracing the Premiership today.

"I read and hear what the likes of Beckham, Owen and Ballack are being paid and think it's outrageous but, then again, I don't think about it for long. Football has changed dramatically over the years, especially since the Premiership was formed, and I just keep my head down and try to earn as much money as I can doing the things I do now.

"I've been in the car warranty business for 22 years but don't have to work so hard at it nowadays, devoting maybe only one or two days a week to it. I also do quite a bit of after-dinner speaking and try to watch as many live games as possible involving Spurs, West Ham and Norwich."

Martin's England career ended in 1974, soon after Ramsey was harshly sacked by the FA following elimination from the World Cup qualifiers at the hands of Polish

Two great footballing brains . . . Martin and Bobby line up a freekick in the late 60s.

keeper Jam Tomaszewski. The thought hadn't eluded Peters that, with the international careers of Moore and Hurst having both ended, he would probably have been captain if Ramsey's team had reached the '74 finals in Germany.

Martin played the last of his 722 league matches in the Third Division for Sheffield United against Gillingham at Bramall Lane on January 17, 1981. A low-key way to end a brilliant playing career but he can look back with very few regrets. And, of course, there are some things that no-one can ever take away from him and the other 10 Boys of '66 whose names are still rightly revered today, perhaps even more so than when they lifted the Jules Rimet trophy at Wembley 41 years ago.

"One thing I've said before, which Geoff Hurst can't get out of his head and he still repeats it at dinners sometimes, is this: If I was playing in the modern era, I wouldn't have won a World Cup medal. That says it all."

Fans of both West Ham and Spurs have been thrilled by the goals scored by Martin Peters throughout the 60s and 70s but the man himself is sometimes saddened by the increasing level of antipathy between the two sets of rival supporters.

"I think the rivalry has got worse and changed for all the wrong reasons over the past seven or eight years," he says.

"I don't recall playing for West Ham against Spurs, or vice-versa, and the crowd being so abusive to the other team as they are whenever the teams meet nowadays. I never had any problems with the Upton Park crowd – I think the worse thing they ever called me was 'Mary', after the 1968 Olympic gold medalist Mary Peters!

"I can guess that the current situation between the two sets of fans has something to do with the number of West Ham players who have left to join Spurs but I think this attitude changed before then – and I hate it.

"I remember sitting up in the stand at Spurs watching the last game of the 2002-03 season and hating it when the fans started cheering the result from Birmingham, which flashed up on the giant screen, confirming West Ham's relegation."

Martin also recalled an unhappy experience when he took his daughter and granddaughter to Upton Park for the Championship match against Preston. "I always take my granddaughter to football on her birthday. On this occasion Preston had scored and then Tomas Repka got sent off for headbutting somebody, so the supporters were upset. It got worse when Preston scored a second goal and some wag behind me started shouting: 'You shouldn't be here, Peters, you've got a lounge at Tottenham'. I didn't hear it myself but Lee Ann and Hannah did, and they were a bit upset by it.

"At Tottenham, they sing 'Stand up if you hate Arsenal', while at West Ham they sing 'Stand up if you hate Tottenham' – and I'd never heard that sung by Hammers fans before.

"When I was invited to attend West Ham's home game against Birmingham, a few days after Ron Greenwood died, and we lined up on the pitch beforehand, I wondered what kind of reception I would get from the crowd. Thankfully, it was really good, which pleased me.

"I think most people perceive me as a Tottenham person, because I used to be on their board of directors (until former manager Glenn Hoddle apparently resented his presence and urged chairman Daniel Levy to remove him in 2002) and still work for the club as a host in their main hospitality lounges on matchdays, which I've done for the past 15 or so years.

"If Tottenham fans ask me who I support, I tell them Norwich!"

Martin can joke about it but it's a sad indictment of the minority of morons that infect every ground in the country that a celebrated World Cup winner, who served his first club with distinction over 11 years, should even have cause to wonder how fans will receive him on his return.

Having spent a good number of years with both the Hammers and Spurs, it's inevitable that he will feel divided loyalties whenever these two fierce London rivals clash. "I do feel that I have to be careful what I say about either club," he admits.

"It's one of the reasons why I never went to the final game of the 2005-06 season at Upton Park. It was a big game for both clubs and I didn't want to be involved.

"I needed to get away for a break, because I'd been very busy beforehand and I knew what was coming up with the launch of my book and the World Cup dinners and reunions, so I decided to get away for 10 days to our apartment in Menorca. We've only had it for a year and for that I have to thank West Ham for buying my memorabilia."

Martin declined to reveal what the club paid for his most prized possessions from his career, including his World Cup and ECWC winners' medal, plus a number of international shirts, but it's fairly safe to assume that it was a much higher price than it cost Tottenham to prise him away from Upton Park 37 years ago.

"They bought my whole package – all my shirts, including those I swapped with other international players, and everything involved in my time at West Ham. To be honest, that has brought me so much security it's unbelievable. I would never have previously considered buying a property abroad but Kathy and I thought about it and we saw that not only would it be good for ourselves, but also our kids and grandchildren, Hannah and Meg. It's solely for use by our family – not for renting – and we don't have a mortgage on the place in Menorca, nor the house we have here, which is brilliant. And I owe that to West Ham for buying all my stuff.

"The sale to West Ham came about because I had been receiving offers for my World Cup medal from abroad. But I didn't want it to go out of this country, so I discussed it with Kathy and we decided to speak to West Ham chairman Terry Brown and his fellow director, Nick Igoe, who were delighted to buy all my memorabilia.

"I used to store everything away in the loft, although the medal has also been kept in a bank and, when we lived at Norwich, in an underfloor safe. I never saw it, no-one could ever view it, so it seemed a waste to have it hidden away like that.

"The only time I got my World Cup medal out was three or four years ago, to show it to the builders who were working across the road. One day they asked to see my medals and after showing them, they built us a barbecue for nothing!

"That medal went on show in West Ham's museum and I think they intend to display the shirts and everything else at some stage. When I've passed on, at least

Martin posing with our popular EX West Ham World Cup Winners' T-shirt when we interviewed him for the magazine in May 2006.

my granddaughter's children and others to follow in our family will be able to go and visit the museum in many years to come and point out what was once mine."

In fact, *EX* magazine's memorabilia expert Tim Crane was consulted by the club to confirm all the details behind Peters' collection – match dates, scorers and opponents who wore the actual shirts on the occasions opponents exchanged them with Martin.

"At our stage in life it's great for Kathy and I to be able to spend time at another home in the sunshine, where we can relax and get away from it all."

Plaistow-born Martin, now 63, will never forget his East End roots, however, and he reveals that Kathy, as well as their daughter, Lee Ann Collins, and her daughter, Hannah, are all fanatical West Ham supporters.

"I was out of the country at the time but Lee Ann and Hannah both went to the 2006 FA Cup final between West Ham and Liverpool and they would probably be season ticket holders if Lee Ann didn't have to work on Saturdays."

To be fair to Martin and the polished diplomat that he is, he does a tremendous balancing act of handling his links with both West Ham and Spurs as adeptly as he used to control and manipulate a football. When he hosted *EX's* 40th anniversary reunion dinner for the 1964 and '65 cup winners in May 2005, he did so with a smoothness and professionalism that characterised his glittering playing career.

Whenever Martin Peters returns to Upton Park in the future, he should always be treated with the respect this gentleman of football deserves.

Chapter 6

BRIAN**DEAR**

"When I look back at myself and the way I behaved in the 80s, I'm ashamed. Anyone would be. But what Natalie said to me was a massive wake-up call. There were plenty of tears but I've never had an alcoholic drink since that day"

BRIAN Dear is in no doubt. Although the Boys of '86 successfully set up their own company to perpetuate and profit from their unique achievement of finishing higher than any other team in the club's history, they are not, according to him, the greatest ever West Ham United team.

Supporters will continue to debate the various merits of sides from different eras. Were the 60s cup-winning teams, spearheaded by Moore, Hurst and Peters, superior to those of the 70s and 80s that also won silverware but achieved more in terms of league points and final position?

The FA Cup and second division title-winning team of the early 80s were, some would argue, also stronger than the side that finished third behind Liverpool and Everton in 1985-86, when they took the first division championship race to the wire before having to settle for third place behind Liverpool and Everton.

Dear respects the Boys of '86, he admires their camaraderie, but you won't persuade him that the golden era of Frank McAvennie and Tony Cottee surpassed the vintage days of the 60s cup heroes he is proud to have been a part of.

Brian said: "It's great that the Boys of '86 have stuck together and it's good for them. The only thing that annoys me is when Frank McAvennie goes on about it being the best-ever West Ham team.

"I'm always going to lean towards the team I played in – and I was only one of the ordinary players. But when you think of some of the class players we had around that time, with Bobby, Geoff and Martin, and towards the end of that period, with Billy Bonds, Trevor Brooking and Pop Robson . . .

"So they finished third in the league in '86. Third! Wonderful, but why mention it in the programme? McAvennie has been quoted as saying that winning cups means nothing, that the league is the only thing that matters.

"We had two guys who won three medals at Wembley in three consecutive years – and another who won two in that time. No other two men did what Bobby and Geoff did at one club, or what Martin did both here and with Spurs.

"With respect to the Boys of '86, McAvennie should sit back and take stock of some of the great players who went before him. They were a good side – a great side – but they were relegated three years later . . . and they don't mention that fact in

Brian flanked by his good mates Bobby Moore and Johnny Byrne, at the airport on their way home from Hammers' European game at Lausanne, Switzerland in 1965.

the programme, do they?"

But Brian goes on to praise certain individuals: "They had probably the best goalkeeper West Ham has ever had in Phil Parkes. Alvin Martin was outstanding and I thought Alan Devonshire was absolutely superb. McAvennie and Tony Cottee scored a lot of goals together for a while.

"I'm pleased that they've kept the West Ham spirit going in the same way that the players I played with in the 60s still have the same camaraderie. You won't see that at West Ham again in the future."

Cut him open, as the cliché goes, and Dear would bleed claret-and-blue. Born in West Ham, he supported his local team since birth and can remember bunking off school to see Johnny Dick score a hat-trick in the FA Cup against Spurs in 1956.

"My dad used to stand on the North Bank and I'd climb up the ladder at the back of the open terrace to help the old boy put up the half-time scores on the board. Then, at half-time, us kids would distract the copper down by the corner of the Chicken Run, hop over the fence, run along underneath the stand and hop over the fence at the other end, to get a better view of the goal we were attacking in the second half!

"I used to get a tanner, a shilling or two bob for 'looking after' people's cars while they watched the matches – even though I'd go in to watch the games myself and only nipped out to stand by their cars 10 minutes from the end! Those who rode to the ground on bicycles would park them in people's front gardens in Priory Road."

Reliving his childhood, the memories continue to trip off the 63-year-old's tongue.

Brian said: "I collected the players' autographs on the back of fag wrappers. They wore those big overcoats and, although they were only young men, they looked so old to me.

"Vic Keeble had back trouble and walked with a bit of a stoop. No wonder – he drove a little sports car, an Austin Healey Sprite, if I remember rightly!"

Brian joined the West Ham groundstaff in 1959. "I bumped into Ken Tucker, who asked me if I used to nick sweets from his mum's shop around the corner. I said: 'Of course I did – we *all* did!'.

"Andy Malcolm was my favourite person, though. Hard as nails, he'd run past you in training and rip a hole in your shorts – and we only had one pair a season! But what a lovely fella. We kept in touch after we both stopped playing and would take a darts team to play at each other's pubs – Andy's in Maldon and mine at Southend."

Brian's first team debut came at Wolves, just before his 19th birthday, in August 1962. But just three league starts in that season and the following one gave no indication of the impact he would soon make. Although a prolific scorer for the youth and reserve sides, Brian could never have dreamed that he would enjoy such a brilliant spell at the end of the 1964-65 campaign that ended in European triumph.

While the senior players celebrated the club's first FA Cup triumph, Brian could only watch in frustration. He started only three league games (as a replacement for Tony Scott) in September '63 and didn't reappear in a first team shirt for another 18 months, when he went on a scoring spree that included his record-breaking five-in-20-minutes blitz against West Bromwich Albion on Good Friday, April 16, 1965.

"It was impossible for Ron Greenwood to change that side. Geoff and Budgie Byrne were doing very well up front and I couldn't get a look in," he recalls.

"You did tend to feel a bit isolated, watching the lads collect their medals. But, deep down, I was really delighted for them, because I grew up with the likes of Jackie Burkett and Ronnie Boyce, who I've known since we were five or six years-old. Ron and me went to Brampton Road junior school together before he went on to East Ham Grammar and I headed for Central Park. We also played together for East Ham Boys, so Boycie is probably my closest friend since my earliest days at West Ham."

Despite scoring 23 goals for the reserves, managed by Ernie Gregory, and being down the first team pecking order, Brian had no thoughts of leaving. "I think Ron Greenwood might have thought about not renewing my one-year contract but I never had any intention of moving elsewhere.

"It was difficult to get in the side on the wing at that time. Johnny Sissons burst through before they signed Peter Brabrook from Chelsea, while Tony Scott was another who was a very underrated player. He was a great crosser of the ball. And then they bought Alan Sealey from the Orient.

"They had also signed Budgie from Crystal Palace. Fifty-eight grand was a lot of money then but it was well repaid. He was quite phenomenal. Ron kept faith with these people, which was understandable."

Injuries did eventually reopen the door for the burly Dear, though, and at an exciting time in the club's history. After his scoring feat against West Bromwich, 'Stag' stayed in the side to enjoy the climax of the European adventure.

"Budgie and Eddie Bov were both ruled out of the final by injury. The only one who could have kept me out of the game was Peter Brabrook.

"I remember a big sore came up on my neck on the day of the final – a reaction to the vaccine injections we'd all just had prior to our end-of-season trip to the States. While I was seeing our physio, Bill Jenkins, about it, I remember Ron asking me if I'd be okay to play in the final, as he had Peter standing by. I told him I was fine. I don't think the game would have been played if I hadn't been in it!

"I had a few chances in the final, hitting the post once. I was our leading scorer in the competition (four goals in five games) but it's unbelievable that Geoff didn't even score one goal in Europe that season. It's fate really, because he and Budgie had been scoring regularly in the league."

Those fortunate enough to be among the 100,000 capacity Wembley crowd that momentous night in May '65 still maintain the Hammers have never played better.

"The Germans were a good side, with plenty of internationals, but everything went good for us that night." continues Brian. "I think our best player was Ronnie Boyce. I watch the video of the final occasionally and you can see Ron making everything he did look so easy. He could go through a game playing two-touch and he was always getting in tackles. He was unbelievable that night and complemented the rest of us ever so well. The way we played suited the European game.

"There were no guv'nors in our team. Yes, we had our little groups – I'd drink with Bobby, Budgie and Boycie, while others didn't want to do that, which was fair enough. But when we played, we were as one."

Sadly, Brian no longer possesses his European medal, which was stolen from one of his former pubs at Southend more than 20 years ago.

"It used to hang from my wife's chain. But thieves broke in one night and nicked it, along with some other chains and gold sovereign rings.

"I asked West Ham chairman, Terry Brown, if there was any chance the club could have another, identical medal struck for me from one of the other ECWC medals they already have in their museum."

Perhaps it would have been safer left in the care of his East End parents, Charlie and Elsie. That's where the match ball from his famous five-goal show against West Brom in '65 remained for years after their son took it to the family's East Ham home.

"Mum kept it in a bag at her place in Hatherley Gardens for years. When she gave the ball back to me it didn't look too good. I was frightened to pump it up in case it fell to bits, but it was okay and now West Ham have it with the intention of putting it on display in their museum," he explained.

Brian was part of the most successful squad in Hammers' history, a club that had won two trophies at Wembley in the space of a year, but instead of building on that success, his career – and life – spiralled downwards.

He is full of honest introspection, saying: "Once you've done something like win a European medal you can't rest on your laurels. I had plenty of opportunity and it's nobody fault other than mine that I didn't go on and do better.

John Cushley, Brian Dear, Eddie Bovington and Dave Bickles at Upton Park in 1967.

"Maybe it was complacency, I don't know. I slung away a playing career really. I was all done at the age of 27, which is criminal.

"I seem to have shoved so much into such a short space of time, but that's life."

Banished back to the reserves at Upton Park, Brian started just 10 matches in 1965-66 and featured in only one of the European ties – the costly 2-1 home semi-final defeat against Borussia Dortmund.

In the following three seasons he was always on the fringes of the first team, making seven appearances (three goals) in 1966-67. He recaptured much of his old form the following campaign with an impressive 16 goals in 30 matches but in 1968-69 he faded again and made only 12 starts (five goals) as young Trevor Brooking emerged to support Hurst in attack.

He tried to rekindle his career lower down the league ladder, joining Fulham in a £20,000 deal in 1969, and then, a year later, Millwall, but neither move worked out.

"They were a nice crowd of lads at Fulham – Budgie was with them by then and Johnny Haynes – but I didn't like it there. I used to travel from Hornchurch to Fulham Broadway on the tube each day and we trained in a park. The trainer, a fella called Gray, used to run us ragged in Richmond Park and manager Bill Dodgin knew I wasn't happy.

"Bill asked if I'd be prepared to go to Millwall in exchange for a bit of money and a couple of players Benny Fenton was looking to offload, so I did. But it was even worse for me at Millwall."

Given a free transfer from The Den, Brian visited Belgium for talks about a possible move to Bruges before he called into West Ham's training ground one day

Not even a broken leg could stop 'Stag' from playing football when he was in his prime.
Inset: Brian and Geoff Hurst boarding the team bus for an away trip.

early in the 1970-71 season and received an unexpected offer.

"I popped in to see the lads when Ernie (Gregory) mentioned that Ron wanted to have a word with me. I thought he was going to tell me to keep away from Chadwell Heath but, instead, he asked if I wanted to come back to West Ham. He could see I was overweight but he told me I was wasting myself. He said that if I trained with the reserves under Ernie and got myself fit again, he'd offer me a contract."

Brian pulled on the claret-and-blue shirt again in October '70, returning for a 2-2 draw against Spurs that attracted the attendance of 42,322 that still stands as a Boleyn record today. He played in the next two first division matches, a 1-1 draw at Crystal Palace followed by a 2-1 home win over Blackpool. Stag would have cause to curse Blackpool, for it was after a humiliating 4-0 FA Cup third round defeat in in the seaside town in January '71 that his second spell with the Hammers ended as abruptly as West Ham's cup run. Greenwood later got wind that Brian, accompanied by Bobby Moore, Jimmy Greaves, Clyde Best and trainer Rob Jenkins, had been at boxer Brian London's nightclub until the early hours of the morning of the match. He stripped Moore of the captaincy and it was only at the behest of the Board that the players and Jenkins were spared the sack. It made headline news at the time but in reality the Blackpool Five were merely enjoying a few quiet lagers (Best didn't drink and was only on orange juice!) and relaxing, and were certainly not drunk.

Having blown his second (and last) chance with Greenwood, Brian disappeared into non-league football for a while with Woodford Town. "Bill Larkin, the peanut boss, got Bob Wheatley, who owned a chain of East End pubs, to sponsor me £100 per week – more than I was on at West Ham! – and I played there with Les Allen. I didn't stay at Woodford long, though, and after I packed up playing I went into the pub game."

Bad move.

Much of the late 70s and 80s were a dark period in Brian's life, when he descended towards alcoholism – the same slippery slope Greaves went down post-West Ham. But he attributed his demise not to missing the buzz that football gave him, or any regrets for having wasted his undoubted goalscoring talent.

He put it down to one simple factor: "I became a publican," he said.

Brian owned or ran five different Essex pubs. "That's when the drink really got hold of me," he admits. "I was in the wrong environment.

"The players used to like a drink after a game but some of us have a bigger capacity than others. I never used to fall over at the bar or roll around drunk. I thought I could hold my drink. But there was nothing for us to do in the afternoons. After training, we'd go to pubs like the Slaters Arms in Romford and have a few lagers.

"But it was once I got into the pub game myself that things turned really bad. It got to the stage where I'd drink any spirits going in the end. And if I was sat upstairs in the pub and there was a bottle around, I'd have to finish it.

"After I came out of the pub game and went to Southend United as bar steward, it was quite well known that I had a drink problem."

Brian's daughter, Natalie, called a family crisis meeting on Boxing Day, 1992, when Brian was given a firm and clear ultimatum: either the booze had to go, or else he did.

He recalls: "Natalie took me to the doctor, where I had some liver function tests. I had an enlarged liver even before the tests, but they didn't show anything and no-one could believe it. But I stopped drinking there and then.

"I weighed just over 20 stone when I first gave up the booze, so I went to Slimmer's World and lost about six stone in the first year. My playing weight was between 12 and 13 stone, although they always used to joke that I was fat!

"It was a doddle to stop drinking – as easy as it was to start in the first place," he says as we chatted just a few feet from the bar at Essex Golf Club, Southend, where Brian was organising the fifth annual Bobby Moore Cancer Fund charity golf day. 'Stag' and friends boosted the charity by around £1,000 on the day – Martin Peters, with his 16 handicap, well up among the front runners – but now Brian prefers to relax with a glass of water rather than a bottle of brandy.

Not that he is ever far from temptation. "I'm bar and catering manager at Southend

United now but I can sit at the bar, visit pubs, or go out to functions where there is booze everywhere, and not even think about wanting another drink. I never weaken. I drink water or coffee, although I don't really enjoy much water so if I'm out somewhere I tend not to drink at all. It doesn't bother me.

"I'm lucky because I never went for treatment, didn't experience the shakes or anything like that. And I've never been to Alcoholics Anonymous either."

Brian got his life back together some 15 years ago thanks to the loving and loyal support of his family. His wife Jan, daughter Natalie and son Jon (a West Ham season ticket holder) and his wife, Theresa, have all been there for him. Now he also has three grandchildren, Alex, Emily and Chloe, to enrich his life.

Brian is also very grateful to two good friends in particular. "Lennie Berry, a lorry driver, would take me out to pubs on a Sunday morning but he'd only buy me a tonic water. Terry Leigh was also a great help to me. And my family, of course. Jon was only young then but Natalie was the real instigator behind my recovery. She took the chair at home that Boxing Day and spelt it all out to me very clearly. She said: 'We've all had enough of you and if you don't stop now, you've got to go'.

"By then, I wasn't a nice person to be around. I was spiteful with people and didn't care. It got to the point where Jan and the kids wouldn't go anywhere with me, because they were frightened of what drinking would do to me, how my mood would swing. There were some hairy moments.

"When I look back at myself and the way I behaved in the 80s, I'm ashamed. Anyone would be.

"But what Natalie said to me was a massive wake-up call. There were plenty of tears but I've never had an alcoholic drink since that day."

In addition to running the bars and catering at Southend United, with specific responsibility for managing the directors' suite and players' food on matchdays, Brian is also working in local schools at Shoeburyness and Canvey Island – a part-time role organised through the football club's community programme.

"They call it mentoring, where I go into schools and work with four different children – youngsters in their final year – for half-an-hour each. I discuss how they are getting on and if things aren't going so well for them, I listen and offer help and advice. I have to write reports on their progress."

Brian appears calm and contended with his life now. He is a regular at Upton Park, where he is grateful for the warm welcome he always receives from staff.

"I've had two second chances in life. One as a player at West Ham, which I didn't take. And the other – giving up the booze – which I did."

Chapter 7

JOHN**SISSONS**

"Once we were going in the players' entrance at Hillsborough when the steward put his arm across the door and said to me: 'Sorry son, you can't come in here'. But Bobby Moore put his arm around me and told the bloke I was a West Ham player, not a young fan!"

JOHN Sissons did everything but score in the European Cup Winners' Cup final, hitting both crossbar and post amid Hammers' second half onslaught and, as he admits, missing an easy chance from close range early on.

It didn't matter, though, because for the fifth time in five visits to Wembley, the young, blond left-winger emerged a winner with another medal to his name.

A year earlier he had made history by becoming the youngest-ever player to score in an FA Cup final, netting the first in West Ham's 3-2 victory over Preston North End.

And before that he had already claimed two World Youth Cup medals as one of England's hottest prospects.

At the age of 19, John Sissons was already a European champion, a first team star and tipped for a very big future in the game.

But Sissons, who starred for England at schoolboy, youth and under-23 level, didn't quite make the step up to full international – though he says that he heard years later that Alf Ramsey had him in mind until advised by Ron Greenwood that it was "too early". Just five years after the ECWC triumph he was on his way out of Upton Park and heading for second division football with Sheffield Wednesday before short-lived spells with Norwich City and Chelsea.

In 1975, after a year in the North America Soccer League with Tampa Bay Rowdies, John and his former wife, Janice, emigrated to South Africa, where he now lives happily with his second wife of eight years, Sandy. Fairly close by are two of his children – John (41) and Jodie (37), on the outskirts of Cape Town.

John's third born, David (25), has been living and working in London for five years and he had joined his father when we met up in the capital for this interview, just a few days before the 64-65 reunion dinner organised by *EX*.

Looking very fit and tanned, John says he can look back on his time at West Ham now with a maturity that he lacked when he was ripping defences apart with his pace and skill in the No.11 shirt back in the 60s. The eloquent John is clearly rueful that he didn't make the most of his obvious talent, a point he had noted from his former team-mate and skipper, Bobby Moore's autobiography.

Johnny Sissons sets Hammers on their way to FA Cup glory with the first against Preston in '64.

So why did his richly promising career fizzle out much too early?

"It was as if there was always somebody there for me if ever I was in trouble," John explains. "Bill Jenkins, our physio, was a fantastic man and like a father figure to me. And on the pitch, I was never in any trouble because Bobby Moore would be behind me, saying: 'Give me the ball, son'. Bobby always looked out for me.

"Once we were going in the players' entrance at Hillsborough when the steward put his arm across the door and said to me: 'Sorry son, you can't come in here'. But Bobby put his arm around me and told the bloke I was a West Ham player, not a young fan!

"And then there was Ron (Greenwood), who always referred to me as 'Young John', even years later when I was one of the senior players."

Now 61, John still is the 'baby' of that triumphant cup-winning team of the mid-60s but he admits now that perhaps more should have been expected of him as the seasons passed and his talent went unfulfilled.

"One of my downfalls after our two cup successes was that I never matured as a person until I left England and moved to Cape Town. I was naive and never felt I ever came out of the cocoon-like world I was in at West Ham. I was so immature and just pleased to be playing in the team.

"And in the early part of my career I was so used to success. By the age of 19 I'd been to Wembley five times and won on each occasion, so I think it all came a little too early for me."

A Chelsea fan who idolised Jimmy Greaves as a young boy, John credits West Ham scout Charlie Faulkner as the man whose persistence persuaded him to join the

Young and talented, John during his early days in the West Ham first team.

Hammers from school, in the face of strong competition from other top clubs, including the Blues and Wolves.

"I was paid £3 per week at first but I wanted to join West Ham because of their history of producing and giving chances to young players."

And he insists it wasn't until after he'd signed for the East London club that a 'gift' of a brand new washing machine turned up at the family home courtesy of his new employers. "Mum was delighted – I think one of the directors, Reg Brandon, owned an electrical store!"

Not that John was exactly spoiled financially by the club. Before the FA Cup final, he earned £15 per week basic, plus £10 appearance money and £10 per point.

"But my basic was doubled at the start of the season following the Cup final – and by that Christmas it went up again to £50 a week. Mind you, I think the World Cup trio were soon earning £100 a week each!"

The most John earned in his career was £150 per week at Chelsea, his last English club, in the mid-70s.

"I used to live on the same housing estate in Hornchurch as Martin and Geoff but after the World Cup they went up in the world by moving to Gidea Park!" he laughs.

Indeed, John can now confess, without fear of reprisal from the FA 43 years on, that the biggest earner for most players who appeared in a Cup final in those days was from the sale of their allocation of Wembley tickets.

He revealed: "We used to get six tickets each for home games and I'd keep two and sell the other four.

"For the '64 Cup final, the players received 20 tickets each but I think most of them went to the well known tout, Stan Flashman. I made about £600 from the

'Sisso' closing down the opposition in the European tie against Sparta Prague.

tickets sold for the Preston final . . . and bought myself a Morris 1100 with it! I was worried that Ron would find out, though."

Recalling his move to Sheffield Wednesday in 1970, 'Sisso' said: "Ron made me promise that I wouldn't breath a word of what we'd discussed to the press and then he called me up that summer to say Sheffield Wednesday had come in for me. Danny Williams had just taken over after moving from Swindon and it was the worst decision I ever made.

"The people at the club were nice but from a playing point of view, it was a disaster – the football was nothing like what I'd been brought up on at West Ham. I had three years there and found out later that Spurs had also been interested in me before I'd signed for Wednesday.

"John Bond signed me soon after he took over at Norwich and my first game for them on New Year's Day was at Upton Park, where we lost 4-2, but the West Ham fans were phenomenal to me on my return. When Norwich were relegated I moved to Chelsea under Dave Sexton. I hadn't been there long when Eddie McCreadie took over and we didn't get on, so I went to play in the States for a year and then moved permanently to South Africa."

John usually makes one return trip to England each year to visit his sister in Surrey and his mum, but he had not seen a game at Upton Park for 11 years when he flew to London in May 2005 and saw Hammers draw 2-2 with Ipswich Town in the Championship play-off semi-final, first leg.

If he had expected to be entertained by the same brand of attacking football that characterised West Ham teams under Greenwood, he was in for a disappointment.

It was one of the team's best performances under Alan Pardew all season, but John said: "I must say I was disappointed with what I saw from both teams and can now see just how big the gulf between the Premiership and the Championship really is," says John, who was left shaking his head at much of what he saw.

"I've never seen a West Ham midfield so lacking in creativity. The full-backs hardly ever got forward on the overlap and yet much of football today is based on full-backs being able to get forward. There was no vision and the two forwards were making the same runs.

"A good first touch was lacking wherever I looked and I couldn't believe I was watching a West Ham team. It was route one football and a little bit sad to see, although I guess that Teddy Sheringham was a big loss to the team."

John had seen Mattie Etherington, the man playing in his old position, create both of Hammers' first-half goals from the left wing, but felt the youngster contributed to his own injury problems in the second half. John speaks as a voice of authority on wing play when he says: "He drifted inside quite a bit and was getting clogged from behind because he couldn't see the Ipswich full-back (Wilnis) coming through him from behind.

"Had he stayed wide, right out on the touchline, he would have known that there was only the white line and the crowd behind him and he would have been able to see where his marker was coming from a lot easier. From that wider position it would have been easier to have seen the challenges coming in and for him to have taken evasive action.

"I like to see wingers use the full width of the pitch anyway, because by drifting inside they are only taking up the space in the channels that forwards should be running into.

"But you can't teach these things to players who are aged 22 and 23 – they should learn them in their teens," added John, who admitted he felt very flattered to be recognised by supporters crowding outside the main entrance before the game.

He admits: "The hairs on the back of my neck stood up as I walked along Green Street towards the ground, having travelled on the tube from Heathrow. No-one recognised me on the train, just as they didn't when I made the same journey regularly across from my old home on the District Line as a young player. But then, as I approached the entrance to the main stand, it was such a lovely feeling for me when people wanted my autograph before the game."

John describes West Brom's Don Howe and Burnley right-back John Angus as the most difficult opponents in his time, with honourable mentions also for Tony Book (Manchester City), Peter Rodrigues (Leicester City) and Bolton hard man Roy Hartle. He also talked of Liverpool's notorious iron man, Tommy Smith, although he saw both sides of the Anfield 'assassin'.

"Tommy and I used to room together with England Youth and got on really well. But once when West Ham played up at Liverpool, he had a very quick word when we arrived at the ground but then said to me that he couldn't stop too long because Bill Shankly didn't like his players talking to the opposition before a game. 'We'll have a drink and a chat after that match,' he said – and then he went right through me as soon as we kicked off!"

Among John's fondest memories are the first-half hat-trick he scored in an epic

7-0 League Cup defeat of a strong Leeds United at the Boleyn in November 1966, all three similarly struck into the bottom corner with his trusty left foot. "Geoff scored a hat-trick himself in the second half and Budgie Byrne was also brilliant that night," he recalled.

He reckons his most important goal, though, was the one he scored with his right foot after a 30-yard run to receive Bobby Moore's through ball in the semi-final, second leg to clinch a 1-1 draw, and aggregate victory, away to Real Zaragoza in 1965.

John says Byrne was the most accomplished footballer he played with in the claret-and-blue. "What an infectious character he was but his knowledge of football was so underrated. He was very aware, tactically, and I thought he could have been the man to take West Ham on after Ron.

"Budgie's man-management skills were fantastic but his reputation as a drinker went before him. Another thing was, he always called a spade a spade.

"After we had both moved out to South Africa he tried to sign me for Hellenic, where he was manager, and I did eventually play a few games for him, albeit at the age of about 38."

John revealed that the last time he had heard *Bubbles* sung, prior to his most recent visit to Upton Park, was at Johnny Byrne's wake in Durban. "It was a very emotional day," says John, "and one felt that he was still there with us, that he had not really passed on. It was hard to believe that Budgie had really died and we all sang *Bubbles* at his wake. He would have loved it."

Although John did some football coaching himself after settling in SA, he never followed his old team-mate Byrne into management. "I got disillusioned with the South African football hierarchy and looked for work outside the game as a salesman, which was about all there was available for ex-pro's like me.

"I went for a job selling overalls but didn't get it, so then I had a spell selling classified advertisements for the local *Argus* newspaper. That led to other things and I ended up having a lot of success selling extended car warranties, which is my forté. We sold out to a big company for a lot of money and now I work for the biggest administrative warranty company in the country, while also retaining interests in a small chemical company in the car industry, as well as a valet firm.

"Sandy and I used to run a guest house, too, but we gave that up and now live on a lovely golfing estate about an hour-and-a-half outside Cape Town, where we both enjoy playing golf. I'm also a keen cyclist and recently competed along with 35,000 others in the annual Argus Cycle Tour for the 19th time, finishing the 104kms course in three hours, 35 minutes.

"The only sad part about our life here is that I had both my West Ham cup winners' medals stolen from home. They were uninsurable and as well as losing those two medals from Wembley, I also lost my two 'Little World Cup' medals and other personal items.

"But I have so many great memories of my time at West Ham and consider myself lucky to have had the privilege of playing for them and with so many great players. The 60s really was a great time to be in football."

John pictured when he returned to England for the EX reunion dinner in May 2005.

"We've got 'Arry, 'Arry, 'Arry, 'Arry Redknapp on the wing . . . " The lower West Side admires a cult hero.

Chapter 8

HARRY**REDKNAPP**

"If we were playing up north, we'd more or less go straight from the train to the dog track at Belle Vue Manchester or Leeds. We'd get someone to take our bags on to the hotel"

THE electronic gates leading to Harry Redknapp's long driveway swung open and there was the former West Ham United player and manager looking as happy as Larry, stood in front of his mansion that is rated by local property experts as the pick of a line of very exclusive homes in the exclusive Sandbanks area of Poole, on the beautiful Dorset coast. Harry and Sandra's dream home is valued at a whopping £8.5million – the same as West Ham's new signing Craig Bellamy!

According to a recent survey by a New York estate agent, the Sandbanks peninsula is the fourth most expensive place to live in the world besides Shoto in Tokyo, Barker Road on The Peak in Hong Kong and Eaton Square, London.

Harry's well to do neighbours include the Computacentre owner Sir Peter Ogden and Body Shop director Ian McGlyn.

"We have bought and sold around 20 houses since we've lived in the Bournemouth area," reveals 'H', making a mockery of the stereotypical 'wheeler-dealer' Del Boy image in which the football media likes to portray him. You won't find Nelson Mandella House anywhere near the Redknapp property portfolio!

Colleague Terry Connelly and I enter the grand looking house and walk past the indoor swimming pool when Harry quips: "We've had it since we moved in three years ago but I've never even been for a swim in it – I leave it to Sandra and her mates to use that and our gym," he laughs.

Less than 50 yards from the home that he and his wife Sandra share with their two Bulldogs, Rosie and Buster, is – well, not so much an annex, but a lovely three-bedroom house within the main grounds.

"No-one uses the place," explains Harry, somewhat disappointingly. "I'd hoped that my Mum and Dad would come down to live in it but after Mum died the other year, I've not been able to persuade Dad to leave his old house in Poplar. He's lived there since I was born and he just won't leave."

Where the Redknapps live now seems a million miles away from the Burdett Estate in London's East End, where Harry grew up, and he certainly appreciates the luxurious lifestyle that more than two decades of football management have brought him. He looks out of the sitting room window towards the shore at the end of his back garden, just as the Sandbanks-to-Swanage ferry meanders across the water. Admiring the view of the red setting sun and pointing out where local fisherman catch bass, he says proudly: "It's not too sad, is it?

"The beach over at Swanage is lovely – it's where I walk the dogs. Mind you, I was shitting myself last year when poor Buster was suddenly attacked by a Staff. It came out of the dark, raced across the car park and grabbed Buster by the throat. I was rolling around on the floor, trying to get between the two dogs, and it took me half-an-hour, and with the help of some passers-by, to force the Staff's mouth open and drag him off Buster. It was frightening – poor Buster spent five days recovering at the vet's.

"But my two . . . they wouldn't hurt anyone."

Harry settles back on his sofa, clutching his mobile phone in one hand, and looks back to his youth and his first ever visit to Upton Park with his father, Harry senior.

"Like my dad, I was an Arsenal fan as a kid and can remember standing behind the goal at Upton Park and seeing West Ham batter the Gunners 6-0.

"I trained with Tottenham as a schoolboy and I could also have gone to either Arsenal or Chelsea, but once I met Wally St Pier and Ron Greenwood I chose West Ham. Ron was at every youth team match and he'd make a point of talking to the young players' parents after games. I could see it was a family club and when you looked at their record of producing youngsters compared to the other London clubs, West Ham got more first team players than anyone through their youth team. I knew it was the place to play.

"Colin Mackleworth, my big mate from East London Schoolboys, signed for West Ham as well. Charlie Faulkner was the scout who worked for Wally and they'd also signed the likes of Johnny Sissons, Peter Bennett and Trevor Dawkins.

"There was a great atmosphere about West Ham, it was full of local boys, and I knew it was a club that would give us a chance. I'd only been there about a week when we went off to play in the *Blau Wit* under-19 tournament in Amsterdam. I'd only left school the previous Easter, aged 15, and they took me with them.

"But while all the other players went off with different families in their cars, I happened to stay with Eddie and Iki Oostergaard – who only owned a moped! Eddie ended up driving me halfway round Amsterdam on the back of his moped, with my case and a bag, and me hanging on the back for grim life!

"I'll never forget Martin Britt telling me how they were all planning to meet up again in the main square at seven o'clock that night. I'd never been away from home before, so I took a taxi to meet the others and then realised that I'd left the piece of paper, giving details of the address where I was lodging, back at the house . . . and I didn't have clue where I was meant to be staying!

"I was late getting to the meeting and all the others – most of them 18 or 19-years-old, including Martin Peters – had all gone off without waiting for me. I was still wandering around at 11pm, trying to find somebody I knew, when luckily I bumped into Roger Hugo, who said I could spend the night at his digs.

"It was terrific to be at a club among so many other young lads who had all had the same upbringing. We got on great together and it was a very good team that won the FA Youth Cup in 1963. We had three 15-year-olds in the side – Colin Mackleworth, Bill Kitchener and myself who were first-year boys – and so it was quite a feat to beat Liverpool in a tournament where the age limit was 18-and-a-half.

"Amazingly, nine of that side were still eligible to play for the youth team the following year, when we were 10-1 on to win it and got beat by Arsenal. We looked certs to win it but lost at Highbury."

Harry says he recalls his senior debut, a 1-1 draw at home to Sunderland on August 23, 1966, when he made an almost immediate impact. It was from the right-winger's corner that Martin Peters headed West Ham in front after four minutes – the first of many such pinpoint crosses that found their target. A fast, if somewhat lightweight, right-winger, many of the headed goals on which Geoff Hurst and Peters built their reputations as world class players came via the boot of the tall, pale-skinned, flame-haired Redknapp in the No.7 shirt.

"Johnny Sissons also put in a lot of crosses," says Harry, underplaying his own contribution. "But it was the same when we played in the youth team and Martin Britt would score near-post goals just like Hurstie did. Martin got four with his head in the second leg of the final against Liverpool.

"I'd first played out wide for East London Schoolboys and stayed in that position throughout my career."

Although he had the pace and trickery to go past full-backs, Harry scored only eight goals in 170 starts and five substitute appearances for the first team between August '66 and his final game, at home to Liverpool on April 15, 1972.

Talking about his most difficult opponents, he says: "Eddie McCreadie of Chelsea was a fantastic player and so was Everton's Ray Wilson, who was very quick. They were both very difficult to get past. The game changed – from the days when players who couldn't run were put at full-back, suddenly they became as quick, or even quicker, than the wingers they were marking.

"Full-backs used to cover right round the back line – look at video footage of the Matthews Cup Final and when Stan receives the ball at his feet, the full-back who is meant to be marking him doesn't even appear in the picture for about 10 seconds!

"But by the time I played in the first team, when a crossfield ball reached me, the full-back would already be positioned very close and then try to whack me up in the air. Full-backs became quicker and suddenly there was no longer any space to play wide, which is why I suppose Ramsey discarded wingers.

"By the mid-60s there were hardly any really consistent wingers around – maybe Mike Summerbee, who was as hard as iron, was one but it was harder and harder to be consistent while playing wide."

Talking of habits that have no place in today's game where the media puts highly paid players under close scrutiny, Harry and his then best mate Billy Bonds would regularly spend the evening before an away match at the local greyhound track. Old habits die hard, though, and this interview is interrupted briefly while Harry checks his telly for the result of a horse race! You can take the boy out of Poplar . . .

Back to Bonzo, and Harry says: "We'd more or less go straight from the train to the dog track at Belle Vue Manchester or Leeds, if we were playing up North. We'd get someone to take our bags on to the hotel. Or if we had enough time to eat before going to bed, we'd order up a prawn cocktail and steak at the hotel for 10pm.

"We'd eat steak before every Saturday game. It would normally be midday but if the coach was late for whatever reason, we sometimes wouldn't eat until quarter-to-one. We'd be eating the fattest fillet steak ever seen, followed by rice pudding. Now if you're telling me that you can run around on that . . . I mean, people today would think you were off your rocker, but that used to be our pre-match meal! Everybody was doing it – and perhaps that's why none of us could run as fast as players do now!"

Harry was certainly not renowned for his aggression, so it was ironic that he should be sent off for the one and only time in his West Ham playing career in October 1968 at Leeds, where Don Revie's great 60s side were anything but shrinking violets. "I dunno what happened there," says 'H', scratching his head. "I think (Billy) Bremner appealed for a goalkick or something, so I told him to 'shut up' and the next thing he got me round the throat. I was sent off for nothing really.

"I remember all the Leeds players circling me, while our lot just stood back and couldn't believe what they were seeing. Mooro just stood on the halfway line and as I walked past him towards the dressing room, he was there with his arms folded, shrugging his shoulders and rolling his eyes at me!

"Meanwhile, Jack Charlton and Norman Hunter were trying to punch me! Leeds were very much a team together, they wanted to win for their lives, and were one of the greatest sides you'll ever see.

"They were great days and, yes, it was a special era to play in. Facing up to the likes of Best, Law and Charlton at Old Trafford was something else – and remember the time they stuffed us 6-1 at home to win the league in '67? 'Macca' (Colin Mackleworth) played in goal and I remember how Sandra and myself, Macca and his girlfriend went out for a meal that night as far away from Upton Park as possible. Macca didn't want to be seen out anywhere near the area and I think we ended up eating at a place in Brentwood.

"United got a penalty after Denis Law made a bad remark to 'Charlo' (John Charles) and tapped him on the side of the face. Charlo pushed him back and the ref gave them a pen."

Harry was choked by the deaths in recent years of his good mates, the Charles brothers, in quick succession due to cancer.

"It was sad losing Charlo and his younger brother, Clive," he said. "I went to to see young Clive when he came over here, just before he died, and I couldn't tell you how brave he was. He was just a bag of bones but he was more interested in other people than himself, especially a young kid he had playing for him back in Portland who he thought would be a good player. Clive knew he had only days left to live but he wasn't thinking about himself. It was unbelievable.

"We had great characters at West Ham – the two Charlos, Dearie, (John) Cushley and Mooro, who was the king. Then you had the coaches, Ernie, Jimmy Barrett and Albert Walker. It was fantastic, a great club."

The closest Harry came to a Wembley appearance as a Hammer was as a beaten League Cup semi-finalist in 1972. His tumble over the arms of Gordon Banks won the penalty for Hurst which was crucially saved by the Stoke City and England goalkeeper in the second leg at Upton Park.

"We were a bit unlucky that night and again when Mooro had to replace the injured

Young Harry (left) was an outstanding product of East London. Right: A first team favourite.

Bobby Ferguson in goal at Old Trafford in the second replay."

Harry doesn't wax lyrical about his own playing performances and had to be reminded that he set up a few goals along the way for Hurst, Bryan 'Pop' Robson and Clyde Best during that thrilling 1971-72 League Cup campaign that brought victories over Cardiff City, Leeds United, Sheffield United and Liverpool.

"I was one of the best young players in the country at 16 and I should have been 10 times better than I was," he admits with a tinge of regret.

With new signing from Hereford United, Dudley Tyler, and young prospect Johnny Ayris vieing for the No.7 shirt, Harry moved to AFC Bournemouth, a haven for ex-Hammers, in August 1972. John Bond paid a Cherries' club record £31,000 for the flying winger who would take the club and town to his heart.

Two years later, Redknapp briefly joined Bond at Norwich City, where the former Cup-winning full-back had progressed up the managerial ladder, but a knee injury wrecked Harry's hopes of his loan move becoming permanent.

Redknapp reveals: "Being uneducated, I didn't know what I was going to do when I finished playing. For a while, I thought seriously about becoming a cabbie."

It doesn't take much imagination to picture Harry behind the wheel of a black cab. But this "uneducated" product of the Burdett Estate in the heart of London's East End had already qualified from the 'University of Life' with a PhD – and he was destined for a much more lucrative living as one of the game's longest-serving managers.

And the magnificent mansion to go with it.

Chapter 9

BOBBY**MOORE OBE**

"He should have been on the West Ham board, someone who would have given the club presence wherever he went, but the directors didn't want to know"

IT still pains Harry Redknapp to reflect on how West Ham, and the English game, turned its back on Bobby Moore while he was still alive and didn't recognise his immense stature for club and country until after his death from cancer, aged 51, on February 24, 1993.

Harry exclusively told *EX:* "The game wasted the greatest opportunity it had. I used to say to Terry Brown, the chairman at West Ham, and everybody else, that when Bobby died they wanted to build statues and name a stand after him.

"But when he was alive, they didn't want to know him. What did they do for him?

"There was a man who should have been a great ambassador for West Ham, like Franz Beckenbaur was for Bayern Munich and Sir Bobby Charlton is now for Manchester United. We had Bobby Moore.

"He should have been on the West Ham board, someone who would have given the club presence wherever he went, but the directors didn't want to know.

"I still tell the story – and people can argue about it all they like but it's true – about when Bobby was actually *thrown out* of the ground at West Ham.

"I went to a game – it must have been in the late 70s – and was sitting next to Frank Lampard's mum, at the back of E Block in the West Stand, when I suddenly noticed that Bobby had come up

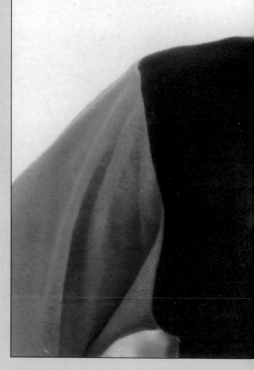

A young Bobby looking as calm and unflappable as ever.
Inset (right): Leading out the Hammers at Anfield.
Inset (left): FA Cup holder in 1964.

Always immaculate, on and off the field.

The players trained at the nearby West Ham greyhound and speedway stadium in Prince Regent Lane, Custom House, because the turf and the size of the pitch there was similar to what they would encounter at Wembley in the Cup finals of 1964 and '65. Alongside Bobby are Alan Sealey, Peter Brabrook and Jack Burkett.

the steps and was sitting a few rows behind us. I looked around, we waved to each other and I shouted to him that we'd get together for a chat at half-time.

"Then I saw a steward approach Bobby and say to him: 'Look Bob, nothing to do with me, but I've been told that you're not allowed in without a ticket'.

"Bobby used to enter through a little side door, just off the main entrance, and then walk through the corridor and up into the main stand. They would open the door for him, let him in and then he'd go up and sit at the back of the stand.

"But when this steward – and I don't blame him, he was only following orders – told Bobby he had to leave, he walked out of the ground and never went back. That's the God's honest truth.

"So it does me in when I see that the club suddenly wants to do things to preserve his name and memory.

"They say it's a family club but when the man was alive they did nothing for him."

One of Redknapp's first acts when he became West Ham United manager in August 1994 was to decorate the walls of the training ground with framed pictures of his old mate, Mooro, and the club's two other World Cup-winning legends.

One wall of Harry's old office at Chadwell Heath was adorned by that iconic image of Moore and Pele exchanging shirts after the epic England v Brazil match at the 1970 World Cup tournament in Mexico.

Redknapp says: "They were put up for everybody to see what had been achieved at the club by those boys. It will never be done again, so having three West Ham players win the World Cup was something we should be proud of.

"Bobby was every boy's dream, someone we would all look up to," he added.

Billy in his first season with the Hammers – thrusting forward from right-back.

Chapter 10

BILLY**BONDS** MBE

"I never had a contract dispute in all my time at the club. In fact, once, John Lyall told me the directors wanted to give me more money! Frank Lampard was the highest earner at the club at the time and they thought it was only right that I was paid the same as him. I think it was Brian Cearns who suggested it, but I didn't ask for an increase. A lot of people would call me a mug, I suppose. I was content, though, just happy to be playing for West Ham"

WHEN West Ham bought Billy Bonds from Charlton Athletic for £50,000 in May 1967, the club had never spent more wisely. Arguably, they have never done a better bit of transfer business since then either (although the £6,000 capture of Alan Devonshire will also take some beating).

After an astonishing, record breaking 795 first team games (including two Charity Shield matches), and having lifted the FA Cup on two of the three occasions Hammers have won it, Billy – now 60 – can look back on a fantastic career with tremendous pride.

Taking us back to where it all began and his first West Ham connection, he told *EX*: "I played for a very successful Sunday boys' team called Moatbridge and our manager, Mr Flowers, somehow arranged for Bobby Moore to come along and present our medals. I was 14 at the time, so Bobby would have been only about 19-20, but he looked immaculate in his suit, like a film star, and he had a beautiful looking girl on his arm – his missus, as it turned out. For me to go from Charlton to West Ham and be playing with Bobby was amazing.

"It came out afterwards that Geoff Hurst had mentioned to Ron Greenwood about signing me, after Charlton were unlucky to lose to West Ham in the final of the London five-a -side tournament. I think Bob Stokoe, who was then manager at Charlton, got into trouble for selling me behind his chairman's back. Bob wasn't too happy with me when I mentioned in our meeting with Ron that there were a couple of other clubs – Leicester City and Sunderland – in for me. Ron actually stormed out and Bob said I shouldn't have upset him by mentioning the other clubs.

"But I think they were doing a bit of a double act on me and I agreed to join West Ham, signing on the last day of the 1967-68 season, when I saw them play Manchester City," recalls Bill.

Although Billy made his official Hammers' debut in the opening game of the following season, a 3-2 home defeat by Sheffield Wednesday, on the same day Bobby Ferguson and John Cushley also made their bows, his first actual appearance in the claret-and-blue had been in Ken Brown's testimonial against a Select XI, on

May 15, 1967.

"I remember it because I came off at half-time with a toe injury. It used to give me a lot of gyp over the years and, in fact, was the reason I missed the whole of the 1985-86 season. The bone in my little toe became infected and I had to have half of it taken off but they reckon the problem could have started almost 20 years earlier.

"West Ham were renowned as a good attacking side but they were also known as a bit of a soft touch. Ron tried to change it a bit but neither Fergie nor Cush really worked out and we never challenged for the title."

Agents were sill unheard of long after Billy crossed the Thames. Not that he ever had cause to regret a lack of financial advice in his dealings with either Greenwood or his successor, John Lyall. "You were just glad to be playing for the club, money didn't come into it," says Bill. "When you're contract was up for renewal, you were given an appointment time with Ron – I'd go in and see him at, say, midday and the next player would be due in for 12.15. You'd go in, Ron would tell you he's giving you a £25 a week rise and a new two-year contract and you'd just say: 'Thank-you, Mr Greenwood'. And that was it. I'd simply go home and tell Lyn, my missus, that we were OK for another two years.

"I never had a contract dispute in all my time at the club. In fact, once, John Lyall told me that the directors wanted to give me more money! Frank Lampard was the highest earner at the club at the time and they thought it was only right that I was paid the same as him. I think it was Brian Cearns who suggested it, but I didn't ask for an increase. A lot of people would call me a mug, I suppose. I was content, though, just happy to be playing for West Ham."

Bill suggests that most fans will remember him more for his days at the heart of the Hammers defence, alongside Alvin Martin, rather than for his buccaneering days as a midfield marauder – Trevor Brooking's so-called 'minder' – or, indeed, the first three seasons he spent as an adventurous, overlapping right-back. Bill is clear in his own mind about the role he favoured most.

"I enjoyed centre of midfield best. I was at my peak playing there in the early 70s," he says without hesitation. "My best years were definitely spent in midfield . . . I could run all day and I was physically powerful. I could influence games from there and I thought I did at times. I absolutely loved that role.

"I can trace my peak period back to around the time of the League Cup semi-finals against Stoke in 1972. Between '70 and '74 I was in my prime as a player."

It says so much about the incomparable leadership qualities of Bonzo and the sheer presence of the great man that he led West Ham to two FA Cup triumphs, racked up a few hundred more appearances and collected a fourth Hammer-of-the-Year award *after* the period in which he considered himself to be at his peak!

Bill made the successful switch from the No.2 to the No.4 shirt in 1970-71, the season after Martin Peters left to join Spurs, which adds intrigue to the former World Cup winner's curious comment to Bonzo at training one day before his departure in March '70. Bill explains: "I can remember the first time Ron tried me in midfield, it was during a training game on a muddy pitch at Chadwell Heath. I enjoyed it but afterwards Martin Peters came over and said to me: 'Don't cut your own throat'. That was all he said but I don't know what he meant by it – I never asked him. Whether he was looking out for me, or he felt I was challenging for his position in the team, I really don't know. I doubt that, because he was a wonderfully talented player. It was a funny thing to say, though.

"I enjoyed playing at right-back, too. Centre-half was the position I liked least, although that's probably the one I'm most remembered for by the majority of fans. I think people outside West Ham saw me as a defender.

"I like to think that Trevor and I needed one and other and that we were good for each other. He needed a Billy Bonds and I needed a Trevor Brooking alongside me. We complemented each other."

Did Bill sometimes believe that he was perhaps a bit underestimated as a footballer who could pass the ball well and also create for others? Was there sometimes more to his game than usually met the eye? "I think you needed to have trained with me and played with me to have appreciated my worth as a player. I never doubted myself."

Bill agrees that the trio of Brooking, Graham Paddon and himself was probably the best midfield combination he featured in. He and Brooking have always been great friends, they enjoyed a mutual respect, but Bill had words of praise for Paddon, too. "It was so well balanced with the three of us. Trevor was a fantastic all round player with great ability, while Graham had a fantastic left peg.

"I loved playing in the mud and many of the pitches we played on in the early 70s were very heavy. My physical strength came through in those circumstances and I always thought Trevor was better playing in the mud, too. He was physically strong, he would stick his backside into people and hold them off. Some of the pitches were diabolical. At Derby, you could barely lift your feet out of the mud.

"Later on, I also played in the same midfield as Trevor and Alan Devonshire – and Dev was a tremendous player, too."

Bill always fully respected team-mates who gave their all, those who showed the same roll-up-the-sleeves type characteristics he embodied throughout his own illustrious career, so it wasn't surprising to hear him single out two in particular.

"I thought Patsy Holland and Geoff Pike were unsung heroes, both terrific players," he said. "I played with Pikey the other day (for the Boys of 86 team) and I thought then, 'Yeah, you can pass the ball all right'. He never gave it away.

"Patsy was a real 110 percent player. His bravery was summed up by the fact that his career was finished by an injury he sustained going for a ball (at Notts County) he had no right to go for. I think we were already winning well up there at the time, but that was typical of him to go for a ball that most players wouldn't have even thought of contesting.

"Patsy would run through brick walls for you – and he had ability, too.

"David Cross was raw when he first came to us but he improved a lot as a player after he joined us. He was a good pro.

"His strike-partner, Pop Robson, was top drawer. I'd have him in my all-time West Ham team, alongside Hurstie. I never saw Budgie Byrne. Pop could score 25-yarders as well as tap-ins."

Bill is reluctant to compare best-ever West Ham teams – the record breaking 1985-86 side against the merits of the early 80s team he led to the second division championship and two Wembley cup finals in a year. Almost half the team actively enjoyed both eras, whereas Brooking and Bonds were out of the picture when John Lyall's team sustained their challenge for the first division league title.

"I saw the 85-86 team all year and some of the one-touch football they played was fantastic. Everybody was on top of their game but, for me, I thought Alan Dickens was outstanding, possibly the best of them all. You couldn't argue with Tony Cottee or Frank McAvennie as Hammer-of-the-Year but Dicko was very instrumental from midfield that season," said Bonzo.

"It's always difficult to compare but I would have thought the '81 side would have beaten them. You can't judge it, though, because a number of players – the likes of Dev, Parksey, Ray Stewart and Alvin – played in both successful teams."

Bill experienced relegation as a player at Upton Park in May 1978 and you have no reason to doubt him when he says that the star players, Brooking, Lampard and himself, never ever considered the possibility of leaving the club to continue playing in the top flight. Okay, so the financial gulf that exists now between the haves and have-nots of the Premiership elite and the Championship did not apply back then. But then neither did that word long gone from the modern-day football lexicon – loyalty.

"It never crossed my mind to move clubs when we were relegated," insists Bill with a comment that belongs to a bygone age. "Trevor and I never even raised the subject. When I was younger I heard talk that Manchester United were interested in me but I never even bothered to enquire about it.

"Going down in '78 was the best thing that happened to us, because we were able to rebuild. John bought well and we came back up much stronger than before, going on to enjoy one of the most successful periods in the club's history.

"The game has changed completely since Bosman, though. Money has changed it. One move and a player can make absolute fortunes. There was a lot more loyalty about in my playing days. Contracts don't mean a thing now. Testimonials are a thing of the past," added the first Hammer to be honoured with *two* testimonial matches.

Bill also bemoans the lack of leaders in the modern game. "Where are they now?" he asks. "Tony Adams has gone. Roy Keane was a leader and I'd say Alan Shearer was, too, but that's it. I love Shearer. He's a man's man and I'd follow him any day."

So how would Bill define his own leadership style qualities?

"I was honest and players knew I expected the same from all of them. I suppose I led by example. I couldn't accept it if players around me didn't give 100 percent. I don't care how much ability a player has, if someone runs past you, you are entitled to run back 10 yards and try to tackle them. I didn't expect Trevor Brooking to win many tackles or 50/50 headers but I *did* expect him to battle back when it was needed, which he did."

You can safely assume that Ted MacDougall, who was famously chinned by Bonzo in the dressing room at Leeds after one particularly lethargic performance by the striker in the early 70s, did not fit into the 'battling' category that day!

"I just didn't like Ted anyway and I don't suppose he liked me either," admits Bill. "I found him to be a bit arrogant off the field. For instance, I didn't like the way he

*Always in the thick of the action, Bonzo unleashes
a shot at the South Bank end.*

Left: He twice lifted the FA Cup.

Billy with Bobby Moore, then of Fulham, the man he succeeded as West Ham skipper.

treated waiters in hotel restaurants – to him, it was as if they didn't even exist.

"I didn't think Ted was putting it in for us at Leeds and I said a few things to him. He said something back to me and it all went off in the bath afterwards – Ron Greenwood's suit got very wet! I think he just thought, 'let 'em get on with it'.

"Ted was one of the few players I didn't get on with. I had rucks with several players – the likes of Alvin, especially when he was much younger, and Mervyn Day – but they'd come to me afterwards and say I was right to say what I did. I slaughtered Mervyn on one trip to Norway but he came up the next day and said I was right. They were as good as gold."

Although he is the proud possessor of two FA Cup-winners' medals and played in the last major European final Hammers reached, in 1976, Bill never questioned West Ham's inability to mount a serious title challenge other than the 85-86 campaign in which he was a frustrated injured onlooker.

"It didn't occur to me to go into the manager and suggest what he ought to be doing. You got paid and went out and played for the club. You did your job. I enjoyed the people I was working with. I had two terrific managers who made me a better player, taught me all kinds of things.

"It was like when Ron asked me to move into the back four, alongside Tommy Taylor. I think it was just before the European Cup Winners' Cup semi-final against

Eintracht Frankfurt. Ron said I would be able to come out with the ball, which he liked his defenders to do. I never questioned moving to the back, I just got on with it and did as he asked."

With his lean but muscular frame topped by a dark beard and longish, flapping hair, and with socks rolled down to his ankles in the days before shin pads were mandatory, Billy Bonds looked every inch the warrior going into battle. A fearsome sight for any opponent. He never flinched from a challenge in his life, every tackle contested full bloodedly. The image of Billy, with head wounds hastily patched up, returning to the scene of the battle to lead and inspire his men like an indestructible general, is enshrined in Hammers folklore.

To fans of other clubs, who perhaps didn't fully appreciate his all round talents, he was pigeon-holed in the 'hard man' category alongside fellow iron men of the era such as Tommy Smith, Norman Hunter and Ron Harris. But Bonzo was sent off only twice in his long career and he insists he was never a dirty player.

"I admire Eddie Bovington's total honesty for what he said in your last issue of *EX* (issue 11) about how he deliberately went through the back of opponents, because that's how it was in those days. But I never went out on to the field to deliberately hurt anyone. I was a good tackler. People say I wouldn't get away with how I played nowadays, and I would still get booked a lot because I was aggressive. Still am at times, according to my missus, it's in my make up. But I could tackle. I won the ball.

"I loved to be physical on the football field, it came quite naturally to me. I didn't have to psyche myself up before a game, although I did nut the occasional dressing room door. Hollow doors – none that were made of oak!

"That's not being dirty, but I loved a tackle. I was sent off once for fighting on the ground with Colin Todd of Birmingham, which nearly cost me my place in the 1980 FA Cup final. And the other time was in 1970, when Simpkin of Hull City gobbed straight in my face, so I nutted him. I remember Ron Greenwood saying something like: 'You shouldn't be doing that, William'. Ron always called me William," laughed Bill.

"I went through people because you were allowed to do it. I went through Cyrille Regis once and got a friction burn on my leg from his shorts!

"I don't like to compare players from the past with those of today, because the rules have changed so much. I'm sure an old-style type centre-forward like Alan Shearer would have been a great player even then, but he would have been beaten up bit. In my day, as a defender you'd have three or four go's at a centre-forward before the referee would even think about the possibility of booking you.

"When I was a full-back, my mentality was: 'It's either you or me today'. Either I was going to have a good game or he would. I didn't go out to hurt anyone but I'd say to myself: 'The first time I go in for a 50/50 tackle with you, I'm gonna give you the lot'. It was a bit like American football. I'd unload on them.

"But sometimes wingers like Eddie Gray or George Best would slaughter me instead. There were so many good wingers about when I played as a right-back.

"As well as Gray, Leeds also had Terry Cooper, a left-back who played like a winger. The first time I played at Anfield, Liverpool had two great wingers in Peter Thompson and Ian Callaghan. There was Johnny Morrisey at Everton; Bestie and

Left: As this picture shows, he was not just a tenacious ball-winner. Right: The sheer intensity of Bonzo.

Willie Morgan for Man United . . . loads of quality wingers around. You had to learn to defend properly and quickly, otherwise you would be taken to the cleaners.

"Harry Redknapp played in front of me on the right side but Harry wasn't the type to get back and help out – he just did things when he got the ball in the attacking half. There wasn't any doubling-up then, wing-backs didn't exist.

"But the art of defending is not about kicking people, it's about tackling. That's why I never respected Vinnie Jones. They called him a hard man, but I didn't think he was. To me, someone who goes in for a 50/50 ball is hard. Patsy Holland would never pull out of a tackle – he wasn't physically strong but he was very brave. He really was hard.

"So, hand on heart, I can honestly say that while I went out to clatter people, I never deliberately tried to hurt anyone, to break anybody's legs or put them in hospital. Even if I had the hump with them, I'd leave them on the floor and say 'get hold of that', but I would never go out to hurt somebody."

Not that the managers Bill played under at West Ham ever preached rough play. "No, definitely not. John wanted us to be aggressive, he loved that about a player, but not to deliberately hurt opponents," said Bonzo.

The former Hammers' skipper says he enjoyed the experience of the 1980 Cup final victory against Arsenal much more than either of his two previous cup final appearances in the mid-70s.

He explained: "I didn't enjoy the '75 final against Fulham much because I wasn't fully fit. I had a groin problem, which I'd been carrying for most of the season, and needed to take tablets and cortisone injections to get through it. It was very worrying and my wife and I even talked about the possibility that my career might be over. I thought about taking a coaching course.

"I also had a bad gash that needed 10 stitches, so I didn't enjoy the '75 final because I was virtually playing on one leg.

"Even after (Dr) Brian Roper operated and fashioned a new socket, I still had shooting pains and couldn't run properly for a time. I just had to run through it, break it down. We were second to Man United in the table when I eventually returned, as a sub against Man City in the sixth game of the season, when Frank (Lampard) scored our winner.

"Apart from the groin problem and the bad toe, the only other bad injury I suffered was when Phil Parkes smashed into me at Sheffield Wednesday, broke two of my ribs and I had to miss the England v Brazil game," recalled one of the best players never to have won a full international cap.

Of his four cup final appearances for West Ham, Bill's saddest memories revolve around the 4-2 defeat by Anderlecht in the European Cup Winners' Cup final in '76 – and not because of the result. Underlining his strong family principles, he explains: "It just brings back bad memories. My mother-in-law was ill with cancer and so I travelled out to Belgium later than the other lads – on the supporters' plane from Luton airport to Brussels. My wife, who had been told her mum had only six weeks to live, was obviously very upset. If Lyn had wanted me to stay at home with her, I would have missed the final. But it was her dad who told me to play.

"I flew in, went to the hotel to hear John's team-talk and then immediately after the game I returned to England with our fans again, while the players went back to the hotel to drown their sorrows. When I got home my wife was crying . . . her mum had died on the night of the game.

"That's why I wanted to enjoy the 1980 final. I wanted to take it all in, because it flies by. Come to think of it, because there were fans on the pitch after our '75 win, I don't even think we were able to do a proper lap of honour. Not many people get a second chance, so I made a point of taking it all in when we beat Arsenal. Even well after the end of the Arsenal game, when everyone had left the stadium and there was just paper blowing around, I walked back out of the dressing room to the edge of the tunnel, to have a last look at the pitch. I thought to myself: 'What's gone on here today? . . . We've won the Cup'. This time I took it all in."

No captain of West Ham United has been able to experience such a magical moment again in the 27 years that have passed since then.

"On the way back to our hotel, Ernie Gregory – who didn't usually drink – was sipping champagne from the cup and he quickly became as pissed as a newt. We had to get him into bed!"

Although not a recognised part of football's drinking culture of the 60s, 70s and 80s, Bill enjoyed a beer like most players. "After the game there would be a pack of beers in the dressing room and I'd help myself to one before heading for home. I didn't like to go into the players' bar – I wanted to shower, then go straight home.

"I couldn't eat when I got home after a game, though, otherwise I would have been physically sick. My missus had to put dinner on hold for a few hours."

In conflict with the modern-day thinking of the nutritionists now employed by all top clubs, Bonzo admits he relished a big, juicy steak (or three) on the day of a game. "At the hotel, I'd eat all my meal and sometimes finish off what one or two of the other lads didn't want, too.

"We didn't eat pasta or anything like that. The first with a new regime was Pop Robson, who ate Corn Flakes with peaches, and he'd also eat a lot of chocolate. That was the nearest any of us came to being scientific! It was always steak or boiled chicken, with a bowl of rice for dessert. Albert Walker, one of the trainers, was an expert at determining the quality of the rice – he'd always give the dessert marks out of 10.

"I'm not saying the way we prepared for a game was right. Who knows, I might have been able to run even quicker if I'd eaten pasta and the other healthy things players eat before a game nowadays.

"A bit later in my career, I'd have a drop of brandy just before a game. Now what would the dieticians of today make of that! Our physio, Rob Jenkins, would pop up to the boardroom to top up his little flask, then Parksey, Pikey and me would have a drop before we went out to play."

When people look back on Billy Bonds' long and illustrious playing career, he will probably be best remembered for his supreme leadership qualities and incredible fitness levels that defied the aging process and put his much younger team-mates to shame. He retained his Peter Pan qualities right up to when he finally hung up his boots for the last time – after his 663rd league appearance at Southampton on April, 30, 1988, four months after a visit to Buckingham Palace to collect a richly deserved MBE.

Bill's lung-busting cross-country runs in pre-season training, his ability to pump iron with the best well into his 40s, is the stuff of dressing room legend at West Ham. So it came as no surprise when he said that he still runs for 40 minutes a week at the gym and routinely manages 1,000 sit-ups (yes, you read it correctly, that's four noughts – one thousand!).

"I've always been able to run all day," he says. "No-one told me how to train or what I should do. I thought that the older I got as a player, the harder I had to work – I ran as well at 38 as I did when I was 18. My missus tells me I look a bit tired after a run now but I still like to do the running, weights and stomach exercises. I think I was 13st 2lbs when I signed for West Ham, I was probably 13st 5lbs when I finished . . . and I'm two pounds heavier than that now.

"I didn't touch weights until I was into my 30s, when I saw Alan Devonshire lifting a stack in the gym.

"My pre-match warm up was very simple – just kicking a ball in the gym for 10 minutes. I hated going out on the pitch for a kickabout. I just wanted to go out there, hear the noise of the crowd and get stuck into the match.

"I was very lucky with injuries really and I generally still feel very fit. The only thing I don't like about myself is that I've got terrible varicose veins in my legs. They don't bother me – my doctor says the exercise is good for them – although I

London Evening Standard Five-a-Side winners in the early 70s. Bobby Howe is next to Bill, with John Sissons, Clive Charles and keeper Peter Grotier at the front.

don't like wearing shorts any more."

Billy never set himself a retirement date as a player. "When I got much older, John Lyall would sense how I felt and he'd say: 'You want another year, don't you?' I'd say: 'Yeah', and he'd be happy for me to continue.

"I did quit at one stage, but then he brought me back. He told me to play with the reserves, teach the kids a few things, and have an influence on them. But then first team players suffered a lot of injuries, so I came back into the side again and had another three or four years or so as a player.

"I think if I'd asked John for another contract at the time I stopped playing in '88, he would have given it to me and, who knows, I might have played on for another year. But my missus used to say to me: 'You're looking a bit tired after games, a bit thin in the face', so I thought about it and decided to pack it in.

"To be truthful, if John hadn't offered me the youth team manager's job, which meant I could stay at the club, I could have gone on to play for at least another couple of years further down the leagues, maybe at second or third division level. No problem.

"The only other option was to take the manager's job which came up at Gillingham, but I turned that down because I wanted to stay at West Ham. Sometimes I look back and regret that I didn't play another 100 games – there is nothing like playing. I loved it – it was like a drug to me."

Big and powerful, Clyde Best was a handful for any defence.

Chapter 11

CLYDE**BEST** MBE

"We didn't look at it that we were three black players in an otherwise white team. It was more a case of, hey, we're all mates together"

TODAY every English Premiership club has its share of talented black players, many of whom have deservedly earned superstar status and the respect and admiration of what is now a multi-cultural nation.

Yet while the racist thugs who first came to prominence on the football terraces in the 60s continued to tarnish the game at grounds up and down the country for most of the next two decades, West Ham did more than any other top club to pave the way for the 'black revolution' in English football.

April 1, 1972 was the historical day that Ron Greenwood became the first club manager to select THREE black players for a first division game. London rivals Spurs were outplayed, 2-0, at Upton Park.

Ade Coker, a livewire teenage striker from Nigeria, scored the second goal but left-back and East End-born Clive Charles – whose elder brother, John, had been the first black player to reach the first team at Upton Park almost a decade earlier – and another forward, Bermudan international Clyde Best, also played their part for the Hammers on that momentous occasion.

Coker would make just 11 senior appearances and disappeared almost as quickly as he had arrived in the spotlight, while the younger 'Charlo' played only 15 first team matches.

The big, burly Best, who developed the build of Sonny Liston, established himself and became a star, the most celebrated footballer to emerge from Bermuda. In a one-club English career spanning seven seasons, from 1969 to 1975, he made 218 senior appearances, scoring 56 goals.

But when reminded of that landmark occasion against Tottenham, Best preferred to play down the significance of it in cultural terms. Speaking from his home in Bermuda, he told *EX*: "We didn't look at it that we were three black players in an otherwise white team. It was more a case of, hey, we're all mates together.

"In fact, a more significant fact about that game was that, once Kevin Lock came on as sub to set up Ade's goal, the average age of our side was reduced to just 21."

Not that Clyde, who will be 52 on February 24, 2008 (the anniversary of former team-mate Bobby Moore's death) and now working full-time in the prison service back home, has nothing to say about the underlying race issues that delayed the development of black players at English clubs around the time he made his West Ham debut, as a 17-year-old against Arsenal in August 1969.

He continues: "I think most English clubs back then were naive and scared to give black players a chance. Some of the best in the world – including Pele and Eusebio – were black but we didn't get the same opportunities in those days that black players do now. We've got good rhythm and movement but very few black footballers were given the credit for that when I first arrived in England.

"But in football, as in any sport or other walk of life, a competitor or a person should always be judged on his or her ability to perform, not by their colour."

Clyde's footballing potential was discovered in Bermuda by English coach Graham Adams, a friend of Ron Greenwood's who was working there. The story of how Best, a raw teenager, turned up in England and was left to roam the strange streets of East London until he found lodgings with John Charles' parents in Canning Town, is part of West Ham folklore.

'Charlo' was an early mentor to Best. "John took me under his wing a bit," confirms Clyde. "He was like a brother to me and taught me at an early age the kind of problems I was likely to encounter from fans at away grounds and how best to block it out.

"I recall a game at Everton in the early 70s when I was getting a lot of stick from the crowd because of my colour. Then I collected the ball on the halfway line and ran past several Everton defenders before sticking it in their net. The fans gave me more respect after that, which proved to me that playing well and scoring goals was the best way to stick it up 'em."

Attitudes have, thankfully, changed for the better in football but there is no room for complacency and Clyde feels strongly that the clubs, as well as the authorities who govern them, must not relax their campaigns to kick racism out of football.

Clyde says: "FIFA need to take stronger action against those who offend and the clubs themselves should definitely take responsibility for their own players."

What if some of the players themselves would rather keep quiet and not draw further attention to the race issues, for fear of being individually targeted? That's understandable – but Clyde is adamant: "There comes a time when you *have* to stand up for what is right and decent. The players who may be victimised today have to think of the guys who will follow on after them."

At 6ft 2ins, Clyde could look after himself on the football field. He started to grow a beard from his early teens and when he first appeared in a Hammers shirt, for the youth and Metropolitan League teams, opponents viewed his inclusion with some suspicion. "I was big for my age and just thankful that God gave me that physique. To me, some of the other kids seemed a bit too young and scrawny!" he laughs.

Playing mainly in a wide, forward position on the right, where he kept Harry Redknapp out of the side for a spell in the early 70s, Clyde showed his ability to impose himself on the game at a time when forwards were not afforded the protection from tough-tackling defenders that they are now.

In only his second season in the first team, in autumn 1970, Clyde starred for West Ham against Brazilian giants Santos in a prestige friendly played in New York. The only two scorers in a 2-2 draw were Best and a certain Pele!

"As well as Pele, Santos were captained by Carlos Alberto and they had Edu on the subs' bench. It was quite an occasion for me, especially at the age of only 19," recalls Clive, who continued to make his mark in the following weeks with the

Left: Clyde's mentor, John Charles, the first black Hammer. Right: Ade Coker, a teenage star from Nigeria.

equalising goal in Bobby Moore's testimonial match, a 3-3 draw with Celtic, and a brace in a 4-2 league defeat at Derby County.

Clyde must have soon realised, though, what a turbulent experience life at West Ham would become. The highs of scoring against one of the world's top sides would be followed, very swiftly, by embarrassing cup defeats to teams Hammers ought to have beaten out of sight. The 4-0 debacle in the third round of the FA Cup at Blackpool in January 1971 was typical of a side that could boast world class individuals like Moore and Hurst (in fact, Geoff didn't play that day) yet go down in the most feeble fashion to lower division teams. Relegation struggles were par for the course.

Ah, Blackpool. An affair that culminated in a blaze of bad publicity and club fines for skipper Moore, Jimmy Greaves, Brian Dear and Best himself. The bottom line from Clyde, who didn't even touch alcohol when the small group went into town for a few drinks the night before the game, is that "it was all blown out of proportion."

While Greaves and Dear were quickly shown the Upton Park exit gates and descended into a long battle with the booze from which they both happily made a complete recovery, Best re-emerged from the Blackpool episode and, a year later, enjoyed his best season at the club.

"Ron didn't hold the Blackpool business against me," explains Clyde, who top-scored for the Hammers with 17 first division goals in 1971-72 – more than twice the total recorded by Hurst. By then, Bryan 'Pop' Robson had signed from Newcastle United and established himself as a firm fans' favourite.

Although West Ham could not rise above mid-table in the league, they reached the fifth round of the FA Cup (Best scoring twice *en route*), while the Big Man added another four in a promising League Cup campaign (including the winner in a third round replay at Leeds) that culminated in a marathon semi-final with Stoke City.

Hammers were favourites to reach Wembley after goals by Hurst and Best gave us a 2-1 first leg victory at Stoke. But after Geoff's penalty kick was brilliantly saved by Gordon Banks in the return leg at Upton Park that ended in a 1-0 defeat, the tie went to a replay. When nothing could separate the sides at Hillsborough, a second replay was needed at Old Trafford.

The images of the players slipping and sliding their way through the Manchester mud is ingrained in the memory, as is the penalty that Bobby Moore saved, only for Stoke to net from the rebound and go on to win a thriller, 3-2.

Clyde reveals that Moore first offered *him* the gloves after goalkeeper Bobby Ferguson was kicked in the head and had to leave the field. He admits: "I was young, very nervous and, besides, I wanted to stay on the field to try and score a goal to put us into the final."

And that cabbage patch of a pitch? "Well, the one we used to play on at Upton Park wasn't much better then. Today's players wouldn't be able to play on it."

Within weeks of that shattering semi-final blow, Hurst was allowed to join Stoke, who beat Chelsea 2-1 in the Wembley final.

"The club got rid of Geoff too early – he still had much to offer West Ham," insists Clyde. "I think Ron Greenwood saw me filling Geoff's role as a target man who could hold up the ball with his back to play, but I was still young and learning the game and I needed to learn more about forward play from Geoff, as well as Pop. The thing is, too, that while defenders were worrying about Geoff and his reputation, they gave me more space."

Robson – "a lovely fella, not at all big-headed" – took over as the main marksmen with 28 league goals in 1972-73 as the team shot from 14th up to sixth position, but Best's personal tally dipped to just seven, despite the continued emergence of Trevor Brooking as the new midfield playmaker. "We were a running. gunning team but we started to put more emphasis on good defensive play," he said.

Clyde also did his bit at the back to earn a 1-1 home draw with Leeds United, when – unlike at the Old Trafford semi – he readily pulled on the gloves after Ferguson suffered another bad knock to his head. "I was a bit older, more confident and I think this time I volunteered to take over from Fergie."

The search for more firepower saw Ted MacDougall signed from Manchester United but he never settled and within 10 months had left to rejoin another of his former clubs, Norwich City. "Ted wasn't one for being involved in the patient build-up football we liked to play at West Ham. He wanted to throw himself at direct balls into the box and he wasn't our type," observes Clyde, who recognised the talent in other youngsters at the club.

"We had a guy called Keith Miller who, if it hadn't been for the presence of Bobby Moore, could have become a big star at West Ham. And if it hadn't been for Hurstie and me, Roger Cross could have made it big. These fellas understood the 'West Ham Way'. But, in football as in life, it's about being in the right place at the right time."

In 1973-74, only Billy Bonds (13 from midfield) topped Clyde's dozen league goals but another struggle at the wrong half of the table precipitated further major moves on and off the field at Upton Park, where Greenwood passed the team manager's chair to his protegé, John Lyall, to concentrate on scouting and the acquisition of more new players.

Although Clyde played in all of the first seven league matches of 1974-75, he would start only another five that campaign following the early-season arrival of Keith Robson and Billy Jennings, plus the presence of Bobby Gould, who had signed a year earlier, and the rapid emergence of Cup hero Alan Taylor. Clyde found himself squeezed out of the first team picture and his last-ever first team appearance for Hammers was in a miserable 4-1 defeat at Ipswich Town on April 26, 1975 – just a week before the FA Cup final against Fulham.

If Clyde hadn't already read the writing on the wall, he couldn't miss the large letters staring him in the face when Gould was named as substitute ahead of him at Wembley on the big day. "Although Ron was no longer team manager, I think he wanted John to put Gouldy on the bench instead of me," says Clyde, whose absence from the final squad meant he also missed out on a coveted winners' medal.

As he sat in the stands at Wembley watching Taylor's double destroy Fulham, Clyde inevitably turned his thoughts to a future elsewhere. "I couldn't just sit there at West Ham and take the money without playing, as some squad players at the big clubs seem content to do now," he explains.

He spent a couple of seasons playing for Feyernoord in Holland, where the skills and technique he'd learned at Upton Park stood him in good stead among the Total Football artists illuminating the Dutch game in the mid-70s. "A fantastically technical league," enthused Clyde, clearly proud to have rubbed shoulders with the likes of Wim Jansen, Ari Haan and Ruud Krol.

Then Clyde turned his attention much closer to home and the North American Soccer League, where some legends of the game – including Moore, Pele, George Best and Franz Beckenbauer – were at the forefront of the initial NASL boom Stateside. He played in Portland, Oregon and Toronto between 1975 and 1982 before hanging up his boots at the age of 31.

While in America, Clyde qualified as a soccer coach. Like most young players at West Ham at the time he was there, he was encouraged to teach kids football in local East London schools in his spare time, so the foundations for becoming a coach had been laid many years earlier.

Between 1997 and 2000, he enjoyed success as Bermudan national coach until he became disillusioned with the politics and interference of the president of the FA that employed him. His career path then took a completely new direction.

Still resident on his native island, for the past seven years Clyde has worked full-time at the Westgate Correction Centre, a halfway house for prisoners who are being rehabilitated back into society. He is employed by a US company who are linked to the Bermudan government.

Clyde explains: "We don't have lots of murderers here but there's a big drugs problem and it's my job to work with the prisoners before they are released, so that they can hopefully leave here better people and not reoffend.

"I think it's a common sense thing. I just treat people the way I would want to be treated and it definitely helps being able to talk to the prisoners about football. It

Above: Clyde going for goal at the Boleyn.

Left: In more recent times, as coach of the Bermuda national team.

can be very satisfying and rewarding to see someone go straight after they leave us."

Clyde is happy with life back on the sunshine island with Alfreida, his wife of 30 years, and his daughter, Kimberley, 27, who graduated with a law degree and has a good job in investments with the Bank of Bermuda.

"I do miss the East End of London, which still seems like home to me, and the camaraderie of football," says Clyde, who last visited England last year to collect his MBE from The Queen.

Clyde Best can look back with few regrets. He came from obscurity to become a top flight star with the Hammers, his only English club.

"Look at it this way," he says, searching for a good analogy. "There are about 60,000 people on our beautiful island here and, at the age of just 19, I was playing football in front of more people than that for West Ham at Old Trafford! So I have to be very thankful."

Chapter 12

BRYAN 'POP' **ROBSON**

"I scored a lot of good goals for West Ham but most of them were created by the football we played. It wasn't the same at Sunderland – and I knew I'd made a mistake in going there at that time"

BRYAN 'Pop' Robson is among a select group of English strikers who scored more than 250 League goals in their career and West Ham were fortunate to see the best of the little Geordie in two different spells during the 70s.

Strangely, Pop scored 47 top flight League goals in 120 appearances for the Hammers between 1971 and his first move back to the North-East – exactly the same number he accumulated in his second stint between 1976 and 1979.

But before becoming a big crowd favourite at Upton Park, Robson first established his scoring prowess at Newcastle United, where he bagged 82 of his 265 total league goals between his debut in 1964 and that first move to West Ham.

At Newcastle, he was one of the stars of their 1969 Inter-Cities Fairs Cup-winning team, the forerunner to the UEFA Cup. It says a lot about Robson and his contribution to the Magpies in their last golden era that the Tyneside club is still struggling to emulate that European achievement 38 years on.

So how did he come to leave his native North-East in the first place?

"As a local kid at Newcastle I got criticised even though I'd scored 30 goals in one season and 25 the next," he says. "But I didn't have a particularly good start to the 1970-71 season. We'd been in Europe and won the Fairs Cup, and had reached the quarter-finals of that competition again."

Pop enjoyed a very successful forward partnership with the lean and lanky Welsh international centre-forward, Wyn Davies, whom he describes as "magnificent". Davies' strength in the air complemented perfectly the razor-sharp penalty box reflexes of the 5ft 7ins tall Robson but Magpies' fans were not always satisfied and Pop recalls one night in 1970 when he knew that the time was coming for him to leave Toon.

"We'd won 2-0 against Ujpest Dozsa in Hungary in the Fairs Cup but they beat us by the same score at St James', when I missed a penalty in the shootout and we lost the tie."

Stung by more stick from the Gallowgate crowd after that costly penalty miss, Robson requested a transfer . . . which was the cue for Ron Greenwood to make one of his shrewdest signings.

"There was talk of Tottenham signing me but I didn't realise that until after I'd already committed myself to West Ham," recalled Pop.

Left: What a great, little marksman Bryan was. Right: Celebrating a goal with Billy Bonds at Selhurst Park.

"John Lyall took me to a Hammers reserve game before I actually made my debut and I met Spurs boss Bill Nicholson on the stairs afterwards. Bill and Ron were very friendly and I think it was agreed between them that West Ham would sign me.

"The Hammers was struggling in the League when I arrived – about third from bottom, I think – but I could tell from my first training session that it was going to be a good move for me. You had only to look around and see the likes of Bobby Moore, Geoff Hurst, Bonzo and Trevor Brooking, to realise there was still a lot of talent at the club even though Martin Peters had gone to Spurs. The ball was being played around, one and two-touch, and, as a striker, I knew I would get four or five good scoring chances a game.

"At Newcastle, we didn't concede too many goals and most of our play was based on hard work and organised defence. But at West Ham the emphasis was always on attacking. We used to concede goals but we'd win games by 4-3 or 3-2.

"Jimmy Greaves was my hero as a kid – and he was playing for us in midfield on the night I made my debut against Nottingham Forest."

Greaves was, by then, however, a rapidly fading force. The greatest goalscorer of his generation was facing a new battle to beat the booze instead of defenders. Robson arrived less than two months after the infamous Blackpool nightclub affair, when Greaves and Moore, in particular, had appalled Greenwood with their late night revelry. It was time for a new hero to emerge . . . and Pop was that man.

Signed for a club record £120,000, he marked his debut against Forest, on February 24, 1971, with a typically acrobatic flick from a Harry Redknapp cross to score spectacularly in a 2-0 home win. Further important goals in consecutive 2-1 Upton Park victories over Manchester United and West Brom in early April did much to help the Hammers narrowly avoid relegation that season.

There's nothing like a debut goal to win over new supporters but Pop also discovered immediately that West Ham fans would not always give the players unconditional support.

"I remember on my debut, I was buzzing about all over the place, chasing balls from one part of the pitch to another and generally trying my hardest to impress. After about 20 minutes, I made a good tackle and knocked the ball over the touchline in front of the Chicken Run. It was dead quiet in the crowd until this bloke piped up: 'C'mon, Robson, f****** liven up a bit'. That was absolutely brilliant!

"Greavsie was the first to congratulate me on my debut goal, which meant a lot because of what he stood for in football. As I said, he was a big favourite of mine as a kid and a really nice fella, too.

"He was obviously not as serious about his football by then but I didn't know he had a drink problem when we were together at West Ham. I didn't mix socially with Jimmy – my friends were Billy and Trevor, who were in my age group.

"London seemed massive to me but I had no problems settling in because the lads made me feel so welcome. There was a great atmosphere among the players even though the team was struggling in the League when I joined them. Bobby Moore was still England captain but he was as good as gold.

"I remember one Christmas, we had no relatives nearby to spend time with after I'd signed for West Ham, so Geoff and Judith Hurst invited us over to their place at Chigwell on Christmas Day. Our kids were nicking their two little girls' toys! The Hursts were really friendly to us and we actually went on holiday with them to Mijas one year.

"Geoff was fantastic to play with. He'd drop his shoulder and go short and then hold the ball up for others. He had great touch for a big player and would score with either foot. I think he learned a lot from Johnny Byrne. Wyn Davies was magnificent for me at Newcastle but Geoff was the best forward I played with.

"I played with Johnny Sissons for England under-23s but when he used to tell me about the West Ham way of playing, I never really understood what he meant. It wasn't until I arrived at the club that I fully appreciated how, and why, Geoff Hurst made the runs that he did, and the reasons why it worked so well for the benefit of him and the team.

"The first thing I learned when I came to West Ham is that you had to do everything on the half-turn. We were taught to receive the ball sideways-on, not square-on. West Ham made me more creative and I learned how to link the play between defence, midfield and attack."

Nine league goals in 1971-72, as Hammers climbed six places to 14th, helped Robson to enhance his reputation as a sharp penalty box predator capable of scoring with either foot. His personal highlight was scoring a League Cup fifth round hat-trick in a 5-0 home victory over Sheffield United, which set up the marathon semi-final epic with Stoke City. Earlier in the competition, Hammers had won a thriller at home to Liverpool, thanks to a Robson strike, and also a replay against Leeds United at Elland Road. Leeds were champions at the time and Clyde Best's winner in Yorkshire represented one of the shock results of the season.

"As we came off after the drawn first game at Upton Park, Jack Charlton said: 'Wait till we get you lot back to Elland Road', but we played really well up there, where few teams managed to win in those days.

"And when we beat Sheffield United by five under the lights at Upton Park, they were also going well in the top division at that time, so it was another great result against a decent side.

"I remember coming back from Stoke after winning the first leg of the semi-final, 2-1, and seeing the Twin Towers of Wembley as our train made its way in to Euston station. I thought to myself: 'We could be going there soon . . .'

"I know we would have got there if Gordon Banks hadn't saved Geoff's penalty in the home leg but we just didn't perform well that night. We were expected to go through but I don't remember us creating much and I didn't have a particularly good game myself. We weren't under-prepared or complacent, it just seemed that fate was against us. Especially when you consider how Fergie (Bobby Ferguson) got injured in the second replay at Old Trafford and Bobby had to go in goal and face a penalty.

"It was as if Stoke were destined to reach Wembley that year."

Capped twice for England under-23s, Robson never came closer to playing at Wembley than the 3-2 League Cup semi-final defeat in the Manchester mud.

But, as he points out, despite his deserved reputation as a prolific scorer, Greenwood in fact played him in a deeper midfield link role on a number of occasions, especially early on in his first spell with the Eastenders. Burly Bermudan Clyde Best (17 goals) led the line well, while Hurst played alongside him in his last season before joining Stoke City.

A selfless, energetic worker, all his team-mates say Robson was a delight to play with. But, on the other hand, he is the first to acknowledge the quality of service he received from those around him.

Of Brooking, who was fast emerging as a gifted midfield talent in the early 70s, Pop says: "We had a really good link up. Trevor had this ability to receive the ball and no matter how many opponents were around him, he'd just shape it around people. He didn't have to beat people because he could put the ball where he wanted it to go.

"For me, he was easy to read, he had great vision and always knew where you were. He was always a pleasure to play with.

"Trevor hadn't played that many games for the club when I first arrived but he quickly became more and more influential, and his link up play with Kevin Keegan for England was brilliant.

"Trevor was the most creative player I ever played with," says Pop.

"He did the same thing every time from our throw-ins, but no-one could stop him from letting the ball run across his body before turning to build up the play. If we got in trouble, we just used to give the ball to Trevor. He'd say to Bonzo in the dressing room: 'Just fill in when I go forward', and it happened all the time. Bonzo did all the chasing down for Trevor and me.

"There was no side to Bonzo. He came in, did his training, then went home. You'd try to keep up with him in training but he'd just kick on and he'd be away from you.

"But even our defenders could play. I mean, with Bobby Moore, it was a case of 'how do you want it?' He'd drop the ball short for you and put it on a sixpence. Sometimes, he played in midfield, just in front of the back four, because he was very capable of doing that. They were really accomplished players.

"Our full-backs – Frank Lampard on the left and Johnnie McDowell on the right – liked to bomb forward whenever possible and the supply of crosses was great. Harry Redknapp used to cross them in from the right at first but Trevor would also get wide and curl crosses in. He'd wrap his foot around the ball and his delivery was spot on.

"It was strange, though, that we had a mixture of really good players and some bad ones. I don't want to mention names but we had World Cup winners, and other quality players like Bonzo, Brooking and Lampard, but I wondered about some of the others who they were playing with.

"The club should have achieved more than it did considering the top players we've had. I was involved with the best football of my career at West Ham."

Pop admits, however, that he would like to have played more matches as a pure striker, rather than as a more deep-lying link man.

"For some reason, Ron always fancied me as a midfield player. I used to work hard from that position but it wasn't really me, although it seemed to work okay for a while. I scored about 14 goals playing in midfield, then on the left for a while, but I was always pushing to play in my preferred position up front."

With Hurst having moved on to see out his twilight years at Stoke, Pop got his wish to lead the forward line for the 1972-73 season – and how magnificently he responded. His tally of 28 top flight goals (equalled only in the Football League that season by Exeter City's Fred Binney) is a West Ham scoring record unsurpassed in the last 34 years. And with the team achieving the dizzy heights of sixth position, this was to be the most successful period of Pop's two spells as a Hammer.

He needed more support, though, and says: "We had problems trying to replace Hurstie. Although he scored quite a few goals, Clyde Best was playing wide-left a lot of the time, and then Ted MacDougall even had a spell out there when he came."

Illness caused Pop to miss almost half the league programme in 1973-74, when he netted seven times in 22 appearances as Hammers fought yet another battle to avoid the drop, finishing just fifth from bottom. At 29, the balding striker pushed for a move back to the North-East and his home-town club, Sunderland, but not for football reasons.

For the first time since he left the club, Pop revealed to *EX*: "I had an illness during my first spell at West Ham. I had a swollen testicle, which had twisted, but for a while they thought it might be cancerous.

"I was rushed into hospital for an operation but, thankfully, it turned out to be nothing more than a virus. I missed a lot of football and left West Ham for the first time after that.

"My wife, Maureen, had to cope with the two kids while I was in hospital and we

Left: Pop loved playing with Trevor Brooking. Right: Pop greets another great goalscorer, Tony Cottee.

didn't have any family around us, so we started to miss home and our families.

"But I shouldn't have left West Ham then," admits the softly-spoken Geordie. "The club wanted me to stay but Maureen and I wanted our young 'uns, Louise and Stephen, who were just three and four, to start their schooling back home," he explained.

"I had also started to wonder how much longer I had left in the game and whether someone would still be prepared to buy me if I'd stayed there for a few more years. It was a mistake to leave, though. I joined Sunderland a year after they had won the FA Cup and a season after I left the Hammers, John Lyall's team won the trophy!"

It wouldn't be the last time Robson's usually impeccable timing on the field would desert him when it came to transfers.

He won a second division championship medal and the divisional Golden Boot award at Roker Park but says: "I realised Sunderland weren't playing the type of football I had thrived on at West Ham. I scored a lot of good goals for West Ham but most of them were created by the football we played. It wasn't the same at Sunderland – and I knew I'd made a mistake in going there at that time."

Pop did not sever all links with West Ham, however, and by keeping in touch with friends like Brooking and Bonds part of him still belonged at the Boleyn. Indeed, in October 1976, after two years away, he rejoined Hammers in an £80,000 deal that proved astute business by manager Lyall.

It was like home from home for the Robsons – quite literally. Pop explains an extraordinary property trail: "We bought Peter Eustace's old house in Malburn Drive, Woodford Green when we first came down south and then, when I returned to West Ham after two years in Hexham, we moved back into exactly the same place again! We'd kept in touch with the next-door neighbours who told us our old house was back on the market, so we were delighted to snap it up for a second time.

"The story gets better, though . . . when I came back to play in London for a third time, with Chelsea, we moved into Malburn Drive again!"

Playing alongside cup-winners Billy Jennings, Alan Taylor and namesake Keith Robson, Pop proved that, even in his mid-30s, he still possessed the Midas touch in front of goal. His 14 goals in 30 games saw him back at the top of the club's scoring charts in 1976-77, when a brace in the thrilling final home match, a 4-2 win against Man United, ensured Hammers' safety for at least another year.

Although his tally of nine, and a promising new partnership with David Cross, couldn't avert relegation the following season, Pop's experience was underlined again as he amassed 24 goals in the second division.

He relished the chance to play under Lyall, a person and coach he very much admired and respected. It was John who encouraged Pop to pursue coaching experience while he was still a player, advice that stood him in good stead when he finally hung up his boots and decided to stay in football.

"Some of the things I'd do now as a coach, like little passing movements and third man running, are the same things I first learned under John," he says. "When you enjoy what you are doing, you produce better results.

"Crossy was a good target man, someone I could play off, like Geoff Hurst. He was a good, intelligent lad and we both wanted each other to do well – we laid on goals for each other. David's son, Bobby, came to me when I was running the centre of excellence at Man United, but he was also a canny cricketer and I think he went on to join Lancashire youths."

But rather than stay on at Upton Park and continue to lead the quest for a return to top flight football, Pop again decided to return to his North-East roots at the end of the 1978-79 season. He rejoined Sunderland before spells with Carlisle United and Chelsea, who, under John Neal, were then in Division Two. Pop spent only a season at Stamford Bridge and was not enamoured with their outspoken chairman. "Ken Bates? Well, he wasn't anything like Reg Pratt or the Cearns brothers!" he laughed.

Pop joined Sunderland for a third time as player-coach and was still playing in the old first division aged 38.

Yet again, though, for the third time in his career, he had just missed out on a glorious cup-winning campaign and the promotion party that followed a year later. For in the season after he joined Sunderland for a second spell, Hammers went on to lift the FA Cup again!

He was also somewhat unfortunate to miss out on full England honours, much to the disappointment of the man who first brought him to East London. Ron Greenwood reflected ruefully in his autobiography that Robson would have become a senior international had he joined the Hammers earlier in his career – and Pop is entitled to wonder what might have been.

"Ron said a funny thing to me when I was about to leave West Ham the first time. He asked me: 'Why don't you stay? You never know what's going to happen...' It was as if he was trying to tell me that he would soon become the next England manager."

Pop made history at Carlisle United when, during a brief though unsuccessful nine-game spell as player-manager, he turned out against Shrewsbury Town aged 39

Pop pictured when EX interviewed him in October 2004.

years and 321 days in September 1985. Even after finally retiring as a player, he continued to make his mark in the game as a coach with Carlisle, Sunderland and Manchester United, where he played a significant role in the development of some of the country's brightest, young stars.

He performed similar sterling service as assistant academy director at Leeds United before the club plunged itself into the financial crisis from which it has still to recover.

In recent years, Pop has worked as a part-time scout for the Republic of Ireland and Birmingham City and is now employed in the same capacity by Chelsea, covering the North-East of England as well as Scotland.

Now 61-years-old, Pop last returned to Upton Park as the special guest of Tony Cottee in the hospitality lounges, prior to the Carling Cup tie against Southend United in autumn 2004. He enjoyed being back among old friends and West Ham United clearly still holds a special place in his heart.

"I can't have any regrets," added Pop, "because I've been lucky to enjoy a career doing something I loved doing – playing football, scoring goals and getting a lot of credit. I was very lucky.

"I should have stayed at West Ham and gained even more recognition," he added.

Chapter 13

BILLY**JENNINGS**

"When I met Ron Greenwood for the first time that day, it was a case of 'where do I sign?' I just wanted to join a big club and, being an East Ender, it was a dream come true to move to West Ham"

WHEN the 22-year-old Billy Jennings sat down in Ron Greenwood's office at Upton Park, eager to sign his new contract, the Hackney-born striker could have done with a smart agent by his side.

A trusted advisor would almost certainly have pushed for a clause in his young client's contract that would have rewarded him handsomely for goalscoring exploits in the top flight, after he had shot to prominence with 26 for second division Watford the previous season.

An added bonus if Hammers won the FA Cup and qualified for Europe would undoubtedly have added a few more noughts to his take-home pay.

Billy knows better than anyone that he and his colleagues were probably undervalued as players – because he is now back in football working as an agent himself!

But back in September 1974, he was just like any other rookie grateful for the chance to prove himself among the game's elite.

Little could he have known then that he would settle into first division football like the proverbial duck to water, scoring on his debut – a 2-1 home defeat by Sheffield United – and adding another dozen in 32 league appearances.

Billy also scored a vital FA Cup fourth round goal in a 1-1 home draw with Swindon Town as the Irons battled their way to Wembley and a final victory against Bobby Moore's Fulham in the 'Cockney Cup Final'.

"I was a bit surprised how quickly I settled in at West Ham after my move but then that's what happens when you've got very good players around you. They make it easier," says Billy, now 55, speaking from his family's wonderful cottage on the rural outskirts of Brentwood, Essex.

"I look back now and think how eager I was to sign the contract Ron Greenwood put in front of me but agents weren't around in those days and young players like me didn't question what we were earning. We just wanted to play football and do our best for the club.

"You wouldn't think of asking for a goals incentive bonus, as we do now on behalf of some of our clients at Premier Management. If I was representing myself today, I would have been looking to build creative incentives into the contract, which wouldn't harm the club but would reward the player if he achieves. Scoring goals, winning the FA Cup, qualifying for Europe – they would have been obvious

Jubilant fans carry Billy around Wembley after the 1975 Cup final. Inset: the programme cover and match ticket for the final against Fulham.

'carrots'," he points out.

"Some clubs still won't agree to offering a player a goal bonus but it makes strikers hungrier. One of the best goal-based incentive deals ever done was when Wimbledon bought John Hartson from West Ham. He earned a fortune, thousands per goal, for the Dons. And it worked well for Wimbledon, too, because they later sold him on to Coventry for big money.

"A lot of forwards expect a goal bonus in their contracts while, on the other hand, goalkeepers ask for a clean sheet clause in theirs.

"But when I met Ron Greenwood for the first time that day, it was a case of 'where do I sign?' I just wanted to join a big club and, being an East Ender, it was a dream come true to move to West Ham."

After initial interest from Portsmouth came to nothing, Watford manager Mike Keen – father of former Hammer Kevin – informed Billy that West Ham were in for him and after a guided tour of the Boleyn Ground from John Lyall, who was in the process of taking over the team management from Ron, Hammers had their man. Graham Paddon has been brought in the season before and very soon after Billy arrived, Alan Taylor and Keith Robson were added to a new-look line-up.

"It all seems so long ago now," continues Billy, struggling to recall the finer details of his impressive career at West Ham that still means so much to him.

"I think the European games stand out for me even more than the Cup final, which wasn't a good game." Although he missed the earlier rounds of the European Cup Winners' Cup, in Finland and the old Soviet Union, due to injury, he certainly made a big impact on the 1975-76 competition.

West Ham were 4-0 down against Den Haag in Holland, staring a quarter-final exit in the face, until Billy netted two second half goals to turn the tie on its head. It made him a Hammers hero. In the second leg at Upton Park, West Ham won 3-1 to clinch a remarkable 5-3 aggregate victory which set up the glorious semi-final win over Eintracht Frankfurt before going on to the ill-fated final against Anderlecht in Brussels.

"All I can remember about Den Haag is that we got absolutely battered in the first half. John had a few words at half-time, urging us to do ourselves justice, and we scored early in the second half. I think one of my two goals was a header. At least we walked off at the end with a bit of pride and gave ourselves a chance in the second leg.

"They were fantastic times. Coming up against European teams, we were introduced to a different way of playing and different cultures. It seems a lifetime away now, because so much has happened to me since then.

"My time at West Ham went by very quickly. I was a single lad then – Keith Robson and I were the only two who weren't married at the time – and we enjoyed ourselves. It was a great club, very friendly and an easy place to settle into.

"We were not unlike the West Ham side of today. We would entertain and score lots of goals but we also conceded plenty. And we always seemed to be in the bottom half of the table."

To underline the point, after defeats to Sheffield United and Spurs in his first two matches, Hammers then rattled in 14 goals in their next three games, with Jennings

Billy fires in a shot during the 1976 ECWC final in Brussels. Inset: Billy pictured early in 2004.

netting in all three, against Leicester City (two in a 6-2 home slaughter), Birmingham City (3-0 at home) and Burnley (5-3, away). Lyall's revamped and revitalised team went on a run of 17 games that included just one defeat between mid-September and the end of the year, as the new signings quickly made their mark. Billy appreciated the service he and fellow strikers, Taylor, Robson and, occasionally, Bobby Gould, received from the illustrious midfield trio behind them.

"We couldn't fail to improve with Trevor Brooking, Billy Bonds and Graham Paddon supplying us," he enthused. "We usually played 4-3-3 and as well as the great service we got from midfield, we had flexibility up front. Keith would normally play wide on the left but he could also pop up on the right. Alan had sheer pace, like a whippet, and although I wasn't as quick as him, before my bad injury I had a burst of pace to get away from defenders. I was happy coming off my marker to receive the ball at my feet, or looking for the ball played over the top.

"It worked well and that is probably why Trevor also liked to play 4-3-3 when he became caretaker manager at West Ham. He specialised in playing near-post crosses and if you were prepared to gamble and make the right runs, it often paid off for us.

"Graham was always steady and would crack home the occasional 30-yarder, while Bonzo was a much better all round player than he was given credit for. Sure, he could tackle and hustle and bustle, but he could also play and was usually the star of the five-a-sides in training.

"Our back four could all play, they liked to play the ball on the ground, so perhaps it's no surprise that we were prone to concede a few.

"And above all, we played football with a smile."

A run of defeats at the end of the 1974-75 season, when the team was distracted by success in the FA Cup, meant a modest 13th place finish. But Billy was relieved to make Wembley at all, as he explains: "We were battered by Ipswich in the semi-final at Villa Park but managed to hold out for a replay. In the second game at Stamford Bridge we were one up, once again against the run of play, when I netted the only own goal of my career.

"I was marking at the near post on a corner when the ball skidded off the snowy surface, glanced off my leg and into our net. I was so relieved when we made it 2-1 to go through!"

Billy recalls with more affection scoring goals in rare league victories at Old Trafford – "a near-post header" – and Highbury, as well as a hat-trick against Stoke City and England keeper Peter Shilton at the Boleyn in front of the TV cameras in December '75.

But 13th position in the table was as high as Hammers would ever finish during Billy's time at the club. Despite making it all the way to the European final in May '76, Hammers could finish only 18th that season. And after a rise of just one place in 1976-77, their repeated flirtation with relegation finally took its toll when the team went down in May '78.

Who knows what difference a fully fit Billy Jennings would have made, because a serious Achilles tendon injury restricted him to just two appearances and his season was finished by September of '77.

Ask anyone who saw Billy play regularly, before his injury, to describe his style, and chances are they will mention his uncanny ability to 'hang' in the air. His habit of jumping early to outwit taller markers – Billy stands 5ft 10ins tall – earned him a high proportion of goals for a striker who, at 10st 10lbs, was by no means the biggest around.

"I'd like to be playing up front today, because defenders aren't allowed to clatter forwards from behind any more," he says.

A 12-year career – he played for Leyton Orient and, briefly, Luton Town after leaving Upton Park in '79 – has taken its physical toll on the nippy striker with the trademark immaculately coiffured hair style. He suffers lower back pain today – the possible legacy of a slipped disc from his Watford days – but there are several other battle scars to bear.

As Billy reveals to *EX*, his 'hanging' style and bravery in the penalty box ultimately proved costly. It not only hastened his retirement from the game at the age of 31, but also causes the "terrible arthritic pain" he still suffers in both knees today and which will soon require a complete knee replacement in each leg.

"We were playing QPR at home early in the 1977-78 season," he explains. "I always pushed off from the ground with my left foot but this time, as I did so, my Achilles tendon just snapped completely. It was only about three or four minutes into the game – I obviously hadn't warmed up enough. It was agony and put me out of football for a year.

"I thought I was finished – and so did West Ham, because they bought two strikers, David Cross and 'Pop' Robson.

"Brian Roper performed my operation and he reckoned that there must have been a slight tear there originally, because the Achilles exploded and ended up at the back of my knee! He told me afterwards that that my left Achilles would never snap again. He did a good job, I managed to play again, but I was never the same player. I couldn't get away from defenders the way I used to. I've still got the wires in my leg from that first operation.

"I've had three knee ops – two on my left and one on my right – and I saw the surgeon, who did my Achilles op, again two years ago. He took scans, looked at old x-rays and confirmed that the arthritis has now reached a stage where I will soon need two knee replacements fitted. Trouble is, they only last about 10 or 15 years and I don't fancy having it done.

"I try to ride a bike at the gym when I get a bit of spare time. The non-weight bearing movement clears the joints a bit but my cartilages have just worn away, there's no soft tissue left."

With Cross having signed around Christmas 1977, and speculation mounting that Robson would soon be returning to the East End to form a new strike partnership, Billy knew his West Ham days were numbered.

"I got myself fit again," he explains, "and thought I did well when I came off the bench to score in both games on tour in Scotland the following pre-season. But then it became obvious that I was surplus to requirements. John Lyall said Orient had come in for me and that the club had accepted their offer of £110,000, which was a lot for Orient to pay. But I was gutted that West Ham were willing to let me go.

"I liked Orient's manager, Jimmy Bloomfield, a genuinely nice guy, but I made the biggest mistake of my football career when I allowed him to sweet-talk me into signing for him there and then, without taking more time to think things through. Jimmy was a good salesman, he really did a number on me.

"Again, it's going back to what I was saying about how an agent today would advise a young player correctly in those situations. Don't get me wrong, Orient had some very good players at that time – Stan Bowles and John Chiedozie – and they were only one league down from West Ham, but I was so unhappy with my situation. I knew, within a month of being there, that I'd made a mistake. The standards were obviously a lot lower than I'd been used to at West Ham.

"After a year-and-a-half at Orient, I also had nine months at Luton under David Pleat. But I didn't play much and was really only there as cover.

"I should have stayed at Upton Park and seen out my contract. Whether I'd have been a regular in the first team again, I don't know, but I would have still got my fair share of games."

Although Billy didn't marry his wife, Shirley, until after he left West Ham, he laid the foundations for his future business activity fairly early on in his adult life. Asked to compare himself to his old mate, Keith Robson, Bill says: "Keith was a nice kid but he'd come down from the North-East and people – so-called friends – took advantage of him. I was young and single, too, and wanted to go out and have a good time just like him, but I was a little bit more sensible than Keith. I bought a house straight away and I think that leaving home when I was 17, to go and live in digs at Watford for three years, stood me in good stead.

"I wasn't the best player in the world but I wanted it badly and was prepared to make sacrifices at a young age. At Watford, I stayed in a lot, did extra training in the afternoons and was dedicated to reaching my goal. I say to young players today, if you want it badly enough, you can get on more than another player in the side who has much more ability than you but isn't prepared to put in the effort.

"Keith gave everything on the pitch, would run through brick walls and spill blood for the cause, but his lifestyle off the pitch caught up with him. It's a shame because he had a fantastic left foot, loads of ability and was as brave as a lion.

"He's a great lad, though, and I was delighted to meet up with both him and Graham Paddon recently in one of the lounges at West Ham."

Their lives have certainly taken an interesting, and at times difficult, path since they were all starring together in Hammers' most successful team of the 70s.

For Billy, life after football has been ultimately successful, although this man of ambition and enterprise has experienced ups and downs along the way. He never much fancied going into coaching, so he indulged his love of fine food and wine instead. Having declined Oxford United manager Jim Smith's offer to join the U's on a two-year deal in the early 80s, Bill first owned a thriving Fleet Street wine bar, 'Daniels', but reluctantly decided to sell it after eight years when 'William's', the two-storey wine bar and brasserie he had converted from a coffee shop in Crown Street, Brentwood, fell victim to the early 90s recession of spiralling interest rates.

Undeterred by financial pressures that plunged him into negative equity on his freehold property, he then took a new lease and opened a classy restaurant, 'Bellinis', in the City near St Paul's. It showed a modest profit before a friendship with an Israeli, first forged during Hammers' tour to Israel following the '75 Cup final, convinced him to sell up and set himself up as a FIFA-registered football agent around 12 years ago.

In partnership with two colleagues, he formed Premier Management International, which, seven years ago, became the first football agency to float on the stock exchange. With his 200 Swiss Francs bond paid and living off the proceeds from the sale of Bellinis, Billy trawled lower division and Premier reserve team matches for eight months, working from his loft conversion at home and renewing old football contacts, before completing his first deal – the transfer of left-back Danny Granville from Cambridge United to Chelsea for £500,000. After 20 games, Granville moved on to Leeds United for £1.7m, joined Manchester City for a further £1m and then Crystal Palace for £600,000. Kevin Phillips and Stephen Carr, both then unknown youngsters at Watford and Spurs respectively, were also among Bill's first clients before they were "seduced" by Premier's competitors.

But the plc continued to expand by buying up three of its contemporaries on the way to building a business that currently employs 15 people (including nine registered agents), with offices in England, Turkey and Hungary.

Billy, now 55, added: "From being very lucrative, the agency business has bottomed out now. There's very little good, young talent coming through in England that hasn't already been snapped up, but the prospects elsewhere in Europe look more encouraging. I now spend a lot of time in Turkey and Hungary."

Keith when he was interviewed by EX in March 2003.

Right: As Boleyn fans will remember the hard man who combined skill and aggression.

Chapter 14

KEITH**ROBSON**

"You can understand how angry supporters must get when they know that players are on thousands of pounds a week and they don't seem to care too much. I feel a bit sorry for the fans, because all they want to see is the players give their all for 90 minutes every game. That's not too much to ask, is it?"

FOR a wholehearted player who never gave less than 100 percent in all of his 87 matches in a claret-and-blue shirt during the mid-70s, Keith Robson is understandably unimpressed whenever he hears from his old friends, who support West Ham, that Hammers' modern day players have not always shown the same appetite for a battle that he and his former team-mates did when the financial rewards were so much less.

"Players have to stand up and be counted," says 'Robbo', who has visited Upton Park numerous times in recent seasons, always hoping to see some of the flair that characterised past West Ham teams but invariably leaving the Boleyn Ground slightly underwhelmed.

"You can understand how angry supporters must get, when they hear that players are on thousands of pounds a week and they don't seem to care too much. I feel a bit sorry for the fans, because all they want to see is the players give their all for 90 minutes every game. That's not too much to ask, is it?"

It was precisely that steely determination with which Keith approached every game he played that led West Ham to pay £60,000 for the then 20-year-old early in the 1974-75 season, shortly after John Lyall succeeded Ron Greenwood as team manager and the latter moved 'upstairs' to focus on scouting and recruitment of new players who would add a hardened edge to Hammers' notoriously soft centre.

Keith says: "In our day, we always got stuck in. Billy Bonds, our captain, would rally the other players and we'd respond to him because he always led by example. If anyone didn't respond, they felt Bonzo's wrath. I heard that Ted MacDougall wasn't pulling his weight at Leeds one day, words were exchanged and Bill sorted him out in the bath after the game. We all respected Billy but, to be fair, we had a workmanlike side in which no-one would hide.

"I find it unbelievable that certain players are out for so long with injuries. Years ago, we got the same injuries as players do today but whereas we'd usually be back playing again within two weeks, nowadays they're out for much longer. That's probably due to the fact that they are being very well paid even when they're not in the team, so they don't tend to rush back.

"Really, I find it frightening that players are earning around 30 grand a week – more than I earn in a year – and yet they still don't give everything they've got for

Keith crossing during the 1976 ECWC final. He didn't want to collect his losers' medal.

90 minutes of every game."

Thirty grand a week? There's hardly a player at Premiership level who would even bother to get out of bed in the morning for that meagre pay in 2007. But it shows how salaries have spiralled uncontrollably skywards in recent years, following even more lucrative contracts with Sky TV, that the above comments were made by Keith in 2003, shortly before the Hammers were last relegated.

Robbo continued: "I went from £50 a week at Newcastle to £100 a week when I signed for West Ham. In my second season I think I got a £25 rise, and we also earned £20 win bonuses.

"The point is, you only received a bonus if you played, or were a substitute, in the days when teams could use only one sub. So it was very important for us to be in the side and playing every week, or as often as possible.

"Bonzo was different class, though. How come he never won an England cap? Billy trained as hard as he played – every day."

Keith, now 53 and living and working in Norwich, where we conducted this interview, looks back on his three seasons as a Hammer with mixed feelings. The pride and passion he always displayed when pulling on the shirt is still there and he talks fondly of a "well balanced" team that grew in stature and, in the space of a year, reached two major cup finals. Indeed, Keith made vital contributions to both the FA Cup triumph in 1975 and the European Cup Winners' Cup campaign of 1976 that, in both cases, left him professionally and personally unfulfilled.

"I vowed when I came to West Ham that I'd win a medal for my dad but it never quite happened," says Keith, barely able to hide the lingering disappointment.

After playing in the first four rounds of the cup, including scoring the fifth round winner against QPR at Upton Park, he suffered a serious thigh injury that ruled him out of the semi-final against Ipswich Town as well as the final against Fulham.

Recalling the injury that almost ended his career, Keith explained: "I collided with John Roberts in a game at Birmingham and suffered internal bleeding in my thigh, which became badly swollen.

"To be fair to John Lyall, he gave me every chance to make the final team and said I'd be playing at Wembley if I came through a reserve game and a first team league match against Arsenal within a week of the final itself.

"But after just one half of the reserve match, the pain returned to my leg and I had to be honest with John and tell him that I wouldn't make it, much as it killed me to say so."

With winners' medals awarded only to the Hammers who played an active part in the final, Keith – who watched the 2-0 victory in the stand along with Clyde Best – admits he was devastated to miss out on the club's biggest success since the European adventure a decade earlier.

"I remember when I complained to Ron Greenwood about not getting a medal, he tried to console me by saying I'd be back to win a European Cup Winners' Cup medal the following year, but that didn't happen either and I couldn't take it."

On top of missing out on two winners' medals, Keith was also badly affected by the death of his father, Thomas, and admits he went off the rails too often for his own good after that. His wildest excesses plumbed new depths when, following a drink-driving incident on one particularly boozy, reckless night in Ilford, he wound up in court. Keith is the first to admit that only the intervention of the smooth-talking Greenwood – "he performed like Perry Mason up there in front of the judge!"– saved the then wayward youngster from a prison sentence.

It speaks volumes for Keith's feelings of despair in the aftermath of the 4-2 defeat by Anderlecht in the Heysel Stadium that he couldn't say exactly where in his house his loser's medal is now gathering dust.

"It's around somewhere, and I'll pass it on to my son, Thomas, when he's older, but who remembers the losers? Immediately after the game in Belgium, I tried to give my medal away to Peter Brabrook's son, Wayne, but he didn't take it from me. I gave my shirt away, though."

I tried, unsuccessfully, to convince Keith that the medal should be displayed with pride, especially as he had scored four vital goals in the competition, including one of the classic strikes in Hammers' history, against Eintracht Frankfurt in an epic semi-final, and also netted what still stands as the last goal by a West Ham player in a major European final.

When fans reminisce about great nights under the Upton Park lights, chances are they will recall the 3-1 victory over the Germans that took the Irons to Heysel. They don't come any better than the thrills served up on that magnificent rain-lashed evening, when the silky skills of Trevor Brooking, who glided across the sodden turf to score twice, and Robbo's rocket from long-distance put the Boleyn crowd on cloud nine.

If ever a goal encapsulated the quality of Keith's cultured left foot, it was that glorious moment when he ran diagonally towards the West Stand, turned his marker and struck the sweetest shot high into the roof of the net in front of the jam-packed

Robbo and Alvin Martin at the 1975-80 Cup final reunion dinner in October 2005. They once shared lodgings.

South Bank terracing.

And yes, it is only right to acknowledge that Robson combined skill and subtlety with the ruthless, aggressive hard-man streak for which he is more commonly remembered. But the 5ft 11ins Geordie couldn't half mix it with anyone crazy enough to take him on.

On one famous occasion at Anfield, Tommy Smith did just that.

Keith laughs as he recalls the incident, within seconds of kick-off at Liverpool, when he clattered the notoriously tough Reds skipper into the advertising hoardings.

"The crowd gasped," he smiles, clearly relishing the memory, "but Tommy was great about it. He didn't roll around like the foreigners do today, whinging for a foul. He just got straight up, tapped me on the knee and said: 'Well done, son'.

"He was looking to 'do' me back as soon as he got the chance, mind!

"But that was the kind of mutual respect players had then. Norman Hunter was another one who'd kick lumps out of you on the pitch but, off the field, he was a nice guy. He did me a big favour up at Leeds one day when the tickets I'd left for my family were taken by someone else and it looked like they'd come all the way down from the North-East for nothing. But Norman stepped in and found them tickets so that they could get in to see me the game."

Keith laments the growing detachment of modern players from supporters, the people who pay their wages. "When I first came to West Ham," he says, "I lived in digs in Lonsdale Avenue, just a short walk from the ground. Sometimes I'd stop off in the Boleyn pub for a few pints on my way home after games, just to mingle with our fans and hear what they had to say.

"You can learn a lot just by listening to fans, because they know a lot more about what's going on at the club than either the players or the management and directors would believe. A lot of the time they can see things the manager can't.

"Up here, Norwich are quite good in that respect, because they have regular question-and-answer forums involving the manager, representatives of the board and supporters, but it doesn't happen as much with Premiership clubs, which is a real shame. But money dominates all aspects of football now, I'm afraid.

"The game has changed so much, it's so high profile that players can't afford to be seen out in pubs and clubs anymore. When I was there, after a home game a crowd of us – Frank Lampard, Graham Paddon, Billy Jennings and me – would go for a few drinks at the William The Conqueror pub in Manor Park, or maybe to one of Frank's own pubs, like the Burford Arms or the Britannia at Stratford. We could relax and chat among ourselves or with the fans without any hassle.

"But there are a lot of jealous people about today and players can't be seen out drinking in public like we were."

When work commitments allow, Keith helps to host one of the hospitality lounges at Norwich City, where he spent a couple of seasons after leaving West Ham in 1977 and an unhappy move to Cardiff City (where he played under former Hammers Jimmy Andrews and his assistant, Alan Sealey) Leicester City and Carlisle United (where fellow Geordie Bryan 'Pop' Robson, on loan from Sunderland, was a team-mate). "It was the early 80s but you could still see Pop's class, his ability to find space and score so many unbelievable goals with his head."

Keith manages to watch the Hammers at Upton Park three or four times a season, usually accompanied by his daughter and West Ham fan, Kelly, 24. "I like to meet up with my old friends and have a few beers with them in the supporters' club, in Castle Street, before the game. I'm always very pleased to have a chat with any Hammers fans while I'm visiting," says Keith, who still enjoys a great affinity with the ordinary people who used to pay his wages.

At the time of this interview, Keith was set to resume the daily grind of full-time employment at the Impress Metal Packaging company near his home, where he had worked as a machine operator for the past 19 years, seven years longer than his career in professional football lasted.

"I've worked 80 hours this week," he said, sipping on a well-earned pint of lager and lemonade top. "Tomorrow (Saturday) I'm on the early 12-hour shift from two o'clock in the morning 'till two in the afternoon."

In 2006 he was made redundant and turned to mini-cabbing to try and eke out a living, but it was still very tough and a far cry from his days as a Hammers favourite.

"Good luck to today's players," he says. "When you're in football, you never think it's going to end. And when it does, it comes as a big shock. Very hard."

But what would any relegation-threatened manager give to have 11 Keith Robsons playing for him every week?

Above: Young Alan before he made the first team breakthrough. Below: Curbs celebrates with Alvin Martin, while Billy Bonds and Paul Brush are on their way to join in.

Chapter 15

ALAN**CURBISHLEY**

"I got stick from the West Ham fans when I was a player, because I was in a relegated team. I was 18 and there was a time when I didn't want to show my face or get involved in things around the club. But it was Frank Lampard who pointed out to me that it was no use hiding myself away. He said: 'As players in these tough situations, you have to front up when it's not going so well. It's no use ducking away from it'. And he was so right."

BORN in Forest Gate, brought up in Canning Town. There really was only ever going to be one club for the talented East Ender Alan Curbishley, who supported the Hammers from birth.

It was almost preordained that the young midfielder, who played in 95 first team games for West Ham between 1975 and 1979, would one day return to his spiritual home as manager – albeit five-and-a-half years after first turning down the chance to manage the club.

One of the first things he did after being appointed as Alan Pardew's replacement on December 13, 2006 was to admit that perhaps he should never have left Upton Park as a player in the first place.

"It was a mistake to want to leave here at the time, but I was young and headstrong," says Curbs, 52, who was one of the most sought-after young teenage players in the country when West Ham talked him out of signing for Chelsea.

The decision to stay east instead of heading west was largely due to his friendship with the Charles brothers, John and Clive, who had both broken into the Hammers first team as full-backs in the 60s and early 70s.

Alan explained to *EX*: "They lived about 50 yards from me in Canning Town and I obviously knew them as West Ham players. Then Clyde Best came to stay in digs with John and Clive's mum, so that was another West Ham connection. Growing up in Canning Town, you just *had* to be West Ham.

"But I was all set to sign for Chelsea as a schoolboy until my mum had a word with Mrs Charles, who told Wally St. Pier, and that's how I came to join West Ham. He intercepted the move and got me to Upton Park instead. When I first joined the club I was coached by Frank Lampard and John Lyall."

Curbishley attended Gainsborough Road School and then South West Ham Tech (now known as West Ham Trinity College) on the Barking Road, where he was coached by Hammers first team stars Kevin Lock and John McDowell. When Alan became a first-teamer, he coached a group of youngsters at Redbridge that included future Hammers midfielders John Moncur and Robert Lee.

As well as starring for Newham Boys, he also shone alongside Glenn Hoddle for

Essex Schoolboys (U15s). He gained eight schoolboy, 10 youth and two U21 international caps for England.

He was undoubtedly a special talent, as former West Ham physio Rob Jenkins realised one Sunday morning.

Rob recalls: "In the early 70s when I was club physio, all games – involving first team, reserves and the Metropolitan League side – were played on a Saturday. I would open my surgery early on Sunday mornings to treat any players who had received a knock the previous day.

"One Sunday, I was just about to close the surgery and head home when I received a call from dear old Wally St. Pier, our famous chief scout. He wanted me to hang about to take a look at a young lad the club was keen to sign – he was playing for Senrab at the time and had taken a hit on his knee.

"I waited around until a fresh-faced 13-year-old with blond tousled hair came in. His name was Alan Curbishley. Wally was very excited about Alan – he rated him very highly."

John Lyall appreciated young Alan's ability sooner than anyone at West Ham. As coach of the youth team at that time, the late and much lamented former Hammers boss also recognised the first signs that his star player might be good management material one day in the long and distant future.

Shortly before his sad death in May 2006, in another of his typically absorbing recollections of his 34 years at West Ham, John said: "Sometimes I would drive the young lads to the youth team matches by mini bus. Alan would always sit near the front, just behind me, asking questions about one thing or another. He was always eager to learn more and more about the game from a very young age and his thirst for knowledge left an impression on me. So I wasn't surprised that he went on to become a very successful manager."

The precocious Curbs was certainly a street-wise kid. He once eclipsed his paltry £8 a week earnings as an apprentice at Upton Park by selling badges and beer at a rock concert given by The Who at . . . Charlton Athletic's Valley ground! Alan and his friend made a small fortune on the night, selling for his eldest brother, Billy, who managed the Roger Daltrey-led band, as well other major acts like Led Zeppelin. The enterprising 16-year-old couldn't have known then that, some 18 years later, he would lead the Addicks back to their famous South London home as manager after half a season spent groundsharing at Upton Park.

It was Ron Greenwood who introduced Alan to the senior team scene at Upton Park. An unused sub against Everton in 1974, he was still only 17-years-old – the youngest West Ham player to make the first team until Paul Allen burst onto the scene – when he made his senior debut. Injury to Billy Bonds paved the way for Curbs to pull on the No.4 shirt in the home league game against Chelsea on March 29, 1975. Unfortunately, Micky Droy's headed winner for the Blues took some of the gloss off an otherwise memorable day for the teenager who had dreamed of following the same path as his claret-and-blue heroes.

"I think Tommy Langley, an old friend of mine, had to go in goal for them. I'd been in the squad a couple of times before then but it was great to finally step out onto the field as a West Ham first team player, having been with the club since I was 12.

"As a fan I used to watch from the North Bank and I was sat up on the rafters when Geoff Hurst scored his six goals against Sunderland in 1968 – or was it five? Didn't he punch one in?

"Later, after I became a schoolboy apprentice, I stood and watched games from behind the dugouts in the West Stand lower. Playing football in the playground, I guess I pretended to be Bobby Moore. He was my biggest favourite."

Growing up in a family steeped in West Ham, Alan recalls watching the Wembley cup final triumphs of 1964 and '65 on television at home in Canning Town.

After his debut against Chelsea, his only other first team appearance in 1974-75 was as a substitute for the injured Graham Paddon in the 2-1 home defeat by Coventry City on April 19. Still, it was an exciting time to be around the club. Three weeks later, West Ham would lift the FA Cup for the second time, beating Moore's Fulham 2-0.

Although not even getting close to the starting line-up at Wembley, Curbs did experience cup excitement that month when the 'kids' were beaten by Ipswich Town in the FA Youth Cup final.

With Lyall favouring a midfield trio of Billy Bonds, Trevor Brooking and Graham Paddon, who provided great balance on the left side of a 4-3-3 formation, young Curbishley had to be patient at the start of the 1975-76 season. It was 10 games into the campaign before he got his next chance – as a replacement for the injured Brooking – in the 2-1 home win against Newcastle United on October 11. Just two minutes into the first division encounter Curbishley drove home the first goal following a cross from the left. A month away from his 18th birthday, he capped an eye-catching performance in front of the BBC cameras by laying on West Ham's winning goal from the head of Alan Taylor. Later that evening, *Match of the Day* presenter Jimmy Hill raved about the impact of the young midfielder who came in to fill Brooking's boots so impressively.

But the return of the maestro meant that Curbs was back on the bench for the next game and it was another two months before he gained another start in the league. As Hammers continued to slip down the first division table, it was clear that their European Cup Winners' Cup adventure had been a distraction, albeit a much welcome one.

The FA Cup final victory over Fulham took the Hammers back into Europe for the first time in nine years and after seeing off Lahden Reipas and Ararat Erevan in the first two rounds, Curbs got his big chance against Dutch opponents Den Haag in a dramatic quarter-final.

"I played in the first leg out there," he recalled, "and came on as sub in the return at Upton Park, when we pulled back a two-goal deficit to go through."

Although not involved in the epic semi-final clash with Eintracht Frankfurt, Alan was at least named among the subs for the final against Anderlecht in Brussels. But the night at Heysel ended in bitter disappointment for him for two reasons. He didn't get on to the field as Hammers went down 4-2 and, to compound the misery, he 'lost' his losers' medal.

"At the end of the game I went up with all the other lads to collect our medals but

Making it happen from the centre of midfield.

I wasn't actually given one. I shook everybody's hand but I wasn't given anything.

"I'd assumed that mine and the other subs' medals would be waiting for us when we got back to the dressing room, but they weren't. Not that we wanted losers' medals, but I've never seen the one I should have been given."

Some 31 years later, Curbs just shrugs his shoulders at the Belgian medal mystery but in a way this symbolised his hunger for a regular first team place that would largely prove elusive at Upton Park.

After a dozen league starts and two sub appearances in 1975-76, he followed it with just eight (plus two as sub) in 1976-77. Alan Devonshire, who arrived as an unknown from non-league Southall and became almost an overnight sensation, damaged Curbs' hopes of nailing down a midfield place after Paddon moved on. Geoff Pike, who emerged from the same youth team as Alan, was also staking his claim for a first team berth at the same time.

Alan enjoyed his longest spells in the side in 1977-78 but after 31 league starts and one outing from the bench, he found himself on the fringes of a relegated team.

And after playing in roughly half of the games in 1978-79, when Hammers narrowly missed out on promotion at the first attempt, his frustration took over.

It's a common misconception among West Ham fans that it was the more artistic talents of Brooking and Devonshire that ultimately denied Curbishley the permanent breakthrough he craved at Upton Park.

But as he explains: "Geoff Pike was also coming through and it was really him that

I lost out to.

"I played the holding midfield role, in a style a bit like Michael Carrick does for Manchester United now, while Trevor was allowed to drift off and do what he wanted. He was such a great player anyway, and then we had Dev playing fantastically well on the left.

"My frustration was that if it wasn't going so well, I was the one who would be moved out of the team – and that's what happened. It got blocked up for me a little bit. Results dictate things and I lost my place for the last half of the (1978-79) season and it just so happened that freedom of contract came in," explained Curbs, who made his final appearance in the claret-and-blue was against Leicester City at Upton Park on March 26, 1979.

"Alvin Martin, Geoff Pike and Paul Brush, who had all played in the same youth team as me, had come up, got into the side and went on to stay in the first team.

"Perhaps, if I'd stayed, I might have been at West Ham for the next 10 or 12 years, like the others were. I look back now and regret it. I wish I'd stayed longer."

Lyall favoured Pike's insatiable drive, energy and bite in the tackle compared to Curbishley's more composed touch and the local lad decided his future lay away from his East End roots.

"Being a bit headstrong was my problem," he reflects ruefully. "I was brought up playing with the likes of Ray Wilkins, Glenn Hoddle, Bryan Robson and Peter Barnes, who all went on and played for England, but I didn't."

Having managed Charlton (initially in tandem with Steve Gritt) in a remarkable 729 matches spanning 15 years between July 1991 and his resignation in May 2006, Curbishley can now fully appreciate John Lyall's point of view. He can clearly see how his first boss tried in vain to handle a difficult situation with a young player who, naturally, only had thoughts for his own predicament.

Curbs admitted, too, that the West Ham crowd were not the easiest to please.

He said: "When it ain't going so well, they do get after you.

"I got stick from the West Ham fans when I was a player, because I was in a relegated team. I was 18 and there was a time when I didn't want to show my face or get involved in things around the club.

"But it was Frank Lampard – and I'll never forget what he said – who pointed out to me that it was no use hiding myself away. Frank said: 'As players in these tough situations, you have to front up when it's not going so well. It's no use ducking away from it'. And he was so right.

"As I mentioned when I came back here last year, I never fulfilled my potential at West Ham as a player and now I hope I can do so as a manager."

West Ham received a fee of £225,000 from Birmingham, who were also in the old second division at the time. And if Alan did have tinges of regret that he had missed out on another cup-winning celebration party in his native East London, there was plenty for him to feel satisfied about as he helped the Blues win promotion back to the top flight in May 1980. He also doubled the £200 weekly pay he'd been on at Upton Park.

He went on to make 153 (+2 sub) league and cup appearances (15 goals) for Birmingham before joining their bitter Midlands rivals Aston Villa, who were

Left: On the ball, with David Cross in support. Right: An unfulfilled talent.

European champions at the time, in a £100,000 deal towards the end of the 1982-83 season.

After four seasons (39 appearances + 2 subs and one goal) in the top flight at Villa Park, Curbs dropped back into Division Two following a £38,000 transfer to Charlton in December 1984. He made 68 (+1) appearances (one goal) for the Addicks before slipping into the third division with a £30,000 switch to Brighton in August 1987. But after 127 (+5) games and 15 goals for the Seagulls, he rejoined Charlton on a free as player-coach in July 1990.

Alan played his final, 522nd league and cup game (42 goals) for Charlton as a sub at Portsmouth on August 17, 1993.

He admits he looks back on his playing days with some regrets. Who knows, maybe injury had denied him a place in England's 1982 World Cup squad?

He says: "When he was England manager Ron Greenwood picked me for the 'B' team and I was probably in his final 40 for the finals in Spain, but then I suffered a bad knee injury. I missed the last two months of that season and the first two months of the following campaign, so I missed out."

Alan remains grateful for the early football education he received at West Ham, as one of its most talented graduates from the 70s academy.

A true East Ender who is West Ham through and through, just like his wife Carol, his brothers and the rest of his family, Curbs is, as Hammers fans like to say, 'one of us'.

Chapter 16

DAVID**CROSS**

"When people say I was a brave striker, I'd say I was more stupid than brave. There is an element of thought process that goes into bravery!"

WHEN you compile a list of West Ham 'hard men', Billy Bonds, Frank Lampard and Julian Dicks will be right up there. So, too, will David Cross, a fearsome striker whose bravery belied his undoubted intelligence, on and off the field.

He wasn't nicknamed 'Psycho' by the West Ham fans for nothing. But as you read this interview, it will soon become obvious that David Cross is also a sensitive, deep-thinking man who speaks with a candour and humility rarely found among today's over-hyped 'stars'.

The trademark beard has long gone but as we talked, the characteristics of the man who made himself so popular in the East End came shining through.

Humility? Well, 'Crossy' doesn't even believe that bravery was among his qualities as one of the most potent and feared strikers of the late 70s and early 80s.

He told *EX:* "I've no idea who gave me the nickname but I think I'm right in thinking it stemmed from a game at Cardiff. One of their players did something to me and I had a dig back at him off the ball. I didn't think anyone had seen the incident but as we walked off the pitch at half-time, one of the West Ham fans caught my eye and said: 'You're a f***** psycho, aren't yer!' I just laughed – because he was right!

"How I behaved on the field was nothing like how I was off it. At certain stages of my career I had to become a different person on a match day. If I hadn't, I wouldn't have been the player I was.

"I was a decent player with a good touch but right from my earliest days at Rochdale, they tried to get me to become more aggressive, which didn't come naturally to me. At one stage, someone said to me: 'If you don't become more aggressive as a forward player, you'll have to walk away from the game.

"I had to come to terms with having to change my approach on the field. So on a Saturday, from around midday onwards, I'd psyche myself up to be a different person, whereas off the field I was meek and mild.

"So that Hammers fan got me right, didn't he? A psycho is a schizophrenic, someone with a split personality. And that's what I had to become. Whoever gave me that nickname was absolutely spot on.

"I'm a very, very patient person but when my temper snaps, everything goes. If somebody wanted to fight me, I'd back away. But if I reached breaking point, I'd want to kill everybody – no matter how big they were!

Main pic: David lets fly at Upton Park.

Above: Men of Iron – Billy Bonds, David and Alvin Martin.

Left: 'Psycho' can't quite believe it.

"So that's why when people say I was a brave striker, I'd say I was more stupid than brave. There is an element of thought process that goes into bravery!

"In one game for West Ham, I dived in where the boots were flying and headed a couple of goals, which people thought was brave of me. But all I saw was the ball. When I watched the goals again later on TV, I saw what they meant by bravery, because *they* had seen the boots flying. But I hadn't. All I saw was the ball. I just didn't see danger, so they were acts of stupidity, not bravery!

"I didn't mind the nickname at all. I thought it was funny, except the odd time when I'd be walking through the centre of London with my girlfriend (he later married Christine), and a fan would suddenly recognise me and shout out 'Psycho!'.

When Hammers signed David on his 27th birthday in December 1977, it was at the third attempt. He explains: "I was at Coventry, realised I was moving out, but I wanted to stay in the Midlands, it was as simple as that. I knew Johnny Giles, the manager at West Brom, fancied me and I was also aware of West Ham's interest. Ron Greenwood spoke to me, it was a very interesting offer, but I had never ever considered coming to play in London – I thought it would bugger me up.

"I was single, aged 26, and I honestly thought that if I came to London I'd go off the rails quite easily. I had the wrong perception of what London was like and, in actual fact, when I did finally join West Ham, I never lived in London anyway. I based myself at Shenfield in Essex, which in some respects was just like living back home in Lancashire.

"So I turned down the move in November '76 and went to West Brom instead. But I lasted only a year there, because Cyrille Regis and Laurie Cunningham got together at that time and it was obvious I'd be moving on. I got injured, Cyrille took my place and he was a young lad, just signed from Hayes and was on peanuts compared to me. That was the start of the black revolution at The Hawthorns.

"I heard that West Ham were back in for me and I was impressed by John Lyall, who by then had taken over after Ron became England manager in '77. I was John's first signing."

But West Ham had initially tried to sign David much earlier than that.

"They tried to sign me when I was 21, while playing for Norwich. John was only the coach then, assisting Greenwood, but they wanted me to come at the same time as Graham Paddon. But the Norwich manager, Ron Saunders, wouldn't agree to sell two players to the same club, so Graham joined the Hammers and that's when I moved to Coventry.

"When I finally signed for West Ham I initially stayed in a hotel at Buckhurst Hill and Essex became my home for the next five years – I never went into London unless it was for a club function. Phil Parkes was my best pal at the club but we never went out socially, because he lived on the other side of London, at Wokingham.

"With due respect to Fergie (Bobby Ferguson) and Mervyn Day, Parkesy was the first top class keeper we had at the club. It was a joke among the lads that we were the only club in the country who had a dedicated goalkeeping coach at that time (Ernie Gregory), yet we had to go out and pay world record fees for TWO keepers (Ferguson and Parkes)!

Not that David was over-impressed on his arrival.

"I thought everything at a London club would be slick and state of the art, but at that time they still had the old cricket pavilion at Chadwell Heath and the training ground looked a shambles. I was amazed, but the lads were great with me. I was particularly looking forward to playing with Pop Robson."

When David signed for a then club record £180,000, it was to play alongside Robson, although there were two other forwards still on the fringe in Derek Hales and John Radford. Radford had won the Double with Arsenal in 1971 but could not score in 30 appearances, spanning two seasons, for the Hammers.

"I wasn't that daft, was I?" laughs David, "because while Halesy had got a few goals, Raddy hadn't scored any – and I knew I'd score goals because I always had done, even when I was playing badly. The fans reading this article will endorse the fact that I didn't always play well, but I always gave everything and my goal ratio was very good.

"So I knew that if I scored after a couple of games, I'd be one up on Raddy anyway!

"Having said that, Raddy was fantastic, even though he knew he would be leaving about a month later. Halesy was also good with me and I played up front a couple of times with him before Pop recovered from injury and got back in the side."

Ironically, David made his Hammers debut at West Brom, where he admits he got a luke warm reception and was never popular with the Baggies' fans, even though his goal ratio for them averaged an impressive one every two games.

"John was pleased that he'd finally signed me and told me to keep doing what I'd always done over the years. He said: 'We've got this image of being a bit soft and not training very hard. I don't know if we're soft, but we certainly train hard'.

"He was right, because I trained harder at West Ham than I'd trained in the previous four years with West Brom and Coventry. We worked more on technique and were a fit side."

Although Lyall played to David's widely acknowledged main strengths – his aerial ability and physical presence – he also earns much credit for developing the lucid Lancastrian as an all round striker who could hold the ball up and cleverly link the play with midfielders and wide players. Tall and rangy, Cross would put the fear of death into defenders who got too close to him. His dark, rugged looks and beard only enhanced his image as one of the game's most aggressive characters, a tough, no-nonsense player who could look after himself.

His fearlessness, allied to improved technique, proved crucial to the team's FA Cup success in 1980, where he played a selfless lone striker's role as Lyall totally outflanked Arsenal with an unexpected tactical ploy that even Crossy himself didn't know about until the day of the final.

David sacrificed possible personal glory for the team cause, although he remains disappointed that he didn't make a bigger impact on that hot day at Wembley. He said: "Realistically, the only chance I had of scoring was just before Trevor's goal itself. I had the first stab at Dev's cross, hitting it on the half-volley. I remember the ball was in the air a long time and as it came over from the left, I wasn't sure whether to slam it, which could have resulted in the ball either rocketing into the net or ending up in the stand.

"So professionalism probably took over and I thought I'd just keep the ball low and guide it back towards the goal, which is what I chose to do. Willie Young cleared my effort off the line, the ball went back out to Stuart Pearson and his shot was headed in by Trevor.

"I had only one other decent chance of scoring, towards the end, but I don't think anyone has ever spotted it. Everyone remembers Young hacking down Paul Allen as he ran towards goal, but I was running just behind Paul when he was tripped and he should really have given me the ball *before* he was brought down. But I was absolutely knackered and, to be fair, even if he'd slipped the pass to me, I don't know if I'd have finished the move effectively."

Recalling the post-Wembley celebrations, David says: "Being single at the time, I was one of the lads who usually liked a drink, but after the final I didn't touch a drop until midnight. I'd played in the '73 League Cup final for Norwich (against Spurs) and remembered nothing from it, so I was determined to take it all in this time. I have vivid memories of '80 Cup final day.

"I was determined not to get drunk too early, whereas Ray Stewart – who didn't normally drink at that time – consumed a whole bottle of champagne in the bath and was violently ill all night. He was spewing up at half-past seven!

"I think I went on Jimmy Hill's *Match of the Day* at half-past 10. He'd backed us to lose, so I had a pop at him.

"I had a couple of beers after midnight and went to bed about two in the morning. And I remember showing off the cup with the lads at East Ham town hall and the parade through the streets the next day. The fans were fantastic."

By the start of the following season, Pop Robson and Stuart Pearson had been succeeded by another front man, diminutive Paul Goddard, who cost a club record £800,000 from QPR and forged a very effective partnership with Crossy. They were the outstanding strike-force who shot Hammers to a record second division title points haul in May 1981, a memorable season in which West Ham reached the League Cup final (losing a replay to the then mighty Liverpool) and the quarter-final of the European Cup Winners' Cup.

How does David compare his two main Hammers strike-partners, Pop Robson and Paul Goddard?

"Pop was a better goalscorer than Paul and he was one of my boyhood heroes, having watched him play for Newcastle as a right-winger when I was a little lad. Pop was a fantastically talented player, as was Paul, but I always regarded Pop as more of a natural finisher who would score goals from three yards or from outside the box, whereas Paul tended to pass the ball into the net.

"They were very similar in many respects – they both linked the play well – but I just felt that, over a very long career, Pop just had the edge on his goalscoring ability.

"But after working with Halesy, Pop and then 'Pancho' (Pearson), Paul Goddard and I formed a very good partnership. Stuart and I were good pals off the pitch, but our partnership on it wasn't that fruitful. I think that was because, like me, he was a face-up type of player who liked playing with his back to goal, knocking the ball back for other people. Trevor Brooking and Alan Devonshire, and all the other really good players I ever played with, couldn't do what I did. I was willing to take all the knocks, chase 50-yard balls pumped up the field and do the best I could."

Just when you think that David might suddenly have developed an ego, he adds: "Whether I'd hold the ball up or knock it one-touch, I'd give it to the lads who could play. All I ever did was look for Giles and Cantello at West Brom; Mortimer and McGuire at Coventry; Paddon and Livermore at Norwich; and then the likes of Brooking, Devonshire, Geoff Pike, Patsy Holland and Jimmy Neighbour at West Ham."

After winning the cup in '80, David experienced his one and only European campaign with the Hammers the following season. A promising run was abruptly ended by the brilliantly accomplished Georgian side, Dynamo Tbilisi, at the third round stage. Although Pearson scored the only goal of the second leg, the damage had already been done at Upton Park – and, typically, David highlighted his guilty part in that defeat to one of the best sides ever to grace the Boleyn.

He recalls: "The lad who played against me – Chivadze, their captain – was fantastic. They stunned us because we were told they'd just had their three-month winter break, no-one had really heard of them and so we thought it would be easy. That was some result when we won at their place, but it would have been better if we'd played the away leg first. We'd have been better prepared but they killed us, 4-1, in the first leg at Upton Park. (David scored in the 54th minute, when we were already two down.)

"I cost us the first goal, when I allowed Chivadze to beat me, run on and score from 25 yards. It was one of the few times I didn't track the centre-half."

Not that Hammers fans would have a bad word said against the northerner with East End fighting qualities.

"I absolutely loved playing at Upton Park – that was a big thing for me," David continues. "I know I wasn't what they'd been used to at West Ham – I wasn't a ball-playing, dropping-off type of centre-forward, but an up and at 'em, smash 'em around sort who got goals. It was my goals that made me popular. The crowd appreciated my effort, but then effort is the very least you should put into any game.

"Although I always loved playing at Upton Park, the stats say that I scored a lot of my goals away (remarkably, 12 out of 16 in the first division in 1981-82) – and that had a lot to do with my popularity.

"If you've scored the winner at Shrewsbury or Bolton, or scored four at Grimsby, and there are only 2,000 or so of our fans there to see it, their long journey home is made more memorable because of your goals," he reasoned.

West Ham fans didn't have to travel home far from Tottenham's White Hart Lane ground on the night of September 2, 1981, but those who witnessed one of the most joyous awaydays in Hammers' history will not forget the contribution of David Cross. He scored all four goals in a superb 4-0 victory – our first away match back in the top flight following the second division title romp.

David recalls all four of his goals in detail: "Up until we scored, we were getting hammered. I used to play on the left-hand side up front, and all I'd done for the first

David with Iain Dowie at Oldham Athletic in October 2002.

25 minutes was chase their right-back, Steve Perryman, back towards our goal.

"But when Jimmy (Neighbour) set up my first goal, the floodgates opened. Jimmy got up the right, crossed it and as the ball came back out to me on the edge of the box, I hit it on the volley. The ball hit Ray Clemence's arm and went into the roof of the net.

"The second one was a cross which I got on the end of. I had a nick at it and, again, it hit a body, which killed Clemence, and I was able to knock it into the empty net.

"My hat-trick goal was a classic volley from 15 yards. Frank Lampard volleyed the ball upfield to Paul Goddard, who volleyed it out to Geoff Pike. Pike then volleyed it to me, and I volleyed it into the net. Bang, bang, bang, bang – in! The ball never touched the ground.

"The fourth goal was scrambled. I think Dev should have scored but his shot came back off Clemence and I just tapped in the rebound.

"I remember most of my goals for West Ham. The third one at Tottenham was probably my best in terms of team build-up. I scored a good curler that went in the top corner at Watford, which was shown on *Match of the Day*, but I suppose I'm a bit perverse in some respects in that I liked scoring a typical striker's goal. I saw my job as scoring in the six-yard box and prided myself on getting in front of their keeper and tapping 'em in from two yards.

"The affection I got from the Hammers fans was staggering, and it was because they took to me so well that I raised my game. I lived by my goals and I always said that whether we won 1-0 or lost 1-5, I wanted to be our goalscorer.

"I desperately wanted to score 100 goals for West Ham. The official records show that I got 98, but I actually netted 99. I went to Wolves on the last day of the 1981-

Joining West Ham made David a much better all round player.

82 season knowing I needed two more for my ton. I got one in a 2-1 defeat and I was a bit sick about that."

David admits that his four-and-a-half years with the Hammers were the happiest and most successful of his career, so why did he leave in the summer of '82, having underlined his scoring prowess on West Ham's return to the first division by top scoring for the club with 16 league goals?

He explained: "I felt, at 31, that after five great years, I'd done as much as I could at West Ham, that if I did one more year things might start to go the other way and the fans would turn against me. I didn't want that to happen.

"I'd been courting the girl who became my wife. That's one of the main reasons I left when I did. Christine came from the same village as me – Heywood – and she had her own business back home. I'd been driving up and down the motorway most weekends for five years. I scored 19 goals in my last season but I still felt I wasn't really living right.

"It was also the first time in my career that I had been able to move completely on my terms, being one of the first players to take advantage of the new freedom of contract rule. John had offered me a good deal over two years, while Manchester City offered me three years. I chose City and the fee had to be decided by a tribunal.

"City turned up for the tribunal totally unprepared. The manager, former Hammers right-back John Bond, couldn't make it, so John Benson and the club secretary came with me. John Lyall was there for West Ham, along with directors Will and Brian Cearns. West Ham wanted 600 grand for me and City offered only £50,000, which was fair enough – that was how it happened. The tribunal would usually meet the clubs somewhere near the middle.

"City argued, off the cuff, that I was 31 and they needed me to replace another player they'd just sold. But West Ham produced a dossier which pointed out that, of all the players who were active, two were way ahead of everybody else in terms of games played and goals scored. Second was Trevor Francis, who Man City had just sold to Forest for £1.2m, and the first was me!

"It was a brilliant dossier and totally flabbergasted City, but in the end I think John got only £130,000 for me, which he wasn't happy about.

"But John was great and didn't begrudge me anything. In fact, when I left that tribunal, in my heart of hearts, I wanted to go back to West Ham – I felt more comfortable with their people. John sensed I'd dropped a bollock but I had to look at the bigger picture. Christine and I got married and had our son, Bobby, after returning to the North-West.

"Manchester City actually went down at the end of that season. They were a club in turmoil. Of all the West Ham people I have come across, I found John Bond the strangest. He was a good coach and good company, but he seemed insecure and that transmitted itself to the players.

"City was full of intrigue, all cloak and dagger, whereas at West Ham everyone was so open and friendly. John was 'John' , not the 'boss', as Bondy liked to be called.

"After City, I had two great years at Vancouver, went back into the first division with West Brom and then on to Bolton. I spent a couple of months on loan to Bury

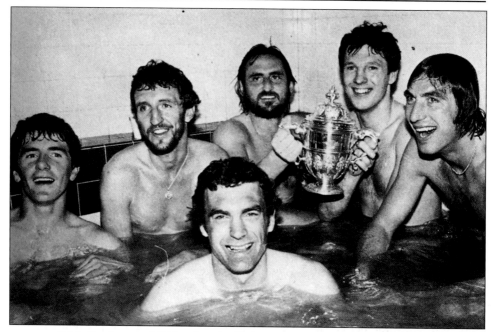

Celebrating the second division championship in 1981. Ray Stewart, David, Frank Lampard, Alvin Martin and Billy Bonds.

but I wasn't a player there that anybody would remember."

Despite his full blooded approach to the game, David suffered few serious injuries, until the one that effectively ended his career.

He says: "They say that if you live by the sword, you'll eventually die by it. I didn't suffer many injuries but I fractured my skull at Bolton and that more or less finished me. I headed the point of somebody's elbow – it was the Bristol Rovers' number two – but I didn't even find out his name. I wasn't bothered. If I'd been a lot younger, I would have come back from it, but I was 35 by then and it knocked the stuffing and the bravery out of me."

When he stopped playing, David earned his living selling life and pensions policies for Allied Dunbar Insurance for nine years, then began working part-time for Oldham Athletic in 1990. After coaching kids and scouting for the Latics, he accepted the youth team manager's job at Boundary Park in 1997, managed the reserves the following season and stepped up to become Iain Dowie's assistant in 2002-03. Within weeks, the two former Hammers strikers plotted West Ham's embarrassing exit from the League Cup at Upton Park in October 2002 but Crossy was to lose his job when Oldham had to make drastic financial cutbacks.

He is still in close contact with the Hammers, though. Now 56-years-old, David stays in touch with the game while working part-time as a scout for West Ham, compiling reports on their future North-West-based opponents.

Chapter 17

DEREK**HALES**

*"It never bothered me going to places like Leeds, Manchester United or Liverpool. A ground's a ground, isn't it? Two goals, one at either end, four corner flags and a load of blokes behind the goal calling you a w*****"*

WHATEVER happened to the bearded footballer? You might find the odd bit of token stubble around the jowls of Lucas Neill or Matthew Upson but, by and large, the modern footballer's chin remains as resolutely hairless as Eggert Magnusson's distinguished dome.

Things were a bit different back in 1977-78, when John Lyall decided the best way to fight a relegation battle was to employ as many hairy players as possible in order to intimidate our opponents into submission.

The ploy failed narrowly when a final day home defeat at the hands of a heavily moustachioed Liverpool outfit condemned us to three seasons in the old second division. But, for six glorious months at least, West Ham boasted the most hirsute squad in the top flight.

Leading the way in the furry fashion stakes was striker Derek Hales, a bewhiskered wonder who was brought in by Lyall for £100,000 from Derby County in September 1977. With his dark, curly hair and beard, Hales was a genuinely scary proposition.

He had the temper to match and, with 23 career sendings off, mainly for retaliation, standing as testament to the maverick, wild man image, the long-since departed bristles were surely a carefully cultivated part of his armoury?

"No, not really, I was just a bit lazy and wasn't a great lover of shaving," said Derek, now 55, neatly shooting down all our nostalgic preconceptions.

"Back in those days there were a lot of beards around. At West Ham, Billy Bonds had one, so did Frank Lampard, Bill Green and then David Cross, so there were a few about, while at Liverpool everyone had a moustache.

"It was just a trend at the time and everyone seemed to have a bit of hair – not that I've got much left now, mind – but you look at modern players and, it's funny, a lot of them haven't got much hair. A lot of them are even going bald."

Derek joined the Hammers when we were right in the mire and one win in eight games meant we were set for a long winter fighting relegation (sounds familiar) on an Upton Park pitch that often resembled a bog.

As a striker of some repute who had averaged a goal every other game in 159 league matches for Luton Town, Charlton Athletic and Derby County, Derek was the man Lyall entrusted with the job of saving our bacon. And, to be fair, he almost delivered.

By the end of a poor campaign, in which we scored as many goals as 13th placed Norwich, but conceded far too many for comfort, Derek had notched a commendable 10 goals in 23 games, a record most current-day front men would glady give a Gucci watch for.

"Even though we got relegated, I enjoyed it. My goals return wasn't bad.

"I'd almost joined West Ham the year before. There were rumours John Lyall had wanted me, Mike Flanagan and Colin Powell, and I'm sure he did enquire, but Charlton wouldn't sell all three at the same time and I ended up at Derby.

"I thought I might be returning to Charlton – even back then Derby were in financial trouble – but John came back in for me.

"West Ham weren't the greatest of sides, although we had some good results. We went to Ipswich when they had John Wark, Eric Gates, Paul Mariner and Kevin Beattie, and were on a roll under Bobby Robson, but we beat them 2-0, so we could do it at times.

"But, where West Ham were the footballing side they'd always professed to be, you couldn't really play it on the pitch at Upton Park.

"At that time, the pitches at Derby and West Ham were the worst in England. The Baseball Ground was always ankle deep, full of sand, and West Ham's was a quagmire.

"Christ, after half-an-hour on West Ham's pitch you were dead and buried, and in the last half hour of games everybody was going through the motions because you couldn't move in the stuff.

"That was a big part of our downfall, but the league table never lies and we just weren't good enough. We used to let in too many goals and sides that struggle are the ones that let in two goals a game."

One thing you could never accuse Derek Hales of was lacking confidence, and even in a relegation-bound team some of his most important goals came away from home, as a late rally came just too late to avoid the drop.

"We went to Leeds and beat them 2-1. Leeds was a bloody intimidating place to go, and I remember going there on the bus and the supporters really giving us hell, which is how they were then.

"We played well that day, when Alvin Martin scored a great goal on his debut and I got the winner after Bonzo had flicked one on for me. We almost got out of trouble, but the side was chopped and changed a bit.

"It never bothered me going to places like Leeds, Manchester United or Liverpool. A ground's a ground, isn't it? Two goals, one at either end, four corner flags and a load of blokes behind the goal calling you a w*****.

"I always got goals – one here, two there – but I was never one to shout the odds, not a strutty, gobby type.

"Yes, I spoke my mind, but I used to respect people who did their jobs. It's like politicians. It's all right gobbing off, but if you do what you've mouthed off about, that's lovely.

"I was always brought up that if you had a bit of mouth you had to back some of it up. If you can't back it up, keep your trap shut. I wish some of today's kids had the same attitude."

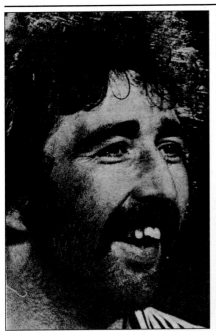 

Left: Derek in his West Ham days and (right) how he looked when he spoke to EX in November 2002.

As a sports master at The Howard Secondary School in Rainham, Kent, just down the road from where he was brought up at Lower Halstow, Derek is well placed to comment on the youth of today – and, in football terms, he does not like what he sees.

"Kids are less fit and totally inactive compared to how we were in my day, when you couldn't keep us off a football pitch. I'm thinner than some of them, even now!

"I don't know where football is going. Most of the Premiership managers are foreigners. Most of the players are foreign, too. We can't call it English football any more, can we?

"In my day, it was every boy's dream to play professional football. But you look at Arsenal, Chelsea and Liverpool now, and they're all full of foreigners, so any kid watching that is thinking 'what chance have I got?'.

"The problem is the big money came into it and clubs want ready-made teams. Look at our top four clubs, how many English players are there? And where does that leave the kids I coach here?

"There are still dreams, but you haven't got a f***** hope in hell. Who in their right mind would send a kid to Arsenal or Chelsea?"

Derek, now 55, spent just one season with the Hammers before being surprisingly sold to Charlton Athletic for £85,000 in July 1978. Twenty-nine years on, he remains mystified by Lyall's decision but still looks back on his short time at Upton Park with satisfaction.

"I thought I was going to be at West Ham for a while and was looking forward to knocking in some goals in the old second division, but it wasn't to be.

"I went in one day during pre-season and John Lyall just asked me: 'Do you want a move to Charlton?'. I wasn't going to argue with anybody, and I got more money, but I enjoyed my time at West Ham and have no regrets."

There really was no finer sight in the 80s than Alan Devonshire in full flow.

Chapter 18

ALAN**DEVONSHIRE**

"To have that taken away through no fault of my own was very upsetting, and it still hurts me to think about it. It's not bitterness – I just wish it had never happened and I would love to know how my career and life would have panned out, because I think I could have gone right to the very top"

HE may have gone on to be an FA Cup winner, England international and one of the greatest individual talents to ever pull on a West Ham United shirt, but it didn't start out as a Roy of the Rovers fairytale for Alan Devonshire. In fact, he was on the football scrapheap at 16, cast into the wilderness like so many other teenage hopefuls, but in the cruellest of fashion.

Having already been released by Crystal Palace as a 14-year-old who was considered 'too small', the former Ealing and Middlesex schools youngster had fought his way back to earn a second chance at Selhurst Park, only for his professional dreams to be shattered once again as he prepared for the step-up to full-time football.

"I was promised by the manager, Bert Head, that Palace would sign me on a one-year professional contract when I was 17, but then Malcolm Allison came in and within two months I was gone," he recalls.

"To be honest, I don't think Malcolm even saw me play, he just let me go without even saying it to my face. I took it badly and more or less packed the game in after leaving Palace. I went off to find work and didn't kick a ball for three or four months.

"In the end, it was my mum and dad who encouraged me to take it up again. My dad took me to a few non-league clubs, including Hayes, where Allan Harris was the manager, but I didn't really like it there and ended up going to Southall.

"I actually bumped into Malcolm when I played for England in a testimonial game at Middlesbrough for a couple of ex-Boro players. He approached me and told me what a good player he thought I was, and how he'd made such a big mistake in letting me go at Palace. That was nice of him, because he didn't have to come up to me and say that."

While he may not have realised it at the time, Dev's rejection turned out to be the watershed that eventually moulded his career. After his father, Les (who had been a professional himself with Palace and Brentford), devoted his time and energy into re-focusing his son's talents, Alan signed for Isthmian League side Southall and, within months, was attracting the attention of several Football League clubs.

"I'm a great believer in fate and, to be fair, the time I had at Southall was my learning curve," says Dev. "A guy called Geoff Taylor was manager and Ron Noades was chairman – they had just taken over when I joined and we went on to enjoy a successful couple of years.

"When I signed for West Ham, people would ask me how I was coping with the physical demands of top level football, and I used to just laugh. Compared to playing with Southall in the Isthmian League, the old first division was like a stroll in the park!

"Yeah, I used to get kicked, but I got a lot more protection from referees at a higher level. In non-league, you didn't get that protection. I remember being carried off at Boreham Wood with blood pouring out of BOTH calves – I'd been studded down the back of each leg in two separate tackles.

"If it hadn't been for the experience I gained at Southall, I might not have become the player I turned out to be. It certainly toughened me up. There wasn't a lot of me, but I had a big heart and I learned not to bother about being kicked. I realised that the more I got kicked, the better I was playing."

One man who certainly noticed that lion's heart and even bigger ability was West Ham United scout Eddie Baily. After watching the slightly-built figure earn a big reputation for himself at non-league level, Baily and his fellow scout Charlie Faulkner advised John Lyall to make his move quickly and, as £6,000 winged its way to the footballing backwaters of Middlesex in September 1976, 20-year-old Dev found himself in the English first division.

Despite the sudden huge leap that would now be unthinkable in the modern game, the new boy was handed a professional debut just weeks after arriving at Upton Park – in a 2-0 League Cup defeat against QPR – before making his league bow just three days later, in a 3-0 loss at West Bromwich Albion.

Isthmian League to the very top in a matter of weeks – it almost sounds impossible, but Dev went on to make 28 appearances in his first campaign with the Hammers and reveals that the step-up was nowhere near as daunting or difficult as he might have expected.

"I thought I was fit when I played for Southall – I didn't drink, didn't smoke and generally looked after myself," he recalls. "But after a couple of weeks of full-time training with West Ham, I was astounded at just how fit I really was.

"Perhaps the biggest surprise, though, was how easy I found the step up. I literally found it easier playing for West Ham than I had done with Southall. I suppose it was down to better pitches, better referees and playing alongside much better players.

"Maybe I was just lucky, but from the word go I seemed to adjust to it, and found it less physically demanding. I still got kicked, but not as badly. And besides, if anyone got too nasty towards me, Bonzo was always there to growl at them!

"I was lucky I went to a club like West Ham, where there were a lot of good people who helped me to settle in and enjoy life on and off the pitch.

"I wasn't a flash or over-confident lad. I was very quiet actually but, inwardly, I knew I had talent and that inner-belief helped me to make the step up pretty smoothly.

"It's hard to explain, but things just seemed to come naturally to me. We had an American guy come over once to study our game and he told me that I was the only player he had seen who had a change of pace when running.

One of the all-time Hammers greats.

Dev was forced to alter his running style but he remained a class act. Inset: Alan today.

"When I asked him what he meant, he said that I slowed down when defenders approached me and then sped up again as they got close. It wasn't something I thought about too much – I would simply slow down to draw them in and fool them into thinking they could get the ball easily, then speed up and accelerate away.

"I can't explain why I did it, but I seemed to *know* when people were going to dive in at me and I found it easy at times to read their game."

It was that spontaneous and instinctive talent that made Dev one of the most feared wingers in the English game during the late 70s and early 80s. A key member of the team rebuilt by John Lyall after relegation in 1978, he was named Hammer-of-the-Year the following season, going on to play an influential role in our 1980 FA Cup triumph. He created the 13th minute winning goal for Trevor Brooking and then starred as we won promotion back to the top flight in record-breaking fashion.

Devonshire illuminated many a match with his dazzling skills and probing runs down the left flank, even though he was in fact more naturally right-footed.

Having developed an almost telepathic understanding with Brooking in the Hammers midfield – those two forming a very creative left-sided triangle with full-back Frank Lampard – Dev was handed the first of his eight full England caps in May 1980 and was unlucky to miss out on Ron Greenwood's squad for the 1982 World Cup finals. He was simply a victim of the embarrassment of riches afforded to England on the left-side of midfield at that time.

Still, as he reached the prime years of his career, there seemed no doubt that the silky winger would go on to achieve plenty more at international level . . . until disaster struck.

It was January 7, 1984, in the 15th minute of an FA Cup third round tie at Upton Park against Wigan Athletic, when Dev saw his dreams of reaching the very top of his profession shattered in one devastating moment.

Sandwiched in a rather innocuous looking challenge, he tore three of the four major ligaments in his right knee, leading to a 19-month spell on the sidelines and a condition that saw 14 out of 15 surgeons advise him to quit the game.

Such was the impact of Dev's talent on the team that Brooking, having originally planned to leave the game at the end of the 1984-85 campaign, brought forward his retirement by a year once he realised that his gifted midfield partner wouldn't be around to enjoy his final campaign with him.

Looking back on the moment that dramatically changed the course of his career, Alan expresses understandable regret and sadness about what might have been.

"I'll always regret my knee injury – always," he says.

"I owe West Ham supporters a lot, because I think they understood that I wasn't the same player when I came back, and accepted that I couldn't do some of the things I used to do.

"It was a tough time for me. I was out for 18 months and, for the first six months, I couldn't even straighten my leg. For a professional sportsman who was used to running every day, that was torture.

"I was very low at one point, crying every day and wondering why it had happened to me. It almost cost me my marriage but, thankfully, my wife Chris was very understanding. I had to spend Monday to Friday at a rehab clinic and only see my son at weekends, but I was determined to get back and play again.

"It upsets me to think about what I could have achieved had I not suffered the injury. A lot of people in the game were talking about me at the time, and at that point I really thought I could have taken my career to the next level.

"Without wanting to sound big-headed, I *knew* how good I was. At 27, I had appeared in three or four England games on the trot and, at the time I did my knee, was playing the best football of my career.

"To have that taken away through no fault of my own was very upsetting, and it

With trademark long hair and moustache in the fantastic 1985-86 season.

still hurts me to think about it. It's not bitterness – I just wish it had never happened and I would love to know how my career and life would have panned out, because I think I could have gone right to the very top."

The fact that he never played for England again after his injury might suggest he is right, but there will still be many Hammers fans who claim that Dev *did* manage to get back to the top. Returning to fitness in time for the start of the 1985-86 campaign, it may have been a slightly slower individual that pulled on the No.6 shirt again, but he certainly proved he had lost none of his old skill as the club enjoyed its best-ever league campaign.

"I had to change my game when I came back and, to be honest, I was surprised that I could still be effective," he admits.

"I don't know whether it was because I had to think about the game more because I'd lost that electrifying pace, but I managed to make an impact and enjoyed a great season in 1985-86.

"Tony Gale and Frank McAvennie always say that I was the best player they ever played with – and that was *after* my injury. I think to myself, blimey, I wish they'd seen me before that!"

Despite his weakened knee and restrictive running style, Dev still went on to enjoy another four years of top-flight football and earn a richly-deserved testimonial. Although, sadly, his final season at the club was one of controversy and turmoil. Following Lyall's departure as manager after 34 years at Upton Park, Lou Macari arrived for a brief and eventful spell, before Hammers legend Billy Bonds took over to steady the ship in February 1990.

By then, Dev had unwittingly played his final game for the club, in the ill-fated 6-0 League Cup semi-final defeat at Oldham Athletic and, while his fellow veteran Liam Brady was handed the chance to enjoy an emotional farewell on the final day of the season in a 4-0 win over Wolves, the 34-year-old walked out on a free transfer that day without having the chance to say a proper goodbye to the supporters who had adored him for over a decade.

After leaving Upton Park, Dev enjoyed a short spell with Watford, making 24 appearances in the 1990-91 campaign, but his time at Vicarage Road ended the following season. He then took his first step into management, leading Middlesex League outfit Osterley to two cup finals.

In 1997, he was appointed manager of Ryman League side Maidenhead United and went on to lead the Kent club to the Premier Division, several cup finals and the most secure period of their history.

After six years with Maidenhead, in July 2003 Dev joined Hampton & Richmond Borough, leading them to promotion to the Ryman League Premier division in his first season.

He has continued to establish himself as one of the most successful managers at non-league level and in May 2007, he guided Hampton & Richmond to the Isthmian (Ryman Premier) League championship.

PENALTY KING: Ray is mobbed by Geoff Pike, Stuart Pearson and David Cross after converting a spot kick at Luton in March 1980. Below: The Mayoress of Newham was there to greet the 1980 FA Cup winners on their return to the Boleyn after defeating Arsenal. Looking a little the worse for wear are (left to right) Pat Holland, Ray Stewart, Stuart Pearson, Bobby Ferguson, Alvin Martin, Jimmy Neighbour and Phil Parkes.

Chapter 19

RAY**STEWART**

"Football was my life and there was no way I could finish like that. Watching the team being relegated and then seeing John lose his job was bad enough, and I felt I owed it to myself to fight back and pull on the shirt again. Looking back, I made the wrong decision and should have listened to the medical experts but, at the time, I didn't want to accept that"

THE phrase 'loyal club man' is sadly an all too rare phenomenon in today's game of inflated wages and egos to match. But, back in the days when football clubs – and West Ham United in particular – boasted several such conscientious individuals, few embodied the title more genuinely than Scot Ray Stewart.

From the moment he arrived at Upton Park as a fresh-faced teenager in August 1979 until the day he ended his claret-and-blue career 12 years later, the versatile defender was a shining example of dedication and commitment – on and off the field.

Not only was he a model of consistency in the No.2 shirt – making more than 430 league and cup appearances for the club (a figure that would have been far greater had he not suffered serious injury towards the end of his career) – Ray was also a first class ambassador for West Ham away from the football pitch.

Rarely a day went by without the affable Scotsman taking part in some charity or promotional event on behalf of the club's commercial department, or simply rounding up team-mates to help out with a good cause. Local hospitals, schools and businesses all benefited from his reliable and enthusiastic co-operation, which in turn developed working relationships and corporate connections that are still in place at the club to this day.

However, if it hadn't been for the fact that young Ray Stewart had an impressively mature head on his schoolboys shoulders, West Ham may well have missed out on such devotion – as he reveals when reflecting on his breakthrough in the professional game up in Scotland in the mid-70s.

"As a schoolboy I had offers from a number of clubs, including Manchester United and Aston Villa in England, while Glasgow Rangers spent many weeks trying to persuade me to sign – even offering my mum and dad money and various other inducements.

"It was very flattering to be chased by some of the biggest clubs in Britain but I had made up my mind to join Dundee United, and the reason was pretty simple. I used to get *Shoot!* magazine and whenever I saw the squad pictures of the big clubs – the likes of Rangers and Man United – they seemed to have 40 or 50 players on

Scottish braveheart Ray never gave less than 100 percent.

Geoff Pike and Tonka show off the FA Cup to West Ham fans after beating Arsenal.

the staff, and that frightened me.

"I gathered that I would have a much better chance of progressing and become an established professional at a smaller club and, when I look back at my career, I think I made the right decision."

Showing remarkable maturity for a 15-year-old football-mad youngster, Ray resisted the carrot being dangled and instead made the short trip from his home in Stanley, Perthshire to Tannadice, the home of Dundee United, where he enjoyed the perfect start to his footballing education and picked up the enduring good habits that would serve him well throughout his career and, indeed, his adult life.

"My dad was a big influence on me but he only gave advice – he left me to make my own decisions. He said to me: 'It's working boots or football boots?' and I chose football as a career. It was all I wanted to do and, even at the age of 14 or 15, I was very determined and clear about the route I wanted to take.

"I felt that Dundee United were an up-and-coming club who gave youth a chance and would offer me the opportunity to prove myself. The manager, Jim McLean, was a massive influence on me from the moment I arrived there.

"Although I didn't live too far from Dundee, he used to insist that all the young players lived within a 15-mile radius of Tannadice, so I moved into digs when I started my apprenticeship and lived in a place called Lochdee with the likes of Billy Kirkwood, Paul Hegarty and Paul Sturrock.

"With the money we got paid, I wasn't able to travel back and forth to home anyway – I'd have had no wages left at the end of the week! We used to claim expenses but there was no taking advantage of it – I remember once putting a newspaper on my expenses sheet and Jim McLean went absolutely mad. He accused me of trying to rip the club off and made me feel terrible."

Such was the impact he made as a young defender at Tannadice that Ray went on to captain Scotland at youth and under-21 level. After just 44 league games for Dundee United, he became Britain's most expensive teenager in August 1979 when John Lyall – who had been tracking his progress for many months – splashed out £430,000 to bring him to Upton Park. And despite his lack of experience in senior football, Ray was more than ready to take the plunge and head south of the border.

"I knew of West Ham's interest – I think John had been up to watch me something like 18 times and the club had rejected a couple of offers, but everything happened quite quickly once a bid was finally accepted," he recalls.

"From my point of view, I just wanted to play football in the best league in the world. When I agreed to join West Ham, I didn't even know they were in the second division! I was just so keen to get down there and show what I could do.

"I wanted to be successful and prove that I was a winner – and I believed that I was the best. Whether I was or not is a different matter but I had that self-belief and desire. It's like when someone does karaoke – they may not be a good singer but, for those five minutes when they are performing and everyone is laughing and clapping, they feel like the best singer in the world.

"And that was how I felt when I joined West Ham."

Thrust into the first team spotlight just a few days after arriving in London, Ray made his Hammers debut in a League Cup second round, second leg tie at Barnsley, playing in the centre of midfield as Lyall's men enjoyed a comfortable passage to the next stage. Four days later – having just celebrated his 20th birthday – he made his league bow in a 1-1 draw at Preston North End, this time as a central defender alongside Billy Bonds.

With his services required immediately, there wasn't really time for Ray to dwell on the enormity of his transfer or reflect on what he had been left behind in Scotland.

"I didn't get homesick. For a start, I was so determined to make a success of myself on the pitch and, secondly, I was made to feel so welcome by everyone at the club. I stayed in the digs run by Roger Cross's mum, Rose, who was a lovely lady. A lot of people who run those sort of set-ups do it for the money, but Rose did it purely to help the club and because she was West Ham through and through.

"She was like a second mum to the lads who stayed there and always made sure that we did things the right way – got to bed at a decent time and ate the right things. If we got up to mischief, she would threaten to tell the manager. Whether she did or not, I don't know, but that was her loyalty to the club and she genuinely cared about our welfare. It hurt me a great deal when I heard that she had died – I'll never forget the part she played in helping me to settle down south.

"It also helped that the other lads were all lovely people. The likes of George

Cowie, John Lynes and Alvin Martin were all in the digs with me and the squad was full of decent, genuine fellas who all cared about each other and the club.

"There was a real togetherness and I was made to feel like one of the lads straight away. You had the leaders like Billy Bonds, Trevor Brooking and Alan Dev, who commanded respect straight away but still treated you as their equal. Then there was Frank Lampard, who taught me all about the East End and made sure I knew what I needed to know.

"I respected every one of them and I can honestly say that I got on well with every player at the club. We weren't best buddies who spent every minute together, but we all mixed well and looked out for each other."

Having made an immediate impact upon his arrival, Ray then settled into a more familiar right-back role and became a permanent fixture in Lyall's rebuilding process that followed relegation from the top flight 18 months earlier. However, even the ambitious young Scot couldn't have predicted the ultimate success of his debut season in English football. He finished second top scorer with 14 goals in 54 league and cup appearances and played an influential part in the team's FA Cup triumph.

His last-minute winner from the penalty spot against Aston Villa in the quarter-final will never be forgotten by all at Upton Park that day.

"For me, the penalty against Villa in 1980 is the one that stands out above all others," he says without a moment's hesitation. "I hadn't been at the club long and that was the night I became a Jockney!

"It was against a top team with a top goalkeeper, and I had the chance to win the game with one kick. I remember just looking up to the sky to say a prayer and then whacking it and hoping for the best. The feeling when the ball hit the net was something else and, as I said, I think that was the moment when the West Ham fans took me to their hearts.

"The penalty against Liverpool in the League Cup final was also a big one, given the enormity of the situation and the fact that it was a Scotsman up against the England goalkeeper. Every penalty I took had pressure on it, though, and I just saw it as my job to take them.

"I'd taken them at Dundee United and I got my chance at West Ham when Geoff Pike missed one, I think. I always felt confident of scoring but it wasn't off the cuff – I used to practice religiously and spent hours on the training ground just striking the ball properly. It got to the stage where, whenever we were awarded a penalty, the fans and my team-mates considered it to be as good as a goal, and I liked being under that kind of pressure.

"As soon as I stepped up, the adrenalin would start flowing and I could sense that thousands of people were pinning their hopes on me. I wanted to rise to that challenge and make them happy."

It was his powerful approach to dead-ball situations that earned Ray his famous 'Tonka' nickname – a moniker that followed him from Scotland.

"I was originally given the name by Hamish McAlpine, the goalkeeper at Dundee United," he reveals. "Then, when I'd moved to West Ham, we actually played a friendly against Dundee United and the lads soon picked up on what my old team-mates were calling me. It stuck for the rest of my career."

And while the vast majority of his 84 goals for the Hammers came from 12 yards out, Ray was also happy to be reminded of a rare strike in open play against Tottenham Hotspur on New Year's Eve, 1983 – a stunning volley that is regarded by many who were present that day as one of the finest strikes ever to grace Upton Park.

"I remember that well," he says. "The ball was crossed from the left and Steve Whitton, who was close by, told me to leave it. If I'd had the time, I'd have told him to f*** off, because there was no way I was going to leave it! I caught it just right and it flew past Ray Clemence into the top corner. One of the finest strikes I ever hit . . . and the fact that it was against Spurs made it even greater!"

But back to 1980. After Alvin Martin had been struck down by tonsillitis, Ray again displayed his versatility by stepping into the centre of defence for the nail-biting FA Cup semi-final replay clash against Everton at Elland Road, producing another faultless display. He then kept Arsenal danger-man Graham Rix quiet in the memorable victory at Wembley, an occasion that he unsurprisingly looks back on with huge pride.

"It was certainly a great way to finish my first season in England and proved to me that I had made the right decision in leaving Dundee United in search of success," he says.

"My brother's daughter was born on the Friday night before the cup final, and he drove down in the early hours of Saturday morning to join the rest of my family who had made the visit, so it was a fantastic weekend for all of us.

"It was the first time I had won anything in senior football and it meant so much to me. The medal still takes pride of place at home and I would never, ever sell it, no matter how much I was offered.

"To me, the FA Cup is still the most prestigious tournament in the world and it is sad that it has been slightly degraded in recent years. Even now, I still get a buzz from thinking about the FA Cup ties we played in and I like to think that the competition will eventually have its romance restored in the future."

Following glory beneath the old Twin Towers at the turn of the 80s, Ray went on to become an integral part of the club's success in the early part of the decade. He missed just one game all season as Hammers romped to the Division Two title in 1981 and fired home another dramatic spot-kick in the final seconds of the League Cup final against Liverpool to earn a well-deserved replay.

At the same time, he broke through on to the senior international scene with Scotland, legendary manager Jock Stein handing him the first of 10 full caps in a friendly against Wales at Swansea on May 16, 1981 – a game that saw Ray play in every position across the back four at one stage or another.

By then, he had established himself as a firm favourite among the Upton Park faithful, who appreciated his steely determination, bravery in the tackle and, of course, his deadly accuracy at dead-ball situations.

For Ray, it was simply a case of repaying the faith the club had shown by paying a record fee for his services, and a desperate willingness to reach the pinnacle of the game – a dream that so nearly came true when Hammers went within touching distance of the League championship for the first and only time in their history.

"All I ever wanted was for West Ham and myself to be successful and that was what drove me on. Even when I was away with Scotland, I felt that I was representing West Ham as much as myself, and I genuinely felt we could be the best.

"At the start of the 1985-86 season, I could see us winning the league, because that was how I felt at the start of *every* season. I couldn't accept that we were going out there for anything other than to win every game and finish as champions.

"It might sound unrealistic, but that was just the way I was. I didn't see the point of playing if you didn't think you could win every game, and I approached each new season with the same attitude.

"In 1985-86, everything just clicked for us and John found the right balance all over the field. There were a group of us who had played in the '81 side and had the experience – the likes of me, Alvin, Parkesy and Pikey – then there were the young lads such as Tony Cottee, Alan Dickens, Frank McAvennie and Mark Ward, who brought youth and enthusiasm to the side. It was a great year but, after going so close to winning the title, I was disappointed that we fell at the final hurdle.

"You have to be gracious in defeat but I always hated losing. Winning was the only thing I was interested in."

Having reached the age of 27 as Hammers threatened to achieve the impossible and end Liverpool and Everton's domination of English football, Ray was at his peak. An automatic name on Lyall's team-sheet and a regular member of the Scotland squad under then new manager Andy Roxburgh, he should have been preparing for the prime years of his career in the mid-to-late 80s.

However, as West Ham failed to significantly strengthen the playing staff following their record-breaking third place finish, the club ended up on the slippery slope that would spell relegation within three years and the end of John Lyall's reign. For Ray, the late 80s were a battle against injury problems that would eventually have just as traumatic an effect on his own career.

Having missed virtually half of the 1986-87 campaign, he returned the following season to prove his versatility once again by filling in at centre-half – and as captain – in the absence of Alvin Martin. Again, though, injury struck at the worst possible time and forced him to miss the final six games of the season as Hammers escaped the drop by the skin of their teeth.

In 1988-89 – a campaign that would ultimately mark the end of an era at Upton Park – Ray managed just six appearances, the last of which came on January 14, when, in a clash against Derby County at the old Baseball Ground, he sustained an horrific knee injury, rupturing the vital anteria cruciate ligament.

In typically fearless fashion, he actually walked off the field in the hope that he had suffered just a minor twist but, once an arthroscopic exam had revealed the dreaded truth, he was forced to face up to the possibility that, with his 30th birthday just a few months away, his playing days might be over.

Added to that the agony of having to watch on helplessly as his team fought an unsuccessful battle against relegation to lose their top flight status after 11 years among the best, and it's little wonder that Ray looks back on the period as the worst of his career. One thing he wouldn't do, though, was throw in the towel.

"I was told by a number of specialists that I should pack it in after I did the knee," he admits. "Brian Roper, the club doctor, advised me to call it a day and said that I would never be the same player. I had the chance to take a big insurance pay-off and set myself up, but I just couldn't do it.

"Football was my life and there was no way I could finish like that. Watching the team being relegated and then seeing John lose his job was bad enough, and I felt I owed it to myself to fight back and pull on the shirt again.

"Looking back, I made the wrong decision and should have listened to the medical experts but, at the time, I didn't want to accept what they were telling me. I never managed to produce the levels of fitness and performance that I had been used to, and it was difficult to accept that my career was over at the age of 31."

Having played no part during Lou Macari's brief spell in charge following Lyall's departure, Ray was boosted by the appointment of old friend Billy Bonds as he continued his gruelling comeback. Throughout his rehabilitation, he remained a loyal and supportive team member, carrying on with the charity work and commercial duties he performed so admirably on behalf of the club – and that dedication was finally rewarded when Bonzo recalled him for a handful of appearances at the back end of the 1990-91 campaign as Hammers secured their promotion back to the top flight.

The long-serving defender also made a substitute appearance in the ill-fated FA Cup semi-final against Nottingham Forest. But there was to be no fairytale ending and, with his contract set to expire, Ray was devastated when the club decided not to retain his services and, instead, handed him a free transfer after 12 years of unstinting service.

While he may reluctantly have finally accepted that his playing days had drawn to a close, the man who had done so much to boost the club's profile thanks to his public relations skills and local community work was surely too important and rare a commodity to discard so easily? Indeed, it was often suggested that Ray would have made a perfect commercial figurehead for the club and he admits that he would have jumped at the chance had he ever been offered such a role.

"The club handed me a testimonial, which was very kind of them, but right up until the day I left Upton Park I clung on to the hope that they would ask me to stay and do a job for them," he says.

"I felt they could have utilised me somehow. Without wanting to blow my own trumpet, I felt I was an ambassador and did a lot for the good of the club. I know some people will say that I did all that for my own gain, but I can put my hand on my heart and say that they couldn't be further from the truth.

"I saw it as my responsibility to give something back to the club and make myself available whenever needed. The likes of Alvin, Parkesy and Galey were the same, we all had the best interests of the club at heart – that was our legacy of playing for John Lyall. I would have done anything for the club and it was sad that I couldn't stick around to help out somehow once I'd stopped playing.

"The thing that hurt the most, though, was what happened on my last day at the

Above: Living up to his nickname, Tonka clearing the danger during the record-breaking 1985-86 season that ended in heartbreak.

Right: The Jockney hero receives the acclaim of the East End faithful who took him to their hearts.

Ray sends Liverpool's Ray Clemence the wrong way to slot the last-minute penalty in the League Cup final.

club. I'd been given a free transfer and everyone knew it was my final day but I walked out of Chadwell Heath without so much as a 'goodbye' or 'thanks' from anyone."

Ray was offered the chance to team up with John Lyall again at Ipswich, but instead opted to return home to Scotland and take up a post at St Johnstone, where he coached youngsters and worked for the SFA as a Community Development Officer in the Perth region.

In the summer of 1997, he took his first steps in senior management as boss of up-and-coming Livingston, whom he led to the Scottish second division title in 1999, only to be harshly fired less than a year later. A difficult two-year spell in charge of struggling Stirling Albion followed, before he took over at second division Forfar Athletic in January 2003.

Again working on a shoestring budget for a board with high expectations, Ray fought admirably for the good of the club and its supporters, yet found himself out of a job again after a sticky run of results – a decision that still clearly hurts the 47-year-old.

"It was a huge disappointment, because I'd worked so hard for the club and really did all I could with the resources we had. The thing is, the money I was being paid didn't match the amount of pressure I was under, and that's the way it is in the lower divisions of Scottish football.

"I didn't do it for the financial rewards, though – I did it for the pride of being a manager and because I love the game. The trouble is, trying to do things the right way doesn't seem to work any more. I was dealing with players barely out of their

Ray in the manager's chair at Forfar Athlletic in 2003.

nappies who were demanding this and that, and telling me to speak to their agents rather than them.

"Agents have far too much importance in the game now, while chairmen and directors only see results and league tables. There doesn't seem to be any appreciation or respect for the job you are trying to do."

Sadly, that's how modern-day football treats decent, honest guys like Ray Stewart, who have so much to offer the game and would put the best interests of their club before personal gain every single day of the week.

It's a sorry state of affairs when someone who gave far more than he ever took from the game as a player is now scratching around trying to find a way back in so that he can pass on some of the coaching skills and methods picked up, first-hand, from principled managers, Jim McLean and John Lyall.

"I've had a break from the game and I miss it, so I'm hoping to become involved again in some capacity soon," says the likeable Scot, whose second wife Jane gave birth to their first child, Mark, in April 2005. With two children from his first marriage – daughter Kerri (18) and son Sam (15) – Ray simply wants the chance to support his family and prove his value to the game.

He has recently been driving a parts delivery truck for Volvo but he admits that he would one day love to return to the club he called home for 12 years.

"I still follow the fortunes of all of my former clubs but West Ham will always be special to me. I like to get down and visit whenever I can because I have so many friends at the club. The fans will always be close to my heart.

"I tell you, if West Ham phoned me now and asked me to help them out, in whatever shape or form, I'd be on the first plane down to London."

Cultured in possession, Tony Gale always looked to create even when he was defending.

Chapter 20

TONY**GALE**

"He treated every player at the club as if they were his own son. If your wife was ill he would send her a bunch of flowers. If you had to go to hospital for any reason after a game, he would go with you. He knew the names of all the schoolboy players and made sure they grew up as good people. Without doubt he was the best manager I have ever played under"

TUNE in to any football-related TV or radio show these days and, the chances are, you'll be listening to the views and opinions of a former West Ham star.

With media coverage of the game now at near saturation point following the Sky TV boom that has exploded in the last 15 years, there has been a growing need for intelligent, considered and constructive comments from the players of yesteryear.

Ex-claret and blue favourites such as Alvin Martin and Tony Cottee have become regular and respected pundits in recent years and it's fair to say that the popular duo were encouraged to build their own careers behind a microphone after witnessing the success of their former team-mate, Tony Gale.

After hanging up his boots in 1997, the classy central defender became known as the voice of London football in his role alongside Jonathan Pearce at Capital Radio, and is now one of the country's most charismatic media personalities, making regular appearances on Sky as well as contributing columns for *The Sun*, West Ham United's official matchday programme and its website at www.whufc.com.

As a player, Gale always enjoyed a good rapport with the press, so the 47-year-old admits he found it easy to make the transition from playing to punditry when his first career came to an end.

"I had done a few bits on the radio during my last season in the game, when I was at Crystal Palace in 1995-96, but I really started to get involved the following year when I packed up at professional level," he says.

"I was playing and coaching for Alan Devonshire down at Maidenhead United, but I didn't train because of an ankle injury, so I had a bit more spare time on my hands.

"Ian Crocker, who is now a Sky commentator, was at Capital Gold then and I knew him anyway because he had previously been the tannoy announcer at Upton Park. I got a bit of work with the likes of him and Jonathan Pearce and Dave Clark – probably because, when I was playing, I was the only one who would talk to them after matches. Everyone else told them to eff off, but I was always nice to them and that gave me a door into radio!

"Seriously, though, I'd always been comfortable with the media side of things – I actually enjoyed it. I had a column in the local *Newham Recorder* for probably eight of the 10 years I spent at West Ham and I think the first ever co-commentating I did was for Sky, covering Farnborough Town before we played them in the FA Cup in 1992. This gave me the opportunity to get to know how it all worked and it was something that interested me.

"In 1997, Jonathan (Pearce) asked me if I wanted to go full-time with Capital. The carrot dangling at the end of it was the chance to spend six weeks in France for the World Cup finals at the end of the 1997-98 season. So I went home, had a chat with the wife, and had to decide if I wanted to carry on with the coaching and try to progress into management or go head-on into the media business. I went for the media and I've never once regretted it."

In a professional playing career that spanned 19 years, the former Fulham, Blackburn Rovers and Crystal Palace defender made around 700 league and cup appearances. He estimates that, in seven years working as the chief co-commentator at Capital, he covered a similar number of games thanks to the station's policy of providing blanket coverage of London clubs, both domestically and European.

"It was hectic, that's for sure," admits Tony. "We were often covering four or five games a week, travelling all over the country and all round Europe for the Champions League games.

"I've actually commentated on every cup final you can think of. I've done the FA Vase and Trophy, the three play-off finals, the League Cup final, the FA Cup final, the European Cup Winners' Cup, the UEFA Cup, the Champions League final, the Super Cup, the European Championship final and the World Cup final. I never played in any of them, though!"

His full-time role at Capital and subsequent success meant that Tony didn't follow the usual route for retiring players into coaching and, although he admits to missing the everyday life at a professional football club, it has been a great career move for him.

"I'm a football addict," he says. "Also, what I found at Capital Radio was that we had that kind of camaraderie and spirit, much like you find at a football club. There wasn't a squad of 20 players, just six of us, but we had this close-knit set-up and enjoyed some great times travelling all over Europe covering the games.

"I was lucky in that I worked with the best radio commentator around in Jonathan Pearce. I was learning off the master and that really made the job much easier for me. He told me when I should come in, when I shouldn't, how to make sure I didn't repeat myself – all helpful hints that allowed me to be more comfortable and relaxed.

"I had a learning spell leading up to the World Cup in '98 and I was flying by then – apart from playing, I don't think anything else could have given me the kind of buzz I got from covering the World Cup in its entirety. I think Jonathan and I covered more games than any other radio station at the tournament and it was a fantastic learning experience for me.

"At the height of it all, we were clocking up thousands and thousands of miles every week. I remember once flying to Romania to cover Chelsea in the Champions League, then leaving in the middle of the night to fly over to Turkey to cover Arsenal's game the next day.

"We also did two Premiership games in one day – Watford v Man United at 11 in the morning, then jumping on a taxi-bike to cover Chelsea v Liverpool at Stamford Bridge in the afternoon."

Having to drive to all corners of the country at weekends and fly to various parts of the continent during the week not only takes its toll physically, though, it can also have a damaging affect on family life. With wives and children left at home on their own, such a gruelling schedule can seriously strain even the happiest of marriages, and Tony admits he is lucky to have a supportive and understanding family behind him.

Son Anthony (23) and daughter Alexandra (16) have become used to seeing dad heading out at the crack of dawn and returning in the small hours, and he insists that the support of his wife Lyndsey has been a vital element.

"I couldn't have done it without Lyndsey – no way. It might sound a glamourous job, and it is in certain ways, but it's not so glamourous when you're getting home from Blackburn at three in the morning after a four-hour drive, and I think it's fair to say that a few commentators have probably lost their marriages because of the work commitments.

"I'm lucky in that Lyndsey isn't interested in football and she only started watching the game when Anthony started playing. That means I can just switch off when I go home and Lyndsey accepts that my job involves a lot of travelling. Without an understanding wife, you just couldn't do it."

Despite the fact that his role at Capital Radio came to an end in 2004 when the station wound up their football coverage in the wake of Pearce's move to the BBC, Galey's impressive and established reputation led to various new opportunities and offers, and he admits that considering a change of career direction isn't an option at present.

"I'm into this," he says. "I've made a little bit of a niche for myself now – I do radio work, stuff for Sky TV, I've got columns in *The Sun* and the matchday programme at West Ham, and I do some bits on the Fulham website, so I've got a bit of a media pie for myself and I'm really enjoying it.

"I suppose it does come quite naturally to me. People have said I have the gift of the gab and I was always a bit of a piss-taker – still am, actually! I've done a bit of after-dinner speaking as well and I just enjoy being with my friends and talking about football.

"Lyndsey always ribs me about not being able to wire a plug, put up a shelf or paint, but my dad (Pete) always said just go and earn the money and pay other people to do it, so that's what I do. It's a good living for me and I'm doing something I enjoy."

The first seeds of that enjoyment were undoubtedly sown during Tony's playing days at Upton Park, when he admits the club's policy of an open and helpful attitude towards the press paved the way for him and his team-mates to build the contacts that have come in handy in recent years.

His former centre-back partner, Alvin Martin, is an established studio pundit and big match radio summariser for talkSPORT, while Billy Bonds and, more recently, Scott Minto have also been regular match day analysts for BBC Radio London.

"I think being at a club like West Ham certainly helped," says Gale. "The club was always media-friendly and we were encouraged to get to know the press boys and co-operate with them, which I was always happy to do anyway.

"Perhaps other teams weren't as media-friendly and the players had to train themselves a bit more to be comfortable talking on TV or radio? We would also talk between ourselves about the game, though, and I think that is why the likes of myself, Alvin and Tony Cottee have been quite successful with it. Even someone like Bonzo, who never did much with the press as a player, got involved with radio work, and I think it has a lot to do with the philosophy we used to have at the club.

"Sadly, that philosophy isn't as evident in the game nowadays. A lot of it is to do with the fact that most players are a different breed now, but I do think that clubs don't really help as much as they could. They don't put their players in front of the press and they're not told to do it, so if they don't want to do it, then they won't.

"I think the fans would be far more friendly and accepting if they saw players going out of their way to talk to them through the press and showing a bit more of a duty towards the club and the supporters.

"It really comes down to how the players are educated when they first walk through the doors of a club as young lads. I personally think they should be given advice on how to deal with the media and encouraged to talk to the press and, although some clubs do that now, I don't think it's something they really place much importance on.

"The thing is, because of the money that players earn now, not many of them will need to consider a career in the media when they retire. So the way they look at it, they don't need to co-operate with us if they don't really want to."

Tony is only too aware of the immense financial changes that have taken place since the advent of the Premier League in 1992 – changes that have created an age where footballers are often millionaires before they are out of their teens.

While he doesn't begrudge England's young stars the fortunes they are now earning, the man who rounded off his top flight career with a Premiership league winners' medal at Blackburn Rovers in 1995 believes that the too-much-too-soon culture of the modern game has its drawbacks.

"Money is difficult to handle when you are that young and a lot of the time it doesn't make for a better person. I'm not saying that these kids are not good people, but they don't live their lives like normal teenagers and that can have a big effect.

"I think a lot of it is to do with how they are brought up by their families. If they have good families supporting them and keeping their feet on the ground, then they stand a good chance of remaining a level-headed person.

"Another thing is that managers no longer get involved in the development of the young players coming through the youth ranks. Sir Alex Ferguson is probably the last of a dying breed of managers who take that sort of interest and have almost complete control over their club. John Lyall was also that kind of manager. When he was in charge here at West Ham, John knew every aspect of the club, inside out.

"Things are so different now, but the game had to change because of the financial boom. Any business or industry that has such a vast amount of money suddenly pumped into it will change. There are better pitches, better stadiums and facilities –

Galey and George Parris combine to dispossess Millwall's Teddy Sheringham in 1991.

everything has changed in that sense.

"The only sad thing is that people have to change, too. I think there were more honest people in the game when there wasn't so much money involved, and money is to blame for a lot of the problems in football.

"That's not to say I'm jealous of players for earning as much as they do now, because I'm not. The financial boom has given *me* a good living in the last few years and I'm grateful for that," he said.

While Tony agrees that certain peripheral aspects are indeed of a higher standard compared to his own playing era, he doesn't believe that the quality of football has improved at a similar rate.

"It's a golden era in the way it's covered but I don't think the actual football is better," he insists. "It's better in terms of comfort for the spectator, facilities and earnings for the players but I will argue all day and all night that it is not a more skillful game.

"It's still two goals and a ball, and can you imagine the football that we would have played on pitches like they play on now? Players may be fitter and more conditioned now, but I still don't think any of them would have beaten Billy Bonds on a 10-mile cross-country run."

Looking back on his time as one of English football's most cultured, and perhaps underrated, central defenders, Tony admits he was fortunate to spend the majority of his career playing for two fantastic clubs at opposite ends of the District Line, and reveals that he turned down the opportunity to play for his boyhood heroes in favour of a switch to Upton Park.

Tony commentating for Capital Gold radio at Upton Park, alongside Ian Crocker.

"I was lucky, because I started out at a very good club in Fulham, and then I came to West Ham, which was a similarly run club but on a bigger scale.

"I remember turning up here and finding out that guys like Billy Bonds, Alvin Martin, Phil Parkes and John Lyall were just normal people. I'd experienced it before at Fulham with George Best, Rodney Marsh and Bobby Moore, who were just the same, but sometimes I thought it must be unique for our club.

"When I left Fulham, I had a choice between Chelsea and West Ham when it came to signing for a new club. Ian McNeil (then Chelsea manager) came to my house to make me an offer, as did John Lyall and Eddie Baily on the same day. I was a Chelsea fan as a boy and lived five miles from Stamford Bridge, but there was no contest when it came to deciding – I was going to West Ham.

"We listened to what John had to say and, when he'd gone, Lyndsey said to me: 'You've got to go with that man'. Nothing against Ian McNeil, who was a nice guy, it was just the impact that John had on us as a family.

"He treated every player at the club as if they were his own son. If your wife was ill he would send her a bunch of flowers. And if you had to go to hospital for any reason after a game, he would go with you. He knew the names of all the schoolboy players and made sure they grew up as good people.

"Without doubt he was the best manager I have ever played under."

After completing that £200,000 move across London in the summer of 1984, it didn't take long for the 24-year-old Galey to settle into his new surroundings and get to know his team-mates – who soon became familiar with the razor-sharp wit and wicked sense of humour that earned him the dubious nickname 'Reggie' – after a similarly wicked and razor-sharp London gangster!

"I was given the nickname by Dave Swindlehurst when I first arrived at the club," laughs Galey. "It only took me a couple of days to get involved with all the chipping and chirping in the dressing-room and I was soon taking the piss out of people.

"Dave just turned round to me one day and said: 'F***** hell, you're as nasty as Reggie Kray'. I'm just glad he didn't call me Ronnie!

"It was all part of the banter and John never discouraged me from having a laugh and winding people up. I never took liberties with him, just like I never took the pee out of Bonzo when he became manager – for fear of getting a right-hander from him!

"It was light-hearted fun and simply a sarcastic sense of humour that, I like to think, all the boys enjoyed and found funny."

While his memories of the team spirit and atmosphere at Upton Park will always be guaranteed to raise a smile or two, Galey admits to feeling a tinge of sadness at the fact that, despite being an ever-present member of the Boys of 86 and playing in three domestic cup semi-finals, his claret-and-blue career ended up trophy-less and an international cap also eluded him.

"It's disappointing that we didn't win any trophies or honours in my time here. Going so close to winning the league in '86 was tough to take, as was not winning a cup of some kind. I played in three semi-finals for the club and was on the losing side each time.

"Most people talk about my sending-off in the 1991 FA Cup semi-final, but that was just a busy referee who wanted to make a name for himself. The two relegation seasons were much harder to deal with and there were some dark days during those periods.

"However, we also had two promotions as well, and they were great times to be at the club. I look back and consider myself lucky to have played at a fantastic club for 10 years with some wonderful players.

"I've also been asked if I was disappointed not to have played for England and I must be honest and say that, yes, there were times when I looked at certain players getting call-ups and thought: 'How are they getting caps and I'm not?'

"John once told me that Bobby Robson was watching me but nothing ever materialised. I always thought that maybe myself and Alvin should have been given a chance as a pairing, in the same way that Terry Butcher and Russell Osman of Ipswich were at that time."

It's fair to say that not all current players or managers have appreciated Galey's observations on both radio and television but he is now a regular and popular fixture with Sky.

He says: "We are there to give an honest opinion and that is all I try to do. The game has become big business now and it's the Sky TV boom that has done that, so managers and players know that their performances and actions are going to debated at length and put under the microscope.

"Having commentated on over 700 games on the radio and probably around 200 on television, I believe I have a considered opinion and, if they don't like it, unlucky. All I'm doing is giving my opinion – and I do it honestly."

Young and talented, Alan had to live with high expectations from the moment he broke into the first team.

Chapter 21

ALAN**DICKENS**

"When it came to contracts, I just used to accept whatever was offered to me. I didn't have an agent and it was just a case of John Lyall spelling out the offer and me signing on the dotted line. I just thought that was the way it worked – it never crossed my mind to ask for more"

MENTION 'Chelsea' to West Ham supporters and it's unlikely you'll get a very polite response – and not only because they are traditional arch-rivals from the opposite side of the capital.

The Blues have become public enemy number one at Upton Park after capturing three of our brightest young homegrown stars in recent times – a situation made all the worse by the West Londoners' limitless spending power throughout the Roman Abramovich revolution.

Since arriving at Stamford Bridge for a combined total of £22.5million, Frank Lampard, Joe Cole and Glen Johnson have all won Premiership title medals and enjoyed great cup success, although the latter has only just returned after being loaned to Harry Redknapp's Portsmouth in 2006-07.

However, the depressing link between our brightest youth prospects and the riches of the Kings Road first reared its ugly head long before the current trio headed from east to west. In the summer of 1989, just after West Ham had been relegated from the top flight, Chelsea swooped to capture Alan Dickens, a member of our 1981 FA Youth Cup-winning team and key part of John Lyall's record-breaking 1985-86 side.

After six years and more than 200 appearances in the heart of West Ham's midfield, the cultured playmaker was snapped up for a tribunal-set fee of £600,000.

Unlike the millionaire lifestyle now enjoyed by Lampard, Cole and Johnson, for Dickens the move to the bright lights of West London wasn't paved with streets of gold.

Had they been, he probably wouldn't be driving a London taxi now. No shame in that, of course, but Alan Dickens is another of yesteryear's heroes who frustratingly missed out by a whisker on the treasure chest of English football that even the most average of players have cashed in on since the Premiership boom took off.

Still living at Barking, Essex with his wife Annika and sons Luke (12) and Sam (10), Dicko remains one of West Ham United's greatest enigmas – a sublime talent who should have gone on to achieve much more than he did in the game.

Speaking to *EX* magazine in another candid exclusive, the 43-year-old admits he finds it hard to comprehend just how much the game has changed since he was making the tentative move that became a joy ride by the time Lampard, Cole and Johnson had their turn.

"I say good luck to them but it's very hard to make a comparison because the game has changed so much and it is just circumstances really," says Alan.

"When I was a young player, we didn't earn enough money and maybe we were held back a bit too much. Nowadays, it's gone too far the other way and young players are earning too much, too soon.

"Looking back, we didn't earn anything at all really. When I was playing regularly in the first team at West Ham, my next door neighbour was a black cab driver and earning much more than me.

"I do feel we could have been looked after a lot better, money-wise, but that is all with the benefit of hindsight and we never realised then how football would go in the future."

A major part of football's evolution has been the advent of agents and their avaricious role in helping to shift the power balance firmly in the direction of the players.

And how Alan Dickens could have benefited had he employed a shrewd agent to maximise his talent and worth. A softly-spoken, shy and retiring person, the Plaistow-born midfielder was never the type to go knocking on the manager's door and demanding a pay-rise at the first hint of personal success – and he admits that his quiet and withdrawn nature cost him dearly when it came to contract negotiations.

"When I was young and breaking into West Ham's first team, the last thing on my mind was earning money – I was just honoured to be playing for the club and living out my dream as a professional footballer," he says.

"When it came to contracts, I just used to accept whatever was offered to me. I didn't have an agent and it was just a case of John Lyall spelling out the offer and me signing on the dotted line. I just thought that was the way it worked – it never crossed my mind to ask for more.

"I was the type of person who needed an agent, and I would advise all young players to make sure they have proper guidance. At the time, I didn't realise it, but I have learned in later life that money really is the be-all and end-all when you have a family and a mortgage.

"I never, ever felt like that when I was playing, but football is such a short career and you can't blame the players now for taking what is on offer to them."

Alan's professional career may have ended sooner than he would have liked but it certainly started quicker than he could have imagined. After earning rave reviews in the youth and reserve teams, he was handed his senior debut by Lyall in December 1982 for the visit to Notts County.

Young Dickens responded by notching the first goal in a 2-1 victory and went on to finish his debut campaign with six goals from 12 appearances – a quite stunning total for a midfielder of that age in the top flight. The 1982-83 season also ended with him wearing the No.10 shirt in the absence of the injured Trevor Brooking, the man many people tipped Dickens to follow as the shining star in the midfields of both West Ham and, ultimately, England.

Recalling his early days at Upton Park, though, Dicko admits the comparison was

Alan going for goal aganst Oxford United, watched by Frank McAvennie and Tony Cottee.

more a hindrance than a help as his professional career progressed.

"I had a fairytale start to my West Ham career, scoring on my debut at Notts County at the age of 18 and, when I first came into the team, all the media attention and comparisons with Trevor were great, because he was still there and playing.

"It became a lot harder when he retired, though. It seemed as though people were expecting me to take over his mantle immediately and produce the kind of displays they had seen from Trevor, which was impossible.

"It was a bit like how people were with Joe Cole when he first got into the team – everyone had heard so much about him and were expecting him to put on an exhibition every time he touched the ball. Sometimes that level of expectation can be a bit daunting and, as a young player, I found it very hard to deal with.

"Trevor never gave me any advice or guidance, which, looking back, was a bit surprising, but young players weren't protected then in the way they are now.

"I had occasional chats with John Lyall about my situation, he was very good to me and knew how to handle me. He was good at lifting you if things weren't going that well and he would always make you understand that things were never that bad and would turn the corner.

"I think, along the way, I could have done with a bit more guidance but that was in the days before agents came along and I was never the type of lad to go looking for help anyway.

"I didn't have any problems in communicating with the other lads, though. I got on with everyone, although my main mates were Tony (Cottee) and George (Parris). We would go out socially and stick together on away trips, that sort of thing, but the senior players were great and never looked down on us. The likes of Bonzo, Alvin and Dev would all spend time talking to you and making sure you were okay – that was all part of the special atmosphere we had at the club then."

That atmosphere was never stronger than in the 1985-86 campaign when, as if you needed reminding, Hammers reached their best-ever third place finish. Ask any of the players from that campaign and they will all tell you that Alan Dickens was a central figure to the success.

Despite starting the season as a substitute, he was given his chance when Paul Goddard was injured at Birmingham on the opening day and never looked back, missing just one match between then and the end of the season. He understandably looks back on the achievement with great pride.

"It was obviously the highlight for me. At the time, I didn't realise it, but I was only 21 and, looking back, it was quite an amazing year.

"It seemed as if that was the way we had always played, and you felt it was always going to be like that, so I didn't think it was one exceptional season. I just expected things to carry on the same way.

"It was a special team, though, and I really enjoy the reunions we have now. It seems strange to be celebrating finishing third in the league but, in a way, it's not really about the football or our final position in the table – more about the characters in that team and the special spirit we had.

"The functions and charity games we have organised have been fantastic and all the fans seem to love it, so it's a nice thing for the lads to be doing.

"All in all, I had some great times at West Ham. My debut was obviously a special memory and the Ipswich home game at the end of the 1985-86 season was fantastic. The 4-0 victory at Chelsea that year was also memorable and I remember having a bit of a scoring spell at the end of my last season, when we almost avoided relegation by winning four on the trot – with me scoring three.

"To be honest, just playing for West Ham was an honour in itself. I was at the club for almost 15 years and I'll always have a special affinity with the place.

"We never won anything while I was there but we always played good football – I really enjoyed it. Perhaps I shouldn't have left West Ham when I did but that doesn't take away what I achieved there. I will always be grateful for that."

His move to Stamford Bridge in 1989 came completely out of the blue following the departure of Lyall, weeks after relegation. And as he recalls that eventful summer, Alan admits he was never entirely happy with the decision he made.

"To be honest, it wasn't a move that was going to give me a big financial boost – the money never came into it," he says. "In fact, I probably didn't earn that much more than I had been on at West Ham – it was just all about circumstances and I didn't even have time to think about the ins and outs of it.

"We'd just been relegated, John had been sacked and I was in complete limbo. My contract had run out and, although the club had lined up a new deal, there was no manager in place and the Chelsea boss Bobby Campbell – who I knew well through his son, Greg, who played for West Ham – was phoning regularly and asking me to go there.

"It was a very difficult time and I just wish now that I had gone to someone for a bit of advice – even if it had been one of the senior players like Bonzo or Alvin. I didn't get any advice, though, and there was no one at West Ham I could talk to.

"I did go and see Lou Macari shortly before I signed for Chelsea – he had just been appointed and I felt it was the right thing to do. He asked me to stay but he didn't say an awful lot more and, as I didn't know him at all, I made the decision to leave.

Dicko with Frank McAvennie at one of the recent Boys of 86 functions.

"If I'm honest, I didn't really know what I was doing. I was just swept along without realising what was really happening. I was so naive. I should have gone back to West Ham for pre-season training and seen how it went. I signed for Chelsea so quickly, though, and that was it.

"The thing is, all I was really comfortable with was playing football. That was when I was happiest, with a ball at my feet. When it came to contract discussions and that kind of thing, I didn't have a clue. That's why I needed someone to give me a bit of guidance."

So would Alan describe the move across the capital as a regret when looking back over his playing career?

"I wouldn't call it regret, it was something that happened and it was still a good opportunity for me. If anything, I just wish I'd made more of it," he says.

"Maybe I should have moved across nearer to Chelsea. I stayed in Barking, though, and some days it would take me two hours to get to their training ground near Heathrow, which was ridiculous. By the time I got round the M25, I felt as if I'd trained before we had even started!

"Saying that, I did really enjoy it at Chelsea early on and I felt as though my football was going to take off again. I was in the side right at the beginning, then I was kind of in and out towards the end of the season. They made big signings the following season, the likes of Dennis Wise and Andy Townsend arrived, and they had young players such as Graeme Le Saux coming through from the youth team.

"I got back in the side the second year and did quite well, finished strongly and carried on with a good start to the following season. But then I made another error with a contract offer – and it turned out to be a mistake that cost me dearly.

"I had signed a three-year deal when I joined and, at the start of my third year, Ian

Porterfield had taken over and they offered me another year. For some reason, though, I didn't sign it.

"Then I got injured, breaking a bone in my foot, and didn't come back until after Christmas. In the March, they gave me a free transfer. If I'd been under contract, I'd have been okay, but I hadn't signed it and so the offer was no longer on the table. It was a real blow – I didn't really know where to turn.

"I was 27-years-old and being shown the door before the season had even ended, at a time when I should have been going from strength to strength. I believe I was the type of player who would have got better as I got older.

"I never really had any pace, so there was no danger of me losing that, and I just thought that, as I grew to understand the game more and more, it would have suited a player of my type.

"I should have been stronger and made it work for myself, though. I can't blame anyone else but myself and I know that, if I could turn the clock back, I would have handled things differently."

On leaving Stamford Bridge, Alan found that the only football direction he could travel was down – and eventually out.

He recalls: "I went to Brentford in the March and spent the last couple of months of the season there. I felt I did well but then the manager, Phil Holder, got the sack in the summer and it was all change again.

"I wasn't on a contract as such, so they let me go and it was back to the drawing board again. In the end I signed a one-year deal with Colchester United – and even they had offered me two years originally!

"I quite enjoyed it there and thought I'd done well but then the manager let me go at the end of the season. If I had been completely rubbish I would have put my hands up and said so, but I had played some good football and coped comfortably at that level, so it was another kick in the teeth.

"Again, if I'd signed the two-year deal they originally offered me, I would have had that bit more security and maybe established myself at the club. In hindsight, it was another poor decision.

"I tried to set something up at a few other clubs but it wasn't working out and, at the age of 29, I made the decision to make a clean break from football.

"Basically, I couldn't face going somewhere and being told again that I wasn't wanted after a few months. That's when I decided to go into non-league and take up The Knowledge.

"I started off with Chesham United and quite enjoyed it. You always come across a good bunch of lads who are playing for the love of the game and have normal working lives during the week, and I made some good friends there.

"I found it very hard to get used to training in the evenings, though. Having been used to playing football during the day, it was a bit of a culture shock, and I did miss the everyday involvement.

"To be honest, I would say it took me two years to come to terms with what had happened. It was such a void not being involved in the game every day, especially at my age, and it was a difficult time for me.

"Annika had just had Luke and we didn't have much money, so I couldn't sit around moping and, while I was doing The Knowledge, I was playing non-league and doing a bit of driving work for my mate."

It seems almost inconceivable that a man who, just a matter of 18 months earlier had been playing at grounds like Anfield and Old Trafford, could then be driving a black cab around London with no further connection to the professional game. But Alan insists that he was never too proud to make such a stark decision.

"What else could I do?" he asks. "I was fed up with the rejection that I had been facing in football, so I wanted to do something where I didn't have to rely on anyone but myself.

"I did okay at school but nothing that was going to get me a good job. That was all there was and I had to do it for the sake of my young family.

"The Knowledge was the hardest thing I have ever had to do and I admire anyone who does it. The only way to do it really is on a moped and I was out in all weathers, at all times of the day, on that stupid bike!

"Honestly, there were times when I was driving along absolutely heart-broken, freezing cold, thinking: 'What am I doing?' That did cross my mind a lot. I was going out in the morning, doing some driving work in the afternoon and playing football in the evening. It was tough but it was either that or go under.

"It took me about two-and-a-half years to get my badge and I've been driving the cab for about 10 years now. I stopped playing football when Luke was about two or three and I really didn't want anything to do with it.

"I had played for Collier Row, Billericay and then Purfleet but I just didn't have the heart for it. I couldn't motivate myself and I turned my back on the game completely."

Eventually, it was the natural progression of his young son that thankfully ensured Alan didn't stay away from the game he loved forever.

"I really had nothing to do with football for about three or four years and, when you are out of it for that long, it is extremely difficult to get back into it.

"To be honest, I didn't even watch it and it wasn't until Luke started showing an interest at the age of six that I began to involve myself with the game again.

"I suppose it's like any line of work, really. The longer you are away from it, the harder it is to forge a career in it again. You really need to be involved all the time once you've stopped playing, or be around people who have a high standing in the game. It is a case of who you know a lot of the time and building up contacts by showing your face, which isn't really my scene."

While he isn't the type to join in with the scout 'networking' that can be witnessed at most youth and reserve team matches nowadays, Alan has begun to step-up his involvement thanks to young Luke's progress.

"Since Luke started playing, I've got really interested in the development of the youngsters, what kind of coaching they did at different ages, that kind of thing.

"I did my prelim coaching badge, just off my own back through the Essex FA, and that was quite interesting, although I haven't got round to starting the UEFA 'B' licence yet, which is the next step if I want to take it further."

His enthusiasm for football revitalised, Alan has managed his son's team, Ascot FC, and also been along to see his old youth team boss Tony Carr, who runs the West

Ham Academy, offering coaching assistance when needed.

Taking a closer look at how things operate in Upton Park's Academy system has given Alan the chance to compare the modern-day set-up with the methods used when he was a young hopeful at the club. He admits that the comparisons are fairly stark.

"It is unbelievable, really. We didn't start until we were under-11s and we just used to go along to Upton Park on Tuesday and Thursday nights for an hour-and-a-half and train in the car-park in front of the ground. If it was bad weather we would go inside and train underneath the old West Stand, next to the dressing-rooms, using crates as goalposts and that kind of thing.

"It really is a different world now. The facilities for the youngsters at Chadwell Heath are fantastic, they've got the all-weather pitch, the indoor-pitch, a gymnasium – everything they need. The system is there so that no-one slips through the net and the kids get the best coaching but I'm not sure if it really makes such a big difference because at the end of the day it is about players. There will never be another like Trevor Brooking, for example, but he didn't have to go all through the Academy system.

"When I look back to my childhood, the most enjoyable football I ever played was with my school, district and Sunday side. You'd meet up with all your mates and it was about enjoying it as much as anything else. That appears to have been taken away from a lot of kids now. They are banned from playing football outside the Academies and the enjoyment factor isn't there.

"It's all so serious and you end up with kids who have no desire to play football, especially when they get a knock-back or are let go by clubs.

"I wish I had played for longer but that was the way it went and I'm not the type of person who is bitter or regretful. I was lucky enough to play for West Ham for almost seven years – and there are a lot of people who would love to do that."

Chapter 22

LEROY**ROSENIOR**

"He gave me his card, which had the initials I.C.F. printed on it. He told me: 'We remember you and how you looked after us, and if there's ever anything you want doing . . . somebody's legs broken, blah, blah, blah . . . then just say so and we'll do it'. I went: 'Oh right,' and I've kept his card. That fan summed it up for me – West Ham is a club that looks after its own"

A S a player, he fought his way back from serious injury to confound the medical experts who said he would never kick a ball again. And now Leroy Rosenior is once again battling to prove a point, this time as a manager looking to get back into football.

The former Hammers striker, who made 65 appearances and scored 19 goals in a three-year spell at Upton Park, was – until being harshly dismissed by Brentford in November 2006 (they were still relegated) – one of only three black managers in the English game, a quite astonishing statistic given the many talented black players who have hung up their boots in recent years and should be taking the first steps on the coaching and managerial ladder. (Another black ex-Hammer, Paul Ince, has since taken his first steps in management with Macclesfield Town and, from the summer of 2007, as boss of Milton Keynes Dons.)

For Leroy, the motivation to carry the torch and break down the barriers stems from the horrific injury nightmare he endured during his playing days with the Hammers – when a surgeon told him, at the age of 25, that he should consider the possibility of a career outside of football.

As he reported for training as usual with Fulham on the morning of Friday, March 18, 1988, Leroy Rosenior had no idea that, just hours later, he would be on his way across the capital to become a West Ham United player.

The 23-year-old, who had only returned to Craven Cottage a year earlier following a brief spell with Queens Park Rangers, was preparing for a Division Three clash against Bristol City the following day, when he was told to get back in his car and drive over to Chadwell Heath to discuss terms with John Lyall for a possible deadline-day move back to the top flight of English football.

Recalling the events that preceded his arrival at Upton Park, Leroy admits that, after a proposed transfer to Watford had broken down weeks earlier, he jumped at the chance to put pen to paper with the Hammers.

"I had been scoring a lot of goals that season and other teams began to show an interest again. It was around February time that I went to speak to Watford but I turned them down. People claimed afterwards that I had been tapped up by West Ham but that wasn't the case at all.

Leroy racing clear of Aston Villa defender Derek Mountfield.

"Watford insisted that all their players lived within 12 miles of the ground and, with a young family, I wasn't prepared to uproot and move right across to the other side of London.

"So I carried on with Fulham, until this one Friday morning I went into training and was told that West Ham were interested in me. I went straight over to Chadwell Heath and agreed the contract in about three minutes.

"I didn't even talk money. I said: 'Yeah, I'll sign for you' and that was it. On Friday morning I had gone to work a Fulham player and by lunchtime I was a West Ham player.

"The next thing I knew, I was sat in the dressing-room at Upton Park on Saturday afternoon, surrounded by all these well-known players, waiting to make my debut against Watford."

And following his sudden arrival in East London, Leroy's impact on the pitch was just as instant. On a run of just one win in 10 matches, Lyall's team sat in 15th place prior to the clash with Graham Taylor's Hornets and were in desperate need of a victory to stop the rot.

The new No.9 immediately captured the attention of the Hammers fans with his powerful presence and athletic determination and, when he raced on to a long pass to fire a low shot through the legs of goalkeeper Tony Coton in the 61st minute, a new Upton Park hero was born.

Reflecting on his debut delight, Leroy says: "I had a good battle with the centre-half, Steve Terry, and scored the goal early in the second half. After that, though, I just collapsed. I think it was all the nervous energy but I just ran out of steam and thankfully we held on for the win.

"I've still got the tape from the game – my kids used to watch it all the time, and I have some pictures of me celebrating the goal. It's great to see the jubilation on the faces of the fans behind the goal and it really was the perfect start for me."

As cries of 'LEEEEEROY!' reverberated around the Boleyn Ground, things were looking up. The unsettled Tony Cottee at last had a permanent strike partner to team up with following the departure of Frank McAvennie to Celtic earlier in the season, and Lyall's side had a new-found belief about it.

The Hammers boss had spent months searching for a replacement for the crowd-pleasing Scot. Chelsea's Kerry Dixon, Luton's Mick Hartford and Wimbledon's John Fashanu were all names linked with possible big-money moves to Upton Park, and it was somewhat of a surprise when just over a quarter of a million pounds was spent on the relatively unknown youngster from Fulham.

The glorious heights of our record-breaking third place finish less than two years earlier certainly seemed a long time ago but, for Rosenior, the pressure he felt had nothing to do with previous events at the club.

"I wasn't aware of all that had gone on before," he admits. "Obviously I knew the position that West Ham was in but I didn't know the history of it. I think the best thing for me was that I signed on the Friday and then scored the winning goal on the Saturday.

"I didn't have much time to think about the situation – it was just straight in and get on with it.

"I had a massive point to prove, though. During my spell at QPR, they had brought Dean Coney in from Fulham to replace me. I knew Dean very well but I didn't think he was better than me and I felt that I deserved more chances at Loftus Road.

"At the end of the day, though, you've always got something to prove. Anyone who says otherwise is a liar. Football is about constantly proving yourself and I knew that I had to do that when I signed for West Ham. There had been stories going around about them paying £1million for Kerry Dixon, yet they signed me for £275,000. At the time, I thought that was cheap and that John Lyall had got a bargain!

"People were expecting me to be just a makeweight but I wanted to prove that I could play and score goals at the highest level."

With a goal in each of his first three Hammers outings, it was clear that Rosenior had the talent to do just that. After his debut strike against Watford, the Balham-born striker found the net with an 81st minute equaliser at Old Trafford a week later, only for Manchester United to snatch victory with two late goals, and then struck again in a defeat at Sheffield Wednesday – a game that was also notable for the debut of Julian Dicks.

He saved his best for last, though – a two-goal strike against Chelsea in the penultimate game of the season that sent Hammers on their way to a magnificent 4-1 victory over the Blues and preserved the club's top flight status.

But the afternoon turned sour when Leroy was shown the first red card of his career following a scuffle with Steve Clarke – an incident that one West Ham history book describes as the striker having 'throttled' the Chelsea defender.

"Yeah, that's about right – and he deserved it!" laughs Leroy. "Steve is a coach at Chelsea again now and we laugh about it but I wasn't too happy at the time. I think we were 3-1 up when he stamped on me, so I just grabbed him round the neck. Unfortunately, that was in the days before football stadiums had TV cameras all around the ground, and the referee only saw me grabbing Steve's neck.

"It took the shine off the day slightly, but I've never known a reception like it after being sent off. I was feeling guilty, thinking I had let everyone down, but the supporters were fantastic – as they were throughout my time at the club."

The new darling of the North Bank headed off for his holidays that summer high in confidence and feeling rightly pleased with his early contribution in a claret-and-blue shirt. Even his former Fulham boss, Ray Harford, who'd once told him that he couldn't trap a bag of cement, admitted publicly that Rosenior now had the potential to go on and play for England.

However, just when it appeared that he would take his career to the next level, disaster struck, in more ways than one. Tony Cottee's £2.05m record transfer to Everton meant that Leroy started 1988-89 as John Lyall's senior striker alongside new signing David Kelly but, with Hammers enduring a dreadful run of form that would eventually see them relegated to the second division, it proved a forgettable year.

Rosenior still managed to impress thanks to his committed determination and uncanny knack of notching important goals, including a superb diving header in a thrilling 3-3 draw with Nottingham Forest and a memorable strike at Highbury that secured an FA Cup third round replay triumph over Arsenal.

His progress was halted in February when a niggly knee injury resulted in a fairly routine cartilage operation. However, with Hammers by then fighting two separate battles – one to save their top flight status and the other to reach a League Cup final at Wembley – Leroy was persuaded to make a premature return to action, a decision that had far-reaching consequences in the long term.

"Looking back now, the advice I got at the time wasn't good," he admits. "I had a cartilage operation and I came back just six days later to play in the semi-final, second leg of the League Cup at Luton. We'd lost 3-0 at home in the first leg, so I wanted to play, and people said I would be okay to play.

"It was a mistake, and I ended up missing quite a few games. The team was struggling, though, and it became clear that we were in a real relegation fight, so I wanted to play and help the team. The surgeon said that my knee would swell up, but I would be all right to play.

"I didn't train in the week, I just did a bit on the Friday and then played on the

Saturday. Towards the end of the season, we went on a bit of a run and I was scoring goals – I got four in the last four games.

"I was in absolute agony, though. They were draining fluid off my knee, it was swelling up and I was having pain-killing injections, but I kept on going out there. If you look back at it, you'll see I was wearing big strappings and limping a lot of the time, but I was scoring goals, we were winning, and we really thought we could stay up.

"We went up to Liverpool for the final game needing to win to avoid relegation. I headed an equaliser but they scored four in the last half-an-hour, and that was it.

"It was during that game that the knee really went. I heard it go crack and so went to hospital for another operation. Afterwards the surgeon said to me: 'So what are you going to do now?'

"I said: 'What do you mean?' and he said: 'Well, you won't be able to play football any more because you've got a hole in your knee the size of a 50 pence piece'.

"I was so upset, but I was also determined to get back. I couldn't accept a pay-out because I wasn't fully insured, but I also wanted to play again because I was only 25.

"It took the best part of two years to get back to something near full fitness again, but I was never the same."

Having made just a handful of appearances under Lou Macari and Billy Bonds during the two seasons Hammers spent battling to get out of the old second division, it eventually became clear that Leroy would sadly never again scale the heights he had reached during his early days at the club. After notching what turned out to be a farewell goal in a 3-1 win over Aston Villa at Upton Park in August 1991, he was handed a free transfer by Bonzo as the club restructured the squad in preparation for another difficult campaign that again resulted in relegation.

It was the end of Leroy's top flight playing career, at the age of just 27, and although he admits to previous feelings of bitterness, he insists that time has been a great healer.

"I got on great with Bill when we played together, then when he was manager I was a pain in the arse to him – I must apologise for that! It's always difficult when you are trying to come back from injury. I just wanted to play but Bill could see that I wasn't fit enough, and he made the decision to let me go.

"At the time, I was young and thought that he didn't know what he was talking about, but he was absolutely right and I can see that now. I still have the utmost respect for him and I always stop for a chat whenever I bump into him.

"Coming back early from injury like that is something a player wouldn't do nowadays, but it used to happen a lot back then and you didn't really think anything of it. I just felt I owed it to the people at the club and the supporters to give it a go.

"I've got no regrets, though. I was very lucky to play and score goals at the highest level and footballers sometimes forget what a privileged position they are in. I may have an arthritic knee now but, when I look back, I wouldn't change it for the world.

"I had fantastic enjoyment out of playing football, experienced something that many people can only dream of, and you can't expect things to always go your way.

"I was bitter at the time, because I was a young man, but over time I've come to terms with it and realised that I was actually a lucky guy. I played for a great club, scored goals and had a fantastic relationship with the people there – and maybe I've got that because of what I put myself through.

"If I was the type who played for the money and disappeared off to Spain as soon as I could, then I probably wouldn't have it. But I cared, and I like to think that the West Ham fans saw that, and appreciated it."

After leaving Upton Park, Leroy made a clean break and headed across London and west to Bristol City, where he was given the opportunity to extend his playing days. Brief success followed but it wasn't long before he began to make strides towards an eventual career in coaching and management.

"I'd gone out on loan to Charlton and Fulham, before Bristol City came in for me and offered me a deal to go down there. I signed with Andy Cole and, it's funny, despite my dodgy knees and him being just a youngster at the time, I used to do all his running!

"City were in relegation trouble at the time but we managed to score goals and keep them up.

"I knew I wanted to coach and I got the chance in 1993. We played against Brentford in the final game of the season and I scored a hat-trick. Afterwards I came in and said: 'That's it – that's my lot.' I was 29-years-old and I thought that it was time to pack it in and concentrate on building my career in coaching.

"Russell Osman took over as manager and I was appointed reserve team manager. I still played for the reserves as well – at centre-half, funnily enough – and it allowed me to develop the kids and learn the ropes. It was a nice transition and I was mentally ready for it, simply because I had been preparing myself for a career away from playing ever since the surgeon had told me that I might never play again."

And so followed a rapid introduction to coaching that saw him spend three more years with the Robins' reserves before taking up the opportunity to manage non-league side Gloucester City, whom he led to the FA Trophy semi-final.

A return to Ashton Gate then followed, as Leroy took over the role of Assistant Director at their Academy, where his son Liam was a promising youngster at the time, before the departure of first team boss Tony Pulis saw him handed his first taste of Football League management as part of a three-man caretaker team alongside Tony Fawthrop and David Burnside.

The trio were handed a Manager of the Month award in February 2000, before former Barnsley boss Danny Wilson arrived as a permanent appointment and decided to retain the services of Rosenior as first team coach.

Another foray into non-league management followed when he took over at Merthyr Tydfil in December 2001, but just months later he was given the opportunity to turn fortunes around at Torquay United, who at the time were floating perilously close to the bottom of the third division.

It was a job he had applied for previously, along with several other vacant positions at one time or another. However, despite gaining experience at every level possible in the lower divisions of the game, the ambitious Rosenior found it extremely difficult to get a job.

Leroy looking to get back into management.

Sadly, it soon became apparent that the kind of prejudices that faced black footballers in the 60s and 70s – such as only being considered as centre-forwards or centre-halves because managers didn't think they would be intelligent enough for other positions – were now coming back to haunt those who wanted to forge a career in management.

Apart from Paul Ince, the only other two black managers currently working at Football League level are Keith Alexander (as Director of Football at Bury) and Keith Curle (Chester City).

"When I gave up playing, I wanted to be the first black football manager," says Leroy. "There weren't any at the time and that was the ambition I held.

"I was applying for jobs and people were saying that I didn't have enough experience, which made me laugh, because I'd coached at every level possible at Bristol City, managed at non-league and managed in the second division of the Football League.

"It is better than it used to be but the problem is still there. There have been times when people wouldn't let me in their boardroom because they didn't believe I was the manager. I don't know if it's racism – I think it's more just ignorance."

After leading Torquay United to promotion into League One, he said: "People tell me that I am the highest ranking black manager in English football – which is ridiculous. It shocks me, to be honest, because, when I think of all the fantastic black footballers there have been, and the talented black coaches that are around, that is quite an amazing statistic.

"People like Luther Blissett, Cyrille Regis and Viv Anderson have got so much to offer but they are not involved in the game, and I find that astonishing.

"Things change, though, and what I'm trying to do, through working hard, is make people take notice of the fact that black footballers can coach as well, in the hope that others will be given a chance.

"I don't like to say I'm just representing black people – I'm representing young coaches who want to do well in the game. I am as ambitious as the next man but it doesn't matter how ambitious you are, you need someone to give you a chance."

Recalling his playing days and an enduring affinity with the Hammers, he continued: "West Ham's result is still the first I look for, and all I would say is that it is a very special place. You don't realise how special it is until you have played for the club. Once you put that shirt on, that's it. The fans want you to do two things: try to play the game the right way, and give 100 percent commitment. I think I did that.

"And what I went through with injury as a player at West Ham has helped me in management – it has helped me become a better person and a better manager of people."

When Hammers fans recall Leroy Rosenior's four years at Upton Park, they will savour memories of his two crucial goals that saved West Ham and sent rivals Chelsea tumbling towards relegation. They will admire his headed FA Cup winner at Highbury and those of us among the faithful few at the Boleyn one night in November 1988, may even recollect his four goals in a 5-2 home win over West Brom in the now defunct Zenith Data Systems Cup.

He says: "I've never been back to West Ham since I left there as a player. I always vowed that I wouldn't return until I go back as a manager – although I might go there to watch if my son Liam is playing. I only went back to Fulham for the first time since my playing days about a year ago to watch him play."

Leroy says that West Ham and Fulham – Cup final opponents in 1975 when he was 10-years-old – are the two clubs forever etched in his heart.

"I thought I'd reached my pinnacle as a player the day I scored for West Ham against United – the team I supported as a kid – at Old Trafford, even though we lost the game 3-1. But that wasn't it.

"The pinnacle was pulling on the West Ham shirt and experiencing that unique and very special atmosphere at Upton Park.

"I was in Bristol years ago when this rough-looking hard man approached me and asked: 'Are you Leroy Rosenior?'

"I took a step back and said: 'Yeah . . .'

"He gave me his card, which had the initials I.C.F. printed on it. He told me: 'We remember you and how you looked after us, and if there's ever anything you want doing . . . somebody's legs broken, blah, blah, blah . . . then just say so and it will be done'.

"I went: 'Oh right,' and I've kept his card. That fan summed it up for me – West Ham is a club that looks after its own. It's a special club," added Leroy, who hopes to return to League management sooner rather than later.

Chapter 23

STUART**SLATER**

"Looking back – and hindsight is a great thing – Billy did everything he could to keep me. He offered me the best contract the club had ever offered a player. But I didn't get an opportunity. My agent just told me point-blank: 'No, we are not signing that'."

"**W**EST Ham have uncovered a gem in the making," declared BBC commentator John Motson to his colleague and pundit Trevor Brooking. "It is always a dangerous thing for a commentator to say, but I do feel we are seeing an England player in the making," he continued as Hammers fans watched in awe as Stuart Slater shone under the Upton Park lights on that Monday night when he almost single-handedly destroyed Everton to steer Billy Bonds' side through to the semi-final of the FA Cup in 1991.

West Ham's Academy had uncovered yet another fledgling star, just as they have from the time of Moore and Brooking to Cole and Carrick. Slater emerged as a star a year before the Premier League was formed, when money quickly became increasingly important and agents were having a visibly influential role in the game.

Slater shot to fame on the national stage with that dazzling display on March 11, 1991, where his 59th minute goal confirmed a 2-1 West Ham victory. Afterwards, Everton manager Howard Kendall told the press that Slater was worth three million pounds and fans began to realise that it was only a matter of time before the club lost its pacy forward.

Cue agent Clinton Durie.

The talented, shy Slater would never win a full England cap – he played at 'B' level as a sub versus Switzerland in May, 1991 – and that had to be due to the unsettling experiences he would endure in the next couple of seasons. Durie sparked a move for his client under the guidance of his best pal, Liam Brady. Liam and Stuart had played in the same Hammers team and in the summer of 1992 decided he wanted him at Celtic, where the Republic of Ireland legend had become manager. Brady would go all out to capture Hammers' prized asset, wrenching young Stuart away from the club he loved and loathed to leave.

"I can remember the day I moved to Celtic and I was crying all weekend. I signed for Celtic but I didn't really want to go. I was such a family guy and I didn't want to leave them," 36-year-old Slater told *EX*.

"My mum, Margot, went up to Glasgow with me because I knew what Liam was going to be like – he was going to persuade me to sign for them. I took my mum because she wanted me to think about it over the weekend.

"But Liam got his way and signed me. I came back on the plane and cried all

Above: Skilful and quick, Stuart Slater shot to prominence with a dazzling display against Everton in the FA Cup.

Left: Stuart in his first season after graduating from the youth and reserve teams.

weekend because I didn't want to leave West Ham.

"I am not knocking agents," reflects Stuart. "They had a plan to get me up to Celtic. What can you say? Liam Brady was the biggest name in football at the time. For him to want to represent me was a big honour.

"For him to want me to be the number one player and to spend big money on me. For him to put his neck on the line . . . it works both ways and it was a great honour.

"I probably got the same wages as they offered me at West Ham. It wasn't the money that took me to Glasgow. The agent had told me: 'I can get you more,' but it wasn't the case."

The £1.5million move to Celtic was inevitable as soon as the unassuming Slater rejected an offer from West Ham that, at the time, was the biggest salary offered in the club's history. From that moment on, Slater knew he was going to leave the club he had been with for 15 years, since his schooldays.

"Looking back – and hindsight is a great thing – Billy did everything he could to keep me. He offered me the best contract the club had ever offered a player. But I didn't get an opportunity. My agent just told me point-blank: 'No, we are not signing that'.

"That's where I wish I had been a stronger person. I wish I could have asked what else was on offer. I wanted to stay at *my* club.

"Billy obviously thought I didn't want to sign. I came back after missing a bit of pre-season. He had a chat with Harry (Redknapp), his No.2, and they decided it was time to let me go.

"I thought at the time that they didn't want me. I had a good idea they were going to sell me a couple of days before it happened, as they had the chairman down. Billy wasn't talking to me. He had seen me during the day and then he waited for me to get home before he phoned me.

"People say it was a sad way to leave but I have the greatest respect and admiration for Billy. I look at it now and see him as the manager whose star player turned down the best possible contract offer and failed to really pledge his future to the club. They must have been thinking: 'Let's get rid of him'. That is what I would have done as the manager in Bill's position."

Slater's failure to impose himself, ceding control of events to his agent, stems from his upbringing in the sleepy surroundings of Sudbury, Suffolk.

"My background was totally different from what my life has been like in the last 10 years when I have been here, there and everywhere. Whereas, back then, I had just been in a small country town and it was a big adventure for anyone from Sudbury to even go to London. You can imagine the way I was brought up – it was very family-orientated.

"I am not having a go at my background – it was a great, stable upbringing. But I think that if we had moved around from area to area it would have stood me in better stead for my footballing career."

Slater made his first team debut in a 1-1 draw at home to Derby County on October 3, 1987 in front of 17,000 fans. Ironically, it was Brady who put Hammers ahead after 24 minutes. In another ironic twist, it was the same week which saw the club lose Frank McAvennie to Celtic for £800,000.

But Slater recalls little of the occasion. "I think I was on the pitch for less than a minute! I can't really remember it. I was warming up and it was the most nervous thing ever. You could hear every chant, everything anyone said. The atmosphere was electric."

Hammers were in the yo-yo years when Slater was at the club. After the despair of relegation in May 1989, it was much more positive in 1989-90, when Stuart completed 49 games and hit the net nine times.

"If I remember correctly, it was the year Lou Macari took over from John Lyall. We beat Bradford 2-0 and I scored two goals within a minute. Afterwards Lou said some nice things about me, saying that he had seen me do things with a ball that no-one else had ever done. I thought, this is a great start to a season."

Slater's ball-juggling ability had onlookers at the training ground captivated as he performed 'keepy-uppy' for hours on end!

"It was under Billy that I started playing wide left. I had played up front throughout my career as a youth team player and also under John Lyall, although I didn't score enough goals. That is what people were saying about me. I drifted out to the left and I remember saying I had never been taught how to play wide. People commented that I played better in the wide position but I recall playing well only once every five games in that role.

"I relied on people to give me the ball, which was fine because we had players at the club – the likes of Bish, Kevin Keen and Paul Ince – who could do that. But as I went on in my career, especially at Ipswich, we didn't have such high quality players. That is where my career really suffered because I played in a team that was quite defensive.

"At West Ham I could play off Frank McAvennie and Tony Cottee. With all due respect, the other players I have worked with at other clubs haven't been in their class.

"It was pure football at West Ham in those days. Tony Carr, the youth coach, knew what John Lyall wanted to bring into the club. They preached playing pure football – pass, one and two touch, angles and movement. That is why Tony has had so much success with youngsters and why he is still doing well for the club today."

Four years ago, Stuart returned to West Ham to coach the club's under-11 squad on a part-time basis, a role he relinquished early in 2007.

He said: "I was fortunate that John thought I had talent. I noticed when I began to coach, albeit at under-11s level, that when you believe in someone and recognise their talent, it goes a long way. Luckily, he thought I had something different."

But Slater's career never lived up to early expectations and faltered. Hampered by injuries and the eventual realisation that his footballing days were numbered, memories of rejection are still fresh.

"There were a few low points," he admits. "Being told that I was not good enough at Ipswich and Watford. A new manager comes in and they want new players. I ended up on a week-to-week contract at Watford, it was pre-season, I injured my Achilles and was out for 12 weeks. They pulled me into the office, offered me two weeks' wages and told me I could leave for nothing.

"When I meet Hammers fans now they say to me I should never have left. They say I left the club in the lurch when we got relegated. But to me, they were the *only* club, despite how massive Celtic are. I loved my time up there – I met my wife, Kirsty, in Glasgow – but it wasn't as big as it is now. In fact we were struggling at that time."

So what was the main cause of the early halt to Slater's career?

"I would say that my Achilles injury was the thing that did most to cut short my career, although obviously you look at the moves I made and they can't have helped either. Even after I left Celtic, I got injured at Ipswich and Watford. In three years at Watford I only played 30 games.

"Graham Taylor was there at the time and he was a great believer that if you are injured, you are a liability rather than an asset to the club."

Which brings us to the man Slater is critical of for the fact that Motty's England prophesy never came true.

He said: "My grudge is probably with Graham Taylor who was England manager at the time. People said that I should have played for England. I used to look at some of the players who were in the team and thought I might have been given a chance – even just to play one game.

Stuart, pictured in 2005, back at West Ham in a coaching role.

"Taylor got rid of me at Watford, too, so he's not my favourite manager!"

Apart from his time at West Ham, Celtic, Ipswich Town and Watford, 'Chopper' also spent a year-long spell in Australia with the Melbourne-based club, Carlton, before they went into liquidation. He went to Cambridge United and Peterborough United but could only play part-time, before non-league spells with Forest Green and Weston Super Mare.

Above: Leading the charge for promotion in 1991.
Below: Celebration time after the Hammers returned to the top flight in 1993.

Chapter 24

IAN**BISHOP**

"I don't think some supporters realise just what a big influence they can have on the success, or otherwise, of the team. They don't realise the affect they can have on their own players"

WHEN West Ham captain Nigel Reo-Coker finally got his wish to leave Upton Park and join Aston Villa before the start of the 2007-08 season, he left the distinct impression that he felt he had been hard done by from a section of Hammers' fans.

The England Under-21 captain didn't believe he was given the respect and appreciation he deserved. Some badly worded comments in the press, during a difficult period when the Boleyn crowd wanted to see more leadership and less sulking from its highly-paid stars, coupled with some ill-timed mutterings by his agent, led to the fans' disenchantment with the young midfielder.

But he would be totally wrong to think that he was the only West Ham player to have ever had a tough time with the crowd. Much better players than Reo-Coker have endured similar struggles – Ian Bishop for one.

A silky midfielder throughout most of the 90s, 'Bish' didn't possess Reo-Coker's energetic running power but he was much more accomplished in possession and had the vision to get the best from his attacking team-mates.

The long-haired Bishop was promoted twice and relegated once in his time with the club, so he knows what life can be like aboard the Hammers' rollercoaster.

He recalled: "Upton Park can be a very intimidating place, even for home players, when the fans are against them. I fully understand that, at times, the supporters have been very unhappy and frustrated with certain performances and individual players, but it does no good to slaughter them.

"I don't think some supporters realise just what a big influence they can have on the success, or otherwise, of the team. They don't realise the affect they can have on their own players.

"I speak from experience when I say that when the fans are on your back, it *does* affect you. It alters your decision-making on the field and players have to be very mentally strong not to let it get to them.

"The West Ham fans are forgiving to players if they see that you are always trying to do the right things. They were even singing my name after we'd been relegated in '92!"

Bishop, who was signed by Lou Macari from Manchester City at the end of 1989, along with Trevor Morley in the £1million deal that took Mark Ward from Upton Park to Maine Road, recalls vividly how he himself suffered at the hands of the East

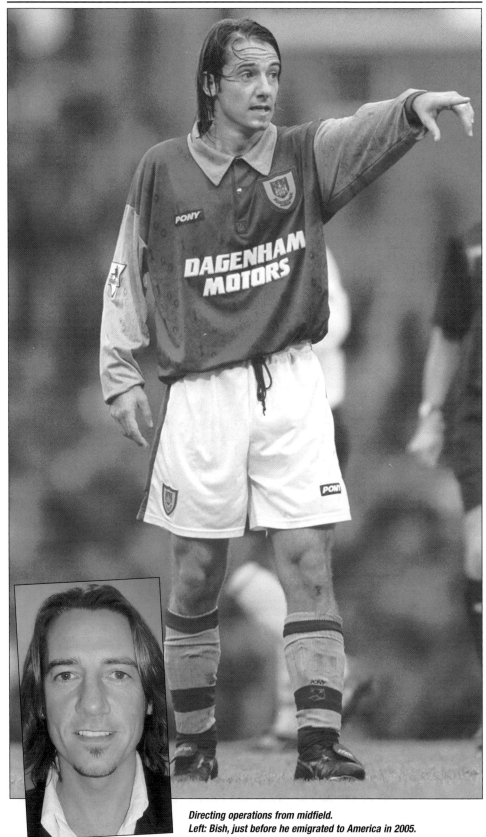

Directing operations from midfield.
Left: Bish, just before he emigrated to America in 2005.

London crowd.

"I must say that the vast majority of fans at both West Ham and Man City were brilliant to me. The two clubs are alike in so many ways and I considered myself very lucky to have played for clubs whose supporters are the most loyal in the country.

"I mean, who else but West Ham fans would still be cheering their team even when they were losing 4-0, as we were in the FA Cup semi-final against Forest at Villa Park in 1991? That was the only regret I have from my time at West Ham – the fact that Keith Hackett denied us the chance to reach the FA Cup final against Tottenham.

"But I did have my moments with the fans. It was a bit nasty when West Ham people booed me every time I touched the ball, after my mistake led to us conceding a goal at home to Chelsea."

It was March 12, 1997 and the first-half mistake made by Bish, which led to Gianluca Vialli's opening goal, did nothing to improve his strained relationship with under-pressure manager Harry Redknapp, who seemed to be fighting a losing battle to keep Hammers in the Premiership.

"I'd run back to the halfway line to retrieve the ball. I knew what I wanted to do with it and – and I'm not blaming him – but I was waiting for Timmy Breacker to give me an angle so that I could roll the ball to him.

"But I put the ball in the wrong place – where I thought Tim should be. Instead, Zola latched onto it, passed the ball to Vialli and they scored – 1-0. It wasn't Timmy's fault – it was down to me, I made the wrong choice – but the crowd really got on my back and booed my every touch until half-time.

"That's when Harry substituted me and I had a massive row with him about it. I called him 'a coward' in front of everyone in the dressing room. He tried to say it was tactical, but it wasn't. I told him that the fans were booing *me*, not *him*, and he was just reacting to the crowd. But I was angry that he wouldn't at least give me the chance to go back out there and prove people wrong in the second half.

"After the game, though, I admitted in front of everyone that Harry had got it right – we'd gone on to win the game, 3-2."

Promotion in May '93 ended a period of hostility at Upton Park, where fans had spent a year and more rebelling against the infamous bond scheme.

"The fans were really directing their anger towards the club's directors, not the players," recalls Bishop, "but, once again, the atmosphere inside the stadium didn't do the team any good. It had an effect, especially against smaller clubs like Wimbledon, who made the most of our situation."

If you believe that the 1991-92 winter of fan discontent was no more than a distracting backdrop to some very dire performances on the field, and the main cause of relegation lay elsewhere, Ian underlined the importance of the Boleyn faithful in lifting the players in claret-and-blue shirts.

"Upton Park was always a very intimidating place for visiting players to come to. They used to speak about the great atmosphere there, especially under the floodlights, and it was no coincidence that West Ham recorded many great victories, often against supposedly stronger teams, in midweek matches played under lights.

"Even when you look back to that relegation season, we still beat Liverpool and Man United under the lights. In '92, when we were heading for relegation, we stopped United winning the title.

"We could beat anyone on our day in those situations, when the fans were right behind us and they didn't have any other agenda."

I must confess to bias here. I have always liked Ian Bishop, a very amiable personality with a razor-sharp Scouse wit who always made time for people and the press. I rated him as a class footballer, a player very much in the traditional West Ham mould, who possessed the subtlety of touch and good passing technique we had come to expect of most of our players.

Okay, so he should probably have contributed more goals than he did from central midfield, but no-one sprayed better diagonal passes to all corners of the park than the long-haired Liverpudlian. He was easy on the eye and you can't say that about two many English midfielders in the Premiership today.

He also showed a great depth of character and good, honest East End bottle in taking responsibility on the field when things were going against the team.

He took over the captaincy for a spell when Julian Dicks suffered his serious knee injury and no matter how good, or indifferently, Bish was playing himself, or how poorly the team performed, he never shirked responsibility.

He says: "Alvin (Martin) was always saying to me that I used to run back too far and too often to help out the defence, by showing myself for the ball and wanting it when I was marked by one or even two players."

Bishop rejoined Manchester City after leaving West Ham on a free transfer in March 1998, having played his final game for the Hammers in a 2-1 win against Chelsea on March 14 of that year.

Summarising his eight-and-a-bit years with West Ham United, Ian says it was a mixture of "highs and lows" but that he was "glad to have been part of it all."

Like so many other former Hammers of Ian Bishop's generation, I guess that their value and the qualities they brought to the club are only fully appreciated with the passage of time. Make no mistake, Bish was an excellent footballer who always tried to be creative when in possession.

After a brief spell as player-coach with non-league Burscough – in tandem with his former West Ham team-mate Mike Marsh – Bish ran a pub at Southport on his native Merseyside. He was always a very approachable and sociable guy, who enjoyed a pint or three away from football.

But at the start of 2005, Ian and his fellow Scouser wife Jane, together with their two children, emigrated to New Orleans in the USA for a fresh start.

Chapter 25

STEVE**JONES**

"I slid on my knees in front of the West Ham fans, who were going absolutely bonkers. We tore Tottenham to shreds and, when we scored the fourth, the home fans cleared the ground and it was just the Hammers boys, singing and dancing round White Hart Lane. That night, I went out with my mates to a pub in Basildon called The Crown. It was absolutely mobbed with West Ham, and I didn't have to buy a drink all night!"

I N these days of multi-million pound contracts, instant demands for success and worldwide scouting networks, it's hard to imagine a top English club ever again delving into the amateur game in search of an undiscovered diamond waiting for his big break.

Gone are the days when an Alan Devonshire, Stuart Pearce or Les Ferdinand could be plucked from non-league obscurity and comfortably make the step up to top-flight football before going on to win full international honours.

Youth academies and expanded scouting systems mean that talented youngsters very rarely slip through the net, while those who do are seldom given a second chance once they drop below the kind of physical levels now reached by players in the top two divisions of English football.

It's therefore likely that West Ham fans will never see another Steve Jones – a lifelong Hammers fan who realised the dream of thousands of us by giving up his day job to pull on the claret-and-blue shirt and go from cheering on the North Bank to celebrating in front of it.

Originally signed by Billy Bonds for the paltry sum of £22,500 from Essex-based non-league outfit Billericay Town – then playing in Division One of the Ryman League (three divisions below the Football League) – the former soap-factory worker may not have reached the heights scaled by the likes of Devonshire, Pearce and Ferdinand, but he certainly made an impact during his two brief spells at Upton Park.

Despite hitting the net just five times in 33 appearances for the club, 'Jonah' forged a reputation as a cult hero among the Hammers fans who considered him to be one of them – a normal, down-to-earth bloke just living the dream and making up for what he might have lacked in ability with plenty of heart and sheer enthusiasm whenever he wore the shirt.

He'd drink in the same local pubs they frequented on a Saturday night, head to the Boleyn Ground for matches on the District Line with his kit-bag over his shoulder, and could often be seen standing shoulder-to-shoulder with the fans on the terraces at reserve matches, or even at first team away games when he wasn't in the squad.

It's no wonder he became one of the most popular figures of the early 90s and is still remembered fondly by supporters from that era. The good news is that he hasn't changed one bit. Now 37, Steve runs his own memorabilia and autograph business, still retains that down-to-earth nature and likeable personality, and was only too keen invite *EX* to his shop in Shaftesbury Avenue – the heart of London's West End theatreland – for a chat about his claret-and-blue memories . . .

The obvious question, when tracing Steve's path from semi-professional oblivion to sudden fame with Hammers is: 'Just how did he avoid the clutches of a professional club while growing up as a prolific youngster in Essex?'

He said: "I played on Sunday mornings for my dad's team, Belhus Colts, and scored hundreds of goals, so I knew that I had ability, but I never really thought about the opportunities that might be available.

"I moved schools quite a lot as a young lad and never really got to play for the school football teams, so I didn't reach district and county level, which is how most pro clubs picked up youngsters then.

"After leaving school I kind of drifted around, turning out for local teams and then ended up playing for Basildon United Reserves. They pulled the plug on all the money there, so they basically used all the reserve players in the first team and I scored a few goals. Billericay Town came in for me and it just went from there."

It wasn't until he reached Billericay that Steve could at last display his talents to a wider audience and the kind of influential people who might be able to open doors for him – including a former Upton Park FA Cup-winner and England international working for Billericay at the time.

"I had scored more than 100 goals in around 70 appearances for Billericay and so people were starting to take notice. I was getting back-page headlines every week in the *Basildon Evening Echo* – their reporter, Dick Marshall, did really well for me.

"I actually had a trial with Sheffield United the week before I joined West Ham but Dave Bassett left a bad taste in the mouth. I went up there expecting to play two reserve games but when I turned up he told me I would just be training. Because I didn't have a professional background, I wasn't the greatest trainer in the world anyway, so I said: 'No thanks' and got on the train straight back to London!

"Thankfully, though, West Ham came in for me straight away. Peter Brabrook was involved with Billericay at the time, and I think he had a word with Billy Bonds and Harry Redknapp. Frank Lampard senior came and watched me a few times and I scored a few goals, but then he saw me play against Wembley, when we lost 2-0, and I had a stinker!

"As I was walking off, though, he said to me: 'Don't worry about today's game', which was a nice touch. A week later I signed.

"I'd been made redundant from my job just two weeks earlier, so things were kind of pushed through a bit sooner – and I think West Ham got me for cheaper dough, too!"

Swapping the Yardley soap factory for the dream life of a full-time professional footballer was manna from Heaven for the tabloid press, who made the most of the corny connections between Steve's old and new employers.

"People made a big thing out of it, and it got on my mum's nerves more than mine

Steve Jones used to be in soaps before he found fame with the Eastenders.

– she hated it!" he laughs. "I just went along with it, though. I did a couple of things in the papers – *The Sun* pictured me blowing bubbles and that type of thing – and it was just a bit of a laugh.

"You'd never get me to do something like that now, but at the time I was new to the fame thing and it was a bit of a novelty. I was only 22-years-old and wanted to make the most of it."

Steve also reveals that his rags-to-riches tale wasn't as lucrative a step-up as some may think. Despite the fact that the newly-formed FA Premier League had just kicked off, he signed his first professional contract at a time when most top football clubs still kept a tight and sensible rein on their finances. And with West Ham having just been relegated from the top flight, the cash certainly wasn't being splashed on wages.

"I wasn't earning big money – no way. I think the most I took home was about £400 a week. I'd been earning about £250 a week at the soap factory, so it wasn't a massive jump but, to be honest, the money wasn't an issue for me. I would have signed for £100 a week – West Ham were my team and it was just a dream come true to join the club.

"I signed on the Tuesday and I was on the bench for the first team the following Saturday, at home to Oxford United. After the game, Julian Dicks took me on a night out, which was a really nice touch. I consider him to be one of the greatest players ever to play for the club, so when someone like that comes up to you on your first day and offers to take you out for a few beers at the weekend, it's a great feeling."

Steve's competitive Hammers debut eventually came in an Anglo-Italian Cup tie away to Cosenza in early December 1992. On a virtually water-logged pitch in southern Italy, the young striker created the winner for veteran partner Clive Allen in his first taste of European football.

"That was a strange experience. It was absolutely flooded and we had to wade through about a foot of water in the tunnel to get on to the pitch! I set up Clive for the winner and, to be fair, it was an amazing goal – he volleyed it into the top corner from about 25 yards.

"I had a one-on-one with the keeper in the second half but he blocked the shot with his legs. It was a good experience, though. Okay, it wasn't a big game, but it was still a European tie and, having played for Billericay just a couple of weeks earlier, it was amazing to be flying off to Italy with West Ham."

He was soon back down to earth, however, as the task of building up his general fitness levels and getting used to the massive jump in class took its toll.

"It took me a long time to get used to it and I would say my first six months at West Ham were probably the toughest of my career. It taught me a few lessons – the main one being that I wasn't as good as I thought I was.

"I remember Alvin Martin marking me in my first training session and I hardly got a touch of the ball. He was an England international, who should have won more caps than he did, and it was just fantastic to be alongside players like him, Clive Allen and Dicksy.

"I gradually began to settle in and build up my fitness, and in the second half of the season Bill gave me my chance."

His league debut came as a substitute in a 2-1 win at Leicester City on January 30, 1993, but it was his contribution seven days later that Hammers fans will remember more. His first start brought his first goal for the club – a close-range effort in a 1-1 home draw with Barnsley.

"It was bit of a lucky goal, off the end of my foot, but it was a great feeling to see it hit the back of the net," he smiles. "I remember running over towards the Chicken Run and jumping on Kevin Keen – I almost flattened him. I also remember looking up and spotting a couple of mates in the crowd, which was pretty bizarre.

"I scored again in the next game, against Peterborough, but then Bill took me off after 55 minutes the following week at Watford and I didn't get in again for the rest of the season. David Speedie came in on loan, which was a bit disappointing for me at the time, but he was an experienced player who did well in the final run-in, and I suppose it was the right decision because we won promotion in the end."

Despite the personal disappointment at seeing his own involvement curtailed so suddenly, Steve admits he was still delighted to be part of the squad that secured our place in the Premier League that year, and also insists that his relationship with Bonzo never suffered in any way.

The Hammers legend had plenty of time for a player who would run all day for him, give 100 percent commitment and get on so well with the fans – despite the fact that he often answered questions about the young striker by using one particular word to describe his talents.

"Yeah, his favourite description of me was 'raw'," chuckles Steve. "I think it was because I was young and a bit rough round the edges. I hadn't grown up at a professional club, so I didn't have the habits or mentality of a pro at first – I was just a normal bloke enjoying myself."

After playing a similar bit-part role early on in the 1993-94 campaign, Steve enjoyed more Premier League action after Christmas, when injuries began to take their toll on Hammers' lightweight squad, and he more than played his part as Bonzo's men fought to retain their top-flight status at the first attempt.

Once again, the statistics suggest a minimal contribution – two goals in eight league appearances (five as sub) – but anyone who was present at White Hart Lane on Easter Monday, April 4, 1994, will vouch for the fact that Steve Jones' contribution was anything but minimal.

"I wasn't really involved early on in the season but after Christmas we picked up a few injuries and I got the odd chance here and there. I played a few times in the FA Cup, scoring against Notts County in the fourth round, and then I scored in the Premier League against Norwich City – a goal that was actually the first scored by a West Ham player in front of the new Bobby Moore stand.

"I was out of the team again after that, though, and Bill was playing a five-man midfield with Trevor Morley up front on his own. Then came the Tottenham game on Easter Monday. I was on the bench and Peter Butler got injured after 20 minutes, and they told me to play on the right of midfield and just get up and down.

"I'd only been on the pitch for about 10 minutes when I did just that. We broke from a corner, I bombed forward and Bish laid the ball into my path on the edge of the box, from where I lashed it past Ian Walker.

"I slid on my knees in front of the West Ham fans, who were going absolutely bonkers, and it just got better and better. We played so well that day, tore Tottenham to shreds and, when we scored the fourth, the home fans cleared the ground and it was just the Hammers boys, singing and dancing round White Hart Lane.

"That night, I went out with my mates to a pub in Basildon called The Crown. It was absolutely mobbed with West Ham, and I didn't have to buy a drink all night!

"I started the following game, against Everton, and had two or three great chances but Neville Southall had an absolute blinder for them and stopped everything. Tony Cottee scored the winner in the second-half and afterwards Bill said a few things about me not being quite ready to play regularly at that level. I didn't get a look-in after that, which was a bit disappointing."

While Steve didn't know it at the time, his memorable strike at The Lane was to be his final goal in a West Ham shirt. After Harry Redknapp had taken over from Bonds in a cloud of controversy in August 1994, Steve made two appearances at the beginning of the new campaign but was soon on his way to Redknapp's former club, Bournemouth, in a £150,000 deal – a transfer that represented a £130,000 profit on the club's original outlay.

He became an instant hit at Dean Court, scoring the goals that kept the Cherries in the second division that season and topping the country's scoring charts for much of the following campaign.

In the summer of 1996, though, came a bolt from the blue, when Redknapp swooped with a £200,000 bid to re-sign the player he had let go less than two years earlier – a move that, although Steve jumped at, still baffles him slightly to this day.

"It was a bit strange, because earlier in the year Leicester City had come in and offered £750,000 for me, but Bournemouth turned it down and said they wanted a million for me. I was like: 'What!'

"Then, just a few months later, they accepted £200,000 from West Ham for me. I still haven't worked that one out!

"But Harry told me that he thought I was a better player and would be able to handle the step up this time. He said: 'I know I'll always get my dough back on you, so why not take a chance?'.

"I came in at the same time as the likes of Raducioiu, Futre and Dumitrescu but I had a decent pre-season, and it was Iain Dowie and me who started up front at Arsenal on the opening day."

The 2-0 defeat at Highbury that day is more famous for one of Harry's future 'after-dinner speech' recollections, when Futre refused to play after being allocated the No.16 shirt and not his coveted No.10 – a dilemma that was eventually solved by John Moncur agreeing to hand the shirt over in return for a free weekend at Futre's villa on the Algarve!

Steve's memories of the Portuguese playmaker are just as unforgettable.

"Funnily enough, I became quite good friends with Paulo during his time there. He was on his last knockings, his knees were shot to pieces but he still had amazing skill and I saw him do things with a football that I'd never seen anyone else try.

"My favourite memory of him, though, was on our first day of pre-season, when we went for the usual cross-country run around Hainault Forest. We were all there loosening up, when all of a sudden this stretch limo pulls up in the car park.

"The window wound down and Paulo was there in his training kit. He took a couple of puffs of a fag, put it out, then got out of the car, did one lap of the forest with us before lighting another fag . . . then got back in the limo and went home! An absolute legend!"

While Futre and his fellow foreign imports brought their own unique style of entertainment, though, the one thing they weren't going to provide was a fighting spirit and strength of character once the going got tough and Hammers had a another relegation fight on their hands. That task was left to Redknapp's British battlers, including the likes of Steve, who found himself in the team once Futre, Raducioiu and Dumitrescu had departed.

"I played only 10 or 11 times but it seemed like I had a different strike partner every game. Mike Newell came in on loan, Iain Dowie was still there, then there were the foreign lads like Radi and Hugo Porfirio – there was a massive turnover of players that year.

"The thing is, I was still young and learning the game, and things might have gone better for me had it been a more settled situation. I think Harry said in his book that we were never gonna stay up with me and Mike Newell up front, but I thought that was a bit harsh.

"He then brought in John Hartson and Paul Kitson, who did well and scored the goals to keep West Ham up, but I think I could have done all right and scored goals alongside someone like Hartson. It wasn't to be, though, and I left for Charlton at the same time as they were arriving."

Again, the club made a healthy profit on Jones – selling him for £400,000 to Alan Curbishley's Addicks – and he headed through the Blackwall Tunnel hoping to at last establish himself as a first team regular in the capital.

Reflecting on his time at the The Valley, he admits: "It was a bit up and down – I started really well but then got dropped after about 15 games. I went out on loan to Bournemouth and scored six in seven, then came back and hit a double against Man City at Maine Road, and scored five or six winning goals in the lead-up to reaching the play-off final against Sunderland.

"I came on just after half-time at Wembley and, had Sunderland's Michael Gray scored his penalty, I would have taken Charlton's next one. I can well understand how he missed it, though, because my legs were like jelly. I don't know how I would have managed to kick the ball. I was absolutely gone.

"Thankfully, Gray was obviously feeling the same way as me and Sasa Ilic saved it. It was the only time I ever played at Wembley – a fantastic experience."

In the summer of 1998, with Charlton just promoted to the Premier League, Steve signed a new three-year contract and went on to make 26 appearances as the Addicks battled in vain to stay up. A few niggling injuries halted his progress and, when Bristol City came in with a £425,000 offer in September 1999, Curbishley suggested he accept the opportunity of a fresh start. However, things didn't go quite to plan.

"I went to Bristol having missed the whole of pre-season through injury, which did me no favours. I wasn't fit, was carrying a bit of weight, and the fans there just weren't impressed with me at all.

"I went out on loan to Brentford, Southend and Wycombe, before going off to America to get myself properly fit. When I came back, Danny Wilson was really good and gave me another chance, and I was doing okay, scoring goals and playing well with Tony Thorpe, until one day we played Brighton and I tore my hamstring – literally ripping it from the bone.

"That more or less ended my professional career. It put me out for five months, I had a year left on my contract and Hornchurch came in for me, so I thought I'd may as well go home.

"I played for a season with them, was top scorer and we got promoted, but the following year my back went and that was it – I haven't played since. I've got four pro-lapsed discs in my back and the specialist told me it just wasn't an option to carry on playing."

Having hung up his boots prematurely at the age of 33, Steve immediately threw himself into an occupation that, until then, had been a spare-time hobby – the collecting of celebrity autographs and memorabilia.

With no footballing fortune to retire on and three young daughters – Stevie (14), Antonia (eight) and Lavinia (six) – to support, he started full-time in the business and opened his own shop, named Lavants, in Shaftesbury Avenue.

"It's something I've always been interested in," he says. "I've got a friend who owns a couple of shops in the Basildon area, and I've known him for about 12 years now. It's hard work but it's enjoyable.

"I enjoyed collecting autographs as a kid – I got a couple from Bobby Moore and have programmes signed from when I went to matches – but it was a lot easier in those days than it is now. It really is big business and footballers and celebrities know that their autographs can command huge amounts.

"I collected a few bits when I was playing – shirts and that sort of thing. I tried to get Beckham's when I played for Charlton against Man United but he wasn't having any of it. I pleaded that I was from the same area as him but it didn't work!

"Strangely enough, though, I'm more interested in music than I am in football. I suppose I started collecting seriously about 12 years ago. One of the first things I bought was Noel Gallagher's hand-written lyrics from 1988. That gave me a buzz and now I'm obsessed with it, as anyone who knows me will tell you!

"I get most of the stuff myself. It's good being based here, because if I hear that someone is in the area, I just shut the shop and go all out to get them. I got Paul McCartney the other day when he was in town for some function, and that was a real coup.

"I've got nice stuff that I've bought from respected collectors – including items signed by Muhammad Ali, Ayrton Senna, Frank Sinatra and Audrey Hepburn – and I also had a Beatles picture signed by all four that I recently sold.

"There are a few bits that I consider to be my own personal collection and would never sell – my Noel Gallagher lyrics, a self-portrait by Ricky Gervais that he did for me when he popped into the shop one day, and a self-portrait by Cold Play lead singer Chris Martin that I got him to do at a hotel when he was on tour.

"I enjoy it but it can be very hard work. I once waited 20 hours for Jon Bon Jovi – and he told me to piss off!"

Despite the knockbacks, Steve certainly isn't living on a prayer, and his fabulous shop is testament to the hard work and dedication he has put into the business.

No doubt there are West Ham supporters who still value a Steve Jones autograph.

"I've got no regrets," he says. "I would have liked to have played as many games

for West Ham as I did for Charlton, and perhaps scored a few more goals, but no-one can take away the memories I have.

"Scoring that goal at White Hart Lane, the relationship I had with the fans – they were fantastic times and I will never forget them."

Steve at his memorabilia shop in London's West End with a signed item from the 1980 Cup final.

Chapter 26

JOHN**HARTSON**

"West Ham will always be special to me because they were the first club where I really started to play well. For that first 18 months or so it was the happiest I'd ever been"

WHEN it comes to the most influential new signings at Upton Park in modern times, it's difficult to look any further than the double capture of John Hartson and Paul Kitson in February 1997.

Others may have enjoyed more lengthy and distinguished careers at the club, but – with the exception of Carlos Tevez at the end of 2006-07 – none have provided the kind of crucial and immediate impact enjoyed by the £5.5million pair when they arrived in the midst of a claret-and-blue crisis a little over a decade years ago.

With just three months of the season remaining, Hammers were virtually at rock bottom. A campaign that had started so promisingly following the arrival of European stars Ilie Dumitrescu, Paulo Futre and Florin Raducioiu had simply disintegrated by Christmas as the expensive foreign flops headed through the exit door, leaving Harry Redknapp famously 'down to the bare bones', as he never tired of reminding the tabloid hacks each week.

Steve Jones, Iain Dowie and on-loan Mike Newell had all tried, and failed, to add firepower to the attack and when Hammers went through January with just one goal and a solitary point to leave them struggling in the relegation zone with 15 matches remaining, the writing appeared to be on the wall. In very large letters.

The final straw had been broken in late January, when second division Wrexham visited Upton Park in an FA Cup third round replay and stunned the hosts with a late winner to send them crashing out of the competition. A post-match pitch invasion followed as angry fans vented their fury at the board in the wake of unfounded rumours that a £25million cash injection from wealthy businessman Michael Tabor had been rejected.

With their Premiership status in the balance and chances of cup glory prematurely brought to another embarrassing end, Redknapp knew he had to act to save the season and, possibly, the club's future.

Under-fire chairman Terence Brown agreed and released the funds for a huge splash (by West Ham's standards) into the transfer market, as Kitson joined in a £2.3million deal from Newcastle United, followed just days later by a club record £3.2million swoop for Hartson, whose move from Highbury would possibly rise to £4.5million depending on his performances at Upton Park.

For many, the signings still represented a major gamble for two players not considered first choice at their previous clubs, but it didn't take long for the pair to

John Hartson signals his goal for the Hammers at Derby in November 1998.

prove the doubters wrong in spectacular style.

The great escape began with a thrilling 4-3 victory over arch-rivals Tottenham Hotspur on a wet and windy Monday night in late February, with both Hartson and Kitson finding the net in what is still considered to be one of the most memorable matches at the Boleyn of the past decade.

That produced a huge surge of confidence and set the tone for an amazing rescue act. Hammers lost just twice in their next 11 games, ensuring safety with an emphatic 5-1 win over Sheffield Wednesday in which Kitson grabbed a hat-trick and Hartson a brace to underline the huge and vital contribution both had provided.

Although Kitson finished top scorer with eight goals – three ahead of his strike partner – it was the burly, young Welshman who stood out as the catalyst in Hammers' turnaround of fortunes. His commitment, raw aggression and desperate will to win clearly rubbed off on team-mates and galvanised the side to such an effect that it provided a platform for the club to go on and enjoy one of the most successful periods in its recent history.

Looking back on the sudden rise to prominence that earned him a reputation as one of the most feared strikers in the Premiership, the Swansea-born hit-man – now with West Bromwich Albion after a spell with Celtic – admits that he never thought twice about swapping relative luxury at Arsenal for a relegation scrap in East London.

"West Ham were struggling, second from bottom with 15 games to go, but it was never in doubt I was going to sign," he recalls. "As soon as I met Harry Redknapp he came across as a nice fella, someone who was honest with his players. I signed and the rest is history.

"It was a desperate time for the club but the good thing was Paul and I never knew much about it. We were both new to West Ham and didn't know much about the history or crowd there. We were fresh to it.

"Kits had had a similar time at Newcastle to what I'd had at Arsenal, so we were both itching for games, desperate to play. I got on great with Paul and we hit it off straight away.

"He was a much underrated player, very quick, held the ball up well, was brave, never hid and an excellent finisher. But his career has been blighted by injuries. It's just a shame that our partnership never went on for three or four years, because you never know what we might have achieved."

Indeed, Kitson's Hammers career never again reached the heights he scaled during his introduction, as an ankle injury sustained just four games into the 1997-98 campaign became the first of a catalogue of problems that blighted his time at the club.

For Hartson, however, his first full season at Upton Park was a completely different story. High on confidence thanks to a goal in each of the first two games – wins over Barnsley and Spurs – the flame-haired striker went on to hit 18 league and cup goals before Christmas as Hammers became the Premiership's surprise-package with a magnificent home record that saw them lose at the Boleyn Ground just twice all year, reach the quarter-finals of both domestic cup competitions and come within a whisker of qualifying for the UEFA Cup.

Hartson eventually finished with 24 strikes in all competitions to place him near the top of the country's scoring charts and he admits that, as a 22-year-old high on confidence, he had the time of his life during that memorable 1997-98 campaign.

"I have some tremendous memories of that season," he says. "We didn't mind Man United coming there. Whoever it was, we knew if we got possession we'd get chances.

"I was young and really up for it. I was happy and very much enjoying being the number one striker at the club, knowing I was going to play every week.

"I was turning up for games thinking: 'How many am I going to score today?' I was confident and had a good relationship with everyone at the club, including the manager. I thrived on the responsibility Harry gave me.

"As a centre-forward I had a great supply, with Eyal Berkovic pulling the strings in the middle of the park, Trevor Sinclair and Stan Lazaridis either side of me and Kits, Iain Dowie or Samassi Abou playing off me."

Sadly, it proved to be the peak of Hartson's Hammers career and the following campaign saw him hit the headlines for all the wrong reasons. There had been a sign

Big John was always up for a scrap.

of things to come when he finished the 1997-98 season on a low note with red cards at Bolton and at home to Derby County that ruled him out of the final four matches.

Returning for pre-season training overweight and unfit later in the summer, his condition forced Redknapp to send him to France for extra fitness work. But matters got worse in October when the Welshman was infamously caught on camera booting team-mate Eyal Berkovic in the head during a training ground bust-up.

Both parties publicly patched things up and attempted to put the incident behind them but, in truth, Hartson's Hammers career had suffered lasting damage and, when Redknapp decided he needed another overhaul of personnel following an FA Cup defeat to Swansea City and poor run of form in January 1999, Hartson was the sacrifice. He moved to Wimbledon in a £7.5million deal as Paolo Di Canio and Marc-Vivien Foe headed to Upton Park.

"I'd had 20 incredible months out of 24 but then I had a strange few months when I came back for pre-season a bit heavy and struggled to get the weight off," he admits. "I didn't have a great start to the season and then came the incident with Eyal. It was just frustration really.

"Whenever I speak to West Ham fans now, they just tend to remember the bad things. What people forget is the incredible time I had before that.

John admits he came back for pre-season training overweight after a fine first full season with the Hammers.

"But there were four poor months, during which came the incident with Eyal and we lost to Northampton and Swansea in the cups. I was playing at centre-forward – the one to score the goals – so I took a lot of the blame. It just left me with a bit of a sour taste in the mouth, which shouldn't really have happened."

Following his surprise move to Selhurst Park, Hartson found himself up against his former club on his debut just a few days later and, although he admits to being hurt by the verbal abuse directed at him that afternoon, he says that a subsequent brush with the claret-and-blue faithful reassured him that his efforts had been appreciated and enabled him to retain some fond memories from his eventful, though brief, stay at Upton Park.

"I was disappointed at the reception I got off the West Ham fans at Wimbledon. I got slaughtered and I thought that was a bit unfair considering I'd scored goals which kept them up.

"They'd paid £3.2m for me and got £7.5m in return, and managed to buy players like Marc-Vivien Foe, Paolo Di Canio and Scott Minto out of the proceeds. So, yes, I was disappointed.

"But then again, I went back to West Ham for the first time about two years after that, with Coventry on a Monday night, and got a great reception. They cheered me on, cheered me off and it was fantastic.

"West Ham will always be special to me because they were the first club where I really started to play well. For that first 18 months or so it was the happiest I'd ever been. It's just a shame in football sometimes that things get broken up, because the spirit we had at West Ham when it was at its best was so good."

Paolo saluting the fans who adored him, with Paulo Wanchope and Igor Stimac in the background.

Chapter 27

PAOLO**DICANIO**

"I was certainly prepared to take a pay-cut with West Ham in order to agree a new contract and play on at Upton Park. No matter that we had been relegated – more than anyone, I wanted to stay and help the club fight back"

AS I travel through the centre of Rome by taxi, on my way to the training headquarters of Serie A club SS Lazio, it isn't hard to recognise that this is Paolo Di Canio's home city.

With lanes of traffic six cars wide, motorists appearing to follow no particular set of rules, cyclists displaying an apparent death-wish and pedestrians risking life and limb just to cross to the other side of the street, it's a scene of madness, disorder, confusion . . . and exhilaration.

Yet, on the other hand, as you pass by the Vatican, the Coliseum, the Trevi Fountain, it's clear that this is also a place of beauty, elegance and majestic pride.

During four-and-a-half eventful years at Upton Park, Paolo Di Canio provided West Ham United and its supporters with an experience that provoked just about every emotion known to man, ranging from the good to the bad, the attractive to the ugly, the intelligent to the absurd, and the brilliant to the unacceptable.

In 142 league and cup appearances for the club, he scored 52 goals – many of them collectors' items – and produced moments of sublime skill that will never be forgotten by those who were lucky enough to witness them.

Having invited *EX* magazine out to visit him in Italy, he is there to welcome me at the gates of Lazio's training ground, based in the small town of Formello, just 20 miles or so north of central Rome. It is close to the home he shares with his wife, Elizabeta, and daughters, Ludovica and Lucrezia.

It's a sunny Saturday afternoon in August 2005, and Lazio are preparing for their crucial Serie A clash against Juventus the following evening. I soon discover that the training headquarters are a world away from West Ham's Chadwell Heath base, which is made to look like an open house compared to the Fort Knox environment in which Paolo and his team-mates prepare for matches.

With gates and walls daubed in anti-Roma graffiti, as well as some anti-Lazio scrawlings left by supporters of their arch rivals who have been brave enough to venture out to Formello, worse is to come as I am checked over by a machine-gun-wielding security guard, whose Alsatian friend looks as though he quite fancies sampling a bit of English meat.

My ordeal over, Paolo shows me to his room – the Lazio squad and backroom staff all spend the night together at the training ground before home matches – and then invites me to watch some training, before offering a guided tour of the complex and then sitting down to reflect on his claret-and-blue love affair.

"I am so happy that you have come out here to talk to me," he says. "It has only been two years since I left, but it seems much longer than that and, to be honest, I still miss life in England."

Gone, but never forgotten. That's how West Ham United fans think of Paolo Di Canio. And it's also how the man himself measures his time in the Hammers' shirt.

In typical Di Canio style, of course, his spell at Upton Park was never going to end in low-key fashion – even if it had appeared that it might well do, right up until the final weeks of the ill-fated 2002-03 campaign.

Having publicly blasted manager Glenn Roeder on the side of the pitch after being substituted early in the second half during our vital 2-1 win at West Brom on February 23, the Italian was simply cast aside as Hammers' relegation battle began to hot up.

It wasn't until Trevor Brooking took over as caretaker manager in the wake of Roeder's illness at the end of April that Di Canio was brought in form the cold – memorably scoring the winner against Chelsea on an unforgettable final appearance at the Boleyn Ground, before signing off with a last-gasp equaliser in the 2-2 draw at Birmingham City a week later, the day relegation was confirmed.

As he reflects on those painful final months at the club, Di Canio admits he is still baffled by the decision to disregard his services during a period when the team needed every bit of quality available to them.

"Before that Chelsea game, I was out of the team for two months – a decision by the manager of the club," he says. "To this day, I still don't really know why.

"Maybe it was something I had said in the press but, even if it was, you should not cast off a player who can maybe offer you something when things are going badly.

"The intelligent thing to do would have been to use me in the matches – especially for that vital one at Bolton – and then say goodbye at the end of the season.

"That was what Trevor Brooking did and it very nearly worked. Of course, I must say, the circumstances that surrounded it all were very unusual and, at the time, the situation with Glenn had a very big impact on everyone at the club. Being human, I was very upset by what happened to him, it was a terrible time for him and his family.

"You have to say, though, that it was only because of the change of manager at the time that I was brought back into the team. We can't say what might have been had I come back earlier, but I certainly wanted to play."

Di Canio insists that he also wanted to stay at the club even after relegation had been confirmed in May 2003. While young striker Jermain Defoe was causing controversy by handing in an ill-timed transfer request less than 24 hours after that fateful result at St Andrew's, the former Celtic and Sheffield Wednesday playmaker had already been informed that he would not be offered a new contract, whatever the outcome.

Despite that being made clear, he clung on to the hope that the club would reverse its decision and offer him a new deal as the likes of Glen Johnson, Trevor Sinclair, Fredi Kanouté and Joe Cole all departed in a fire-sale.

Showing his class on the ball against his old club, Sheffield Wednesday.

A low for Paolo as the Hammers go down in the UEFA Cup against Steaua Bucharest in 1999.

"The bad thing is that a lot of untrue stories came out during my final few months at the club and that is what I want to clear up," he says. "The biggest thing is that I *didn't* want to leave.

"My first choice was always to stay at West Ham. If that wasn't possible, then it was to stay in England and, if no offers came, only then would I have considered returning to Italy.

"I was without a club for three months in the summer, not earning money, and this is the truth, I kept hoping that West Ham would come back to me and ask me to sign again. I knew it was unlikely but I still held on to that dream.

"In the end, I signed for Charlton, for far less money than I had been earning at West Ham, and for less money than I was being offered by some clubs in Italy.

"No-one from the club spoke to me after that final match at Birmingham. There wasn't a single offer on the table – not even one pound a week. I personally didn't think that was very intelligent.

"Fair enough, if it was Arsenal or Chelsea, who could have any player they wanted, but West Ham were losing their best players anyway, and they needed quality for the Championship division. I proved with Charlton the following season that I could still reach a high level in the Premiership, and I believe I could have made a good contribution to West Ham and maybe helped them return to the top flight at the first attempt."

Di Canio, who reportedly took a 50 percent pay-cut to join his beloved Lazio during their financial crisis last year, insists he would have considered a similar adjustment in order to continue wearing the claret-and-blue shirt that he often referred to as a 'second skin'.

"I was certainly prepared to take a pay-cut with West Ham in order to agree a new contract and play on at Upton Park," he confirms. "No matter that we had been relegated – more than anyone, I wanted to stay and help the club fight back.

"At that stage of my career, the money wasn't important to me, just as it wasn't

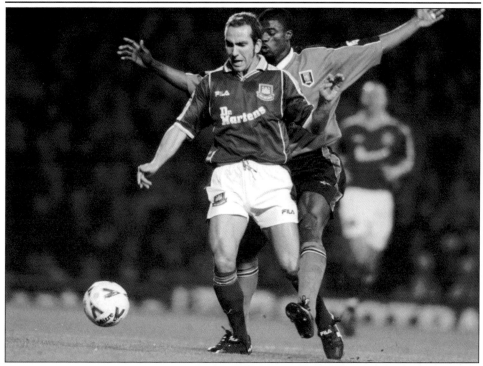

Aston Villa's George Boateng can't stop the Italian maestro.

when I returned to Lazio last year and took another drop in wages. Money cannot buy you happiness and I knew that I would not be able to find the feeling for West Ham and their supporters anywhere else in England.

"I am lucky. I have earned a lot of money throughout my career and it has enabled me to provide a good life for my family. At this stage of my career, I am not playing for money – I am simply playing for the love of the game and because it means so much to me.

"I am a sentimental person. I love to play where I feel that I belong and, at West Ham, I felt I had the perfect situation. I always said that I wanted to finish my career there and I was sad that it didn't happen."

Quite how Di Canio's final season in a West Ham shirt turned into such a nightmare for everyone connected with the club is a question that, two years on, many people still couldn't answer.

After a seventh-place finish in Glenn Roeder's first season in charge, followed by three Hammers making the England squad for the 2002 World Cup finals in Japan and South Korea, things seemed to be heading in the right direction under a bright, new regime at Upton Park.

Just two players were signed that summer – Frenchman Edouard Cisse and Dutch goalkeeper Raimond Van de Gouw – both on free transfers.

However, the effect of the advent of the new transfer window that prevented Premiership clubs buying players during the season – with the exception of a month-long window in January – was seriously underestimated by the West Ham hierarchy. When injury struck to deprive Roeder of Di Canio and Fredi Kanouté – his top two strikers – an uphill battle was always on the cards.

Above: *Playing to the crowd, Paolo gets the Bobby Moore Lower pumped up.*

Right: *Graceful in possession against Osijek of Croatia in the UEFA Cup.*

For Di Canio, though, the true problem was far more deep-rooted, and had begun to surface when confidence among the players was weakened by the disappointing start to the campaign.

"The club also paid the price for not making the squad stronger that year. Sadly, I felt they were more worried about building a new stadium than making sure we had a good team. I remember doing an interview and saying that it was better to play Premiership football with good players in an old stadium than play at Championship level in a brand new stadium.

"I was criticised for that, just like I was criticised when Glenn Roeder took over for saying that we should have appointed a stronger and more experienced manager. It doesn't make me happy to say it now, but when I look back, the things that I said were right."

However, while Roeder and the board of directors took most of the flak for the club's painful slide out of the Premiership, it would be very wrong to suggest the players were blameless. The bottom line was that West Ham had a squad of international, highly-paid, established Premiership stars, who should have been professional enough to get behind the manager and overcome any issues – at least on the pitch.

At the same time, Di Canio was criticised for returning to Italy to receive treatment for a knee injury, with many suggesting that the captain should have remained in England during a difficult period for the team and be treated by the club's highly-qualified medical staff. It is an accusation he refutes.

"I didn't agree with that, because going out to Italy allowed me to recover sooner and return to playing quicker than if I had stayed in England," says Paolo. "I asked the club: 'I am happy to stay in England if you can show me a sports recovery centre here like the one I can go to in Italy.'

"They were unable to – and that is why I went to Bologna.

"At the start of that December I had a serious cartilage problem, but I was back at the end of January and played against Blackburn when we won our first home league match of the season, scoring a penalty. That, to me, showed the value of going to Italy for my recovery."

Di Canio was also at the centre of more controversy during his spell on the sidelines, when a move to Manchester United was reported to be on the verge of going through towards the end of the January transfer window. At the time, it was brushed aside as speculation, with insinuations that the rumours had originated from the player's camp in order to engineer a move. Again, he rubbishes this claim.

"Yes, the move to Manchester United was on, but I can promise you, I told West Ham that I wanted to stay," he insists. "I told them: 'If you want to sell me, then you should tell the fans that and say it in the press.' Instead, they made it sound like I was the one wanting to get away and that they would only sell me for a big price. That I could not understand.

"The thing is, what many football clubs fail to realise is that the most intelligent people are often the supporters. They *know* when something is not right, or when a lie is being told. I had opportunities to leave West Ham before that, to go to places like Chelsea, and, believe me, if I had really wanted to leave, I would have done."

For his part, Di Canio kept a rare and dignified silence during his final days at the club. As West Ham slipped into the second tier, the normally outspoken Italian remained in the background.

"I didn't say much at the time, because I didn't think it was right," he says. "With what the fans were going through, I didn't want to make it any worse for them by talking about all the problems and saying what I thought. It was a horrible time for me and very frustrating.

"My feeling then was just one of sadness. I wouldn't say it was anger. There were some people that I could have been angry with but, honestly, the love and the good feeling I have from the supporters far outweighed the anger I felt about certain individuals.

"My passion for the people was stronger than anything else, and that is why I am now so happy the club is back in the Premiership, where it belongs."

It's the memory of his relationship with the supporters that Di Canio still regards as the greatest legacy of his turbulent time at Upton Park. At the end of our visit, *EX* presented Paolo with a replica West Ham United shirt from that memorable 1999-2000 campaign, with his name and famous No.10 on the back.

That was the cue for him to rip off his tracksuit top, pull on the shirt over his vest and run around the lounge of Lazio's training headquarters singing 'Come on you Irons!' at the top of his voice – much to the amusement and bewilderment of his Italian team-mates!

It's clear that the special bond he shared with the club's supporters is still transparent, and when assured that he is still adored and revered by the majority of Hammers fans, he seems genuinely honoured.

"I am happy if the supporters still remember me, because I can never forget the times we had together," he says. "As you know, Lazio is *my* club, but West Ham will always be so special in my heart. I still wear the claret-and-blue shirt when I play in the garden with my children.

"The memories I have are, football-wise, the best of my career. So many great moments – the two goals against Arsenal, the winner at Manchester United . . ."

Hammers fans will remember the 1999-2000 campaign as being Paolo's best season – the year he took the Premiership by storm and provided so many magical moments. Where does it stand in his career?

"That season was the best of my life. I scored 16 goals and many of them were special ones. I don't remember a really bad game that year, and there were many fantastic ones.

"We played in the UEFA Cup; I scored two goals against Arsenal, the goal-of-the-season against Wimbledon – so many special memories.

"The FA Cup goal against Barthez at Old Trafford and the two against Arsenal were probably the most satisfying goals because of what they meant to the team and the fans. But the goal against Wimbledon was the best in terms of technique," he says of the wondrous right-foot volley past a helpless Neil Sullivan that was voted goal-of-the-season and is, arguably, still the best in Premiership history.

"There was also the 5-4 game against Bradford that year, which I spoke about at the start of my autobiography. That game, for me, probably summed up my career

Di Canio was never slow to let referees know what he thought. Neale Barry gets a verbal volley from the Italian.

at West Ham. I went through every emotion possible in the space of 90 minutes and at the end of the game, I looked around and realised that I had found my true home in football.

"I have a lot of fantastic memories but I would certainly have chosen a different exit, especially with the supporters, because I was so sad with the way it ended. I like to think the fans understand that I didn't want to leave, that it wasn't my decision and that I would have done anything possible to stay.

"My four years at West Ham was an experience I will hold in my heart forever and the supporters gave me something that I have only ever had at my home club, Lazio. For me, it was a fantastic period that I will never forget."

To those of us who had the pleasure of watching him in his majestic prime, Paolo Di Canio was simply unforgettable.

THE END: Paolo Di Canio going down with West Ham in May, 2003.